Screen/Space

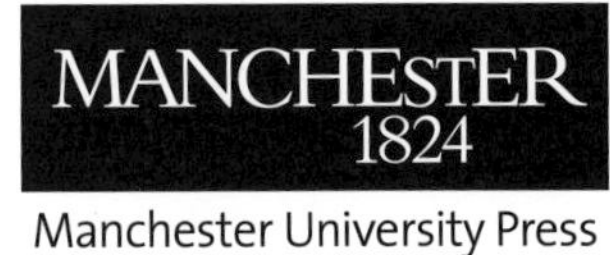
Manchester University Press

rethinking **art's** histories

SERIES EDITORS
Amelia G. Jones, Marsha Meskimmon

Rethinking Art's Histories aims to open out art history from its most basic structures by foregrounding work that challenges the conventional periodisation and geographical subfields of traditional art history, and addressing a wide range of visual cultural forms from the early modern period to the present.

These books will acknowledge the impact of recent scholarship on our understanding of the complex temporalities and cartographies that have emerged through centuries of world-wide trade, political colonisation and the diasporic movement of people and ideas across national and continental borders.

Also available in the series

Art, museums and touch Fiona Candlin

The 'do-it-yourself' artwork: Participation from fluxus to relational aesthetics Anna Dezeuze (ed.)

After the event: New perspectives in art history
Charles Merewether and John Potts (eds)

Screen/Space

The projected image in contemporary art

Edited by
Tamara Trodd

Manchester University Press

Published by Manchester University Press
Altrincham Street, Manchester M1 7JA, UK
www.manchesteruniversitypress.co.uk

British Library Cataloguing-in-Publication Data
A catalogue record for this book is available from the British Library

Library of Congress Cataloging-in-Publication Data applied for

ISBN 978 07190 8462 1 *hardback*
978 07190 8463 8 *paperback*

First published 2011

Typeset in Minion with Myriad display
by Koinonia, Manchester
Printed in Great Britain
by TJ International

Contents

Illustrations

Notes on contributors

NOAM M. ELCOTT is Assistant Professor at Columbia University, New York, where he specialises in the history of modern art and media, with an emphasis on interwar art, photography, and film. Some recent publications include 'Reproduction productive', in *Christian Marclay: Snap!*, ed. Valérie Mavridorakis and David Perreau (Presses Universitaires de Rennes/MAMCO/Les Presses du Réel, 2009), and 'Darkened rooms: a genealogy of avant-garde filmstrips from Man Ray to the London Film Makers' Co-op and back again', *Grey Room*, 30 (Winter 2008). He is currently at work on a book-length study that charts the rise of cinema and media architecture through close analyses of avant-garde cameraless photographs (photograms) and films, in particular those of Man Ray and László Moholy-Nagy. Elcott has been the recipient of Fulbright, Mellon, DAAD, and other fellowships.

AMELIA JONES is Professor and Grierson Chair in Visual Culture at McGill University in Montreal. She has organised exhibitions on contemporary art and on feminism, queer, and anti-racist approaches to visual culture. Her recent publications include the edited volumes *Feminism and Visual Culture Reader* (New York: Routledge, 2003; new edition 2010) and *A Companion to Contemporary Art Since 1945* (Oxford/New York: Wiley Blackwell, 2006). Following her *Body Art/Performing the Subject* (Minneapolis: University of Minnesota Press, 1998), Jones's single-authored books include *Irrational Modernism: A Neurasthenic History of New York Dada* (Cambridge, Mass.: MIT Press, 2004) and *Self Image: Technology, Representation, and the Contemporary Subject* (New York: Routledge, 2006). Her current projects are an edited volume *Perform, Repeat, Record: Live Art in History* (with co-editor Adrian Heathfield) and a book tentatively entitled *Seeing Differently: Identification and the Visual Arts.*

JOANNA LOWRY is Academic Programme Leader for Photography, Moving Image and Sound at the University of Brighton at the University College for the Creative Arts (UCCA) at Maidstone. She was a co-founder with David Campany and David Green of Photoforum, an organisation committed to the promotion of debate on photographic theory and practice, and was co-editor of *Stillness and Time* (Brighton: Photoworks, 2006), a book on the relationship between the still and moving image, based on a conference held at UCCA in 2004. She has written widely on contemporary photographic and fine art practices, both academically and in the art press. Current research interests are the relationship between photography and painting and related issues of medium specificity; the studio as a site of performance, work, and play; technology and the construction of space and subjectivity.

KATE MONDLOCH is Assistant Professor in the Department of Art History at the University of Oregon, where she specialises in art and media since 1960. Her research interests are wide-ranging and include experimental film and video, digital culture, postwar sculpture, contemporary craft, and feminism, as well as theories of spectatorship and subjectivity. She is the author of *Screens: Viewing Media Installation Art* (Minneapolis: University of Minnesota Press, 2010) and has published in a variety of forums, including *Art Journal*, *Afterimage*, *Eikon*, *Leonardo*, and *Vectors*. She is currently working on a book about media art and spectatorship 'after' feminist theory, tentatively entitled *Eye Desire: Media Art After Feminism.*

CHRISTINE ROSS is Professor and James McGill Chair in Contemporary Art History in the Department of Art History and Communication Studies at McGill University. She has recently published *The Aesthetics of Disengagement: Contemporary Art and Depression* (Minneapolis: University of Minnesota Press, 2006) and co-edited *Precarious Visualities: New Perspectives on Identification in Contemporary Art and Visual Culture* (Montreal: McGill-Queen's University Press, 2008). Recent articles include: 'The suspension of history in contemporary media arts' (*Intermédialités*, 2009); 'New media's presentness and the questioning of history: Craigie Horsfield's *Broadway* installation' (*Cinémas*, 2007); 'The temporalities of video: extendedness revisited' (*Art Journal*, 2006); and 'New media art hybridity and augmented reality: a process for the interaction of art, (neuro)science and AR technology' (*Convergence*, 2005).

TAMARA TRODD is Lecturer in European Modernism at the University of Edinburgh. She researches widely in twentieth-century and contemporary art, with a special interest in photography and artists' film. Recent publications include articles on Thomas Demand (*Art History*, December 2009), Tacita Dean (*Art History*, June 2008), and Paul Klee (*Oxford Art Journal*, March 2008), and an exhibition catalogue essay on British video artists Jane and Louise Wilson (*Jane and Louise Wilson: Unfolding the Aryan Papers*, Edinburgh: Talbot Rice Gallery, 2009). She is currently working on a book, *Art After Photography.*

ANDREW V. UROSKIE is Assistant Professor in the graduate programme in Art History and Criticism at Stony Brook, State University of New York, where he specialises in late modern and contemporary art. He is an affiliate professor of cinema and cultural studies, and regularly collaborates with the graduate programme in Art and Philosophy, the interdisciplinary Humanities Institute, and the consortium for Digital Arts, Culture and Technology. His research involves the historical evolution of film, video, and sound technologies within twentieth-century art, and how these durational forms have helped to reframe our thinking about aesthetic production, exhibition, spectatorship, and objecthood in the contemporary era. His monographic study *Between the Black Box and the White Cube: Site, Specificity, and the Emergence of an Expanded Cinema in Postwar Art* is forthcoming from the University of Chicago Press. He has published on artists' film and video in journals and edited collections in several different languages, a list of which is maintained at www.art.sunysb.edu/uroskie.html.

MARIA WALSH is Senior Lecturer in Art History and Theory at Chelsea College of Art and Design, London. She has published essays on artists' film and video and cinema in journals including *Screen*, *Angelaki: Journal of the Theoretical Humanities*, *Rhizomes*, *Senses of Cinema*, *filmwaves*, and *COIL*. Recent relevant publications include interviews with artists Tacita Dean and Angela Bulloch in *Talking Art Monthly* (2007) and book chapters including 'Narrative duration: Tacita Dean's *Disappearance at Sea*', in *Reading Images and Seeing Words*, ed. Rosalind Silvester and Alan English (Amsterdam and New York: Rodopi, 2004), and 'Good girls go to heaven, bad girls go to London. But there is no place like home', in *Sarah Miles No Place* (London: Film and Video Umbrella, 2005). She is currently working on a book on spectatorship, narrative, and duration in film installation.

MAXA ZOLLER is a visiting lecturer in moving image art at Goldsmiths College and Sotheby's Institute of Art. She completed her Ph.D. at Birkbeck College in 2007, where her thesis was entitled 'Places of projection: re-contextualising the European experimental film canon'. She has published widely on film and contemporary art, including a number of articles in *Art Monthly*, and an interview with Malcolm Le Grice in the exhibition catalogue *X-Screen: Film Installations and Actions in the 1960s and 1970s* (Vienna: MUMOK, 2003). She has also curated numerous film screenings at Tate Modern, Berlin Kunstverein and FACT Liverpool, most recently 'Generation Berlin Wall: experimental film from East Germany and West Berlin in the 1980s' in London, 2009. Maxa also runs workshops on experimental film at no.w.here and Oslo Academy of Fine Art.

Introduction: theorising the projected image[1]

Tamara Trodd

What is a projected image?

Projected images in some form or other comprise a large part of contemporary art. The technologies used are diverse and may vary from 16mm film projectors, to slide shows, to works shot originally on film, then transferred to high-definition video (or other digital format) for projection from ceiling-hung data projectors. Yet until very recently there was a lack of scholarly literature paying specific attention to this class of artwork.[2] There are countless books on cinema, of course, and many books on so-called 'art cinema' and cinematic auteurs. There are a number of books and anthologies on video art.[3] There are also books on the history of experimental and independent film, amongst which A. L. Rees's recent *A History of Experimental Film and Video* is an invaluable example.[4] But there is a surprising dearth of books on gallery-based, projected-image art, which has instead often been assimilated on the one hand by film historians, to the wider history of experimental and independent film (on which more below), or, alternatively, by art historians and museum curators, to the broader category of 'installation' art (though this tendency, which was particularly prevalent in the 1990s, is now on the wane). What does this book mean, then, by the 'projected image in contemporary art'? To begin to answer this question, I propose three examples, each of which was shown together in a recent exhibition.[5]

Example (1): Stan Brakhage's now-classic *Mothlight* (1963); a four-minute, looped, 16mm film, projected in a small room with the projector visible and audible in the same space (figure 0.1). The rattle and whirr of the projector mimic the familiar and yet reliably unsettling, amplified sounds of a moth beating its wings against a lampshade. The film seems to pass more rapidly than ordinary films in front of our eyes because its images are supplied by a collage of flower petals, grass stems, and moth wings attached to the film-strip, and the viewer actually sees these individual objects passing quickly through the projector. This feature, too, seems like a mimicry of the insect life which it enshrines, recalling the faster, lighter heartbeat of smaller lifeforms.

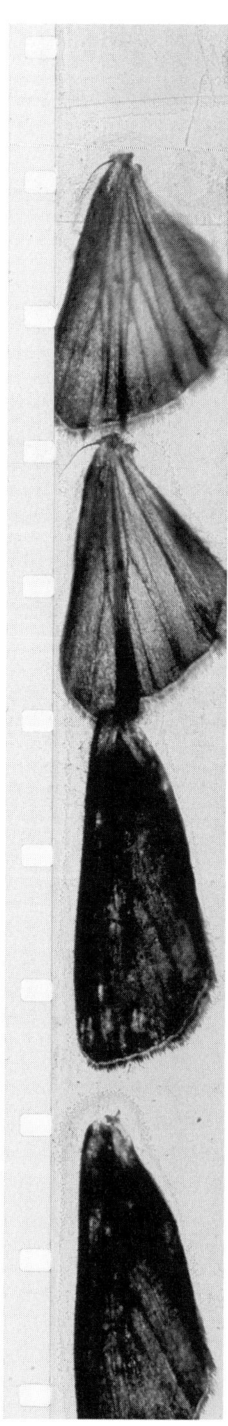

The 'dddrrrrr' trill and stutter of the projector and the rapid attack on our eyesight of the many little objects together resemble a feather-light assault by machine-gun fire. We blink, flutter our eyes nervously, and swallow; our own physiognomies turning moth-like for the few minutes before darkness falls. The projector, too, comes to seem to resemble the insect whose skeleton-structures we see on screen: its large, clumsy shape like the armature of the moth's body, rattled from within by rapid beats, its raised arch of reels like a moth's wings raised; flying towards the light of the screen, a mechanical moth.

Example (2): Mona Hatoum's *Testimony* (1995–2002); a silent, two-minute, thirty-seven second, looped DVD projection of a fixed-viewpoint shot of a man's testicles (figure 0.2).The loop of the projection means that the image appears almost still – the viewer cannot easily see the beginning or ending of the film, but instead is fixed by the camera's viewpoint in a sustained, steady stare. The image shown is plainly bodily, although it may not be easy at first to guess what part of the body is depicted: the viewpoint is so close up to the skin that we see the blood beneath showing through and reddening the skin, and we see also the raised bumps of hair-follicles. Beneath the skin, occasionally, we see a roll and bulge, as the man's testicles move within the ball sac; these ripples are the only stirs of movement in the otherwise still image. A 'projection mask' is used, which shapes the projected image into a circle, and the work is shown at an intimate, bodily scale, low and within arm's reach on the wall.

Whereas *Mothlight* connotes panic, flight, heartbeat, and constriction, and embodies its apparatus via a flight of metaphors, or hysterical mimicry of the insect, *Testimony* mimics the shape of the bodily organ shown in the circular form of the projected image, which at the same time suggests a chain of associations

0.1 Stan Brakhage, film-strip from *Mothlight*, 1963. 16mm film, silent, 4 minutes. Courtesy of the Estate of Stan Brakhage and www.fredcamper.com.

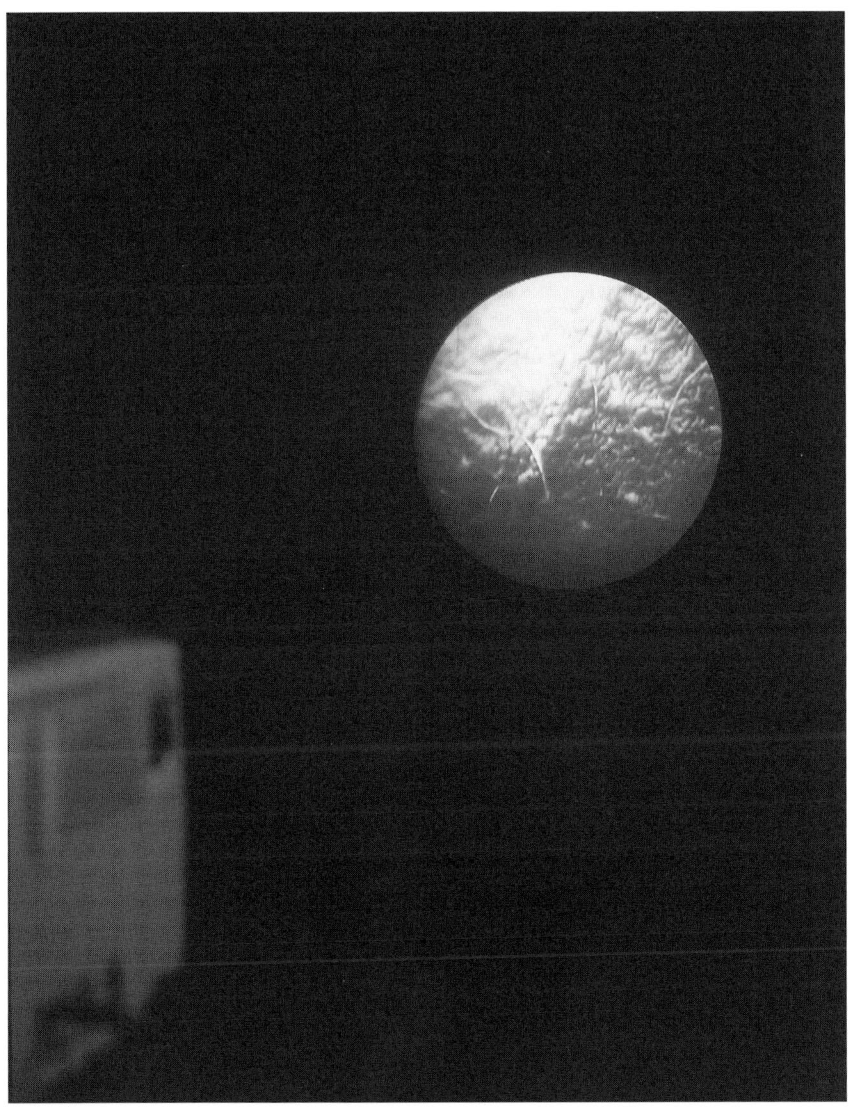

Mona Hatoum, *Testimony*, 1995–2002. DVD projection, colour, silent, 2 minutes 37 seconds, loop, dimensions variable. © The artist. Photo: Arturo González de Alba. Courtesy Laboratorio Arte Alameda, Mexico City, Mexico. **0.2**

to anus, mouth, eye, etc. The small, silent, steady, fixed, and unnerving stare of this work on what may seem at first an unrecognisable object – or an object whose name is 'at the tip of one's tongue' – awakens a de-sublimating, disruptive, and (perhaps) desiring bodily response in the viewer which doesn't rely on words or naming; arising corporeally and viscerally to undo structures of metaphor or language and idealised structures of viewing-response.

My final example: Simon Starling's projected-image work, *Inventar-Nr 8573 (Man Ray), 4m–400nm* (2006) (figure 0.3). Again, the artist has chosen a very specific projection technology for his work: two slide-projectors, inter-linked via a timer, each one timed to fade out just as the other machine's beam brightens. (The two projectors are a little like two eyes which slowly take it in turns to wink.) There are eighty slides in the work, divided equally between the projectors. Each of them shows black-and-white photographs taken from increasingly closer distances of a silver gelatin print photograph by Man Ray (*Geological Field*, c. 1930), hanging in a storage frame in a warehouse rack. We approach the work at first from the other side of the metal grille of the storage rack, so Man Ray's photograph appears initially overlaid by an external grid. This grid sets the appropriate visual tone of measuring and scale-adjustments as gradually we close in, closer and closer to the surface of the work until we begin to examine, using micro-photography, the layers of the image itself at the molecular level.

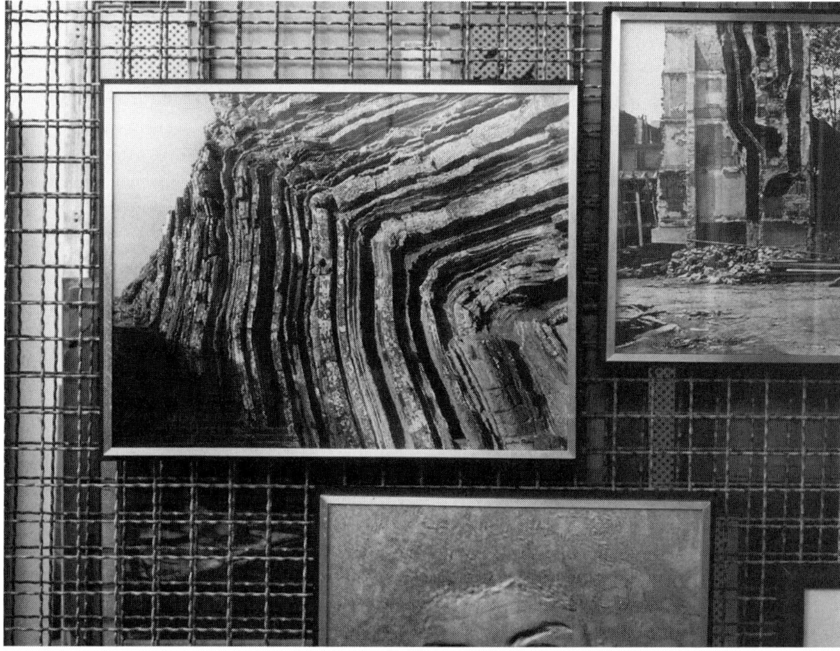

0.3 Simon Starling, *Inventar-Nr. 8573 (Man Ray) 4m–400nm*, 2006. Eighty medium-format black-and-white slides, two medium-format slide projectors, Kodak S-AV unit, CD, dimensions variable. Edition of five. TMI-STARS-00115. Courtesy of the artist and The Modern Institute/Toby Webster Ltd.

This describes what we are seeing, but it does not describe what it is like to see it. Each single projector's beam holds a still image before us for a few seconds which is overlaid or superimposed, just as it begins to fade, for a few moments, with the different still image projected by the other machine. The work thus proceeds via successive layerings, which are superimposed upon each other in transparent dissolves and fluid layers. The liquidity of the way the images dissolve into each other and make new shapes recalls the effects of a Rorschach ink-blot or the swirl of oil dropped on water. The effect is hypnotic, trance-like, meditative. Yet the work is also sensual in its rhythmic fades and quickenings, recalling the effect of sunlight momentarily brightening on a wall when the sun moves out from behind a cloud. This rhythm stirs us to respond, like a touch on the body, or an awakening; but then quietens us again: comprising a steady, calm call and repulse. The work seems to operate at the level of the hypnagogic – the semi-conscious dream forms and transformations belonging to the stage of half-sleeping, half-waking described by Sigmund Freud, where the mind parades before us colours and abstract forms which merge and re-form in our mind's eye just before we fall asleep; or like the motes and sun-dazzle which we see after rubbing our eyes. The trance that falls on the spectator is like the sleep-paralysis that freezes our limbs and prevents us from acting out our dreams when we are asleep.

In their technological diversity, but at their same time, their concentrated material specificity and their attention to the space and apparatus of projection, all three of these examples may be said to typify the material plurality and experiential specificity of the projected-image art discussed by the authors in this book. The solicitation of embodied, sensuous and fantasmatic responses from the viewer, and the importance of Surrealism as an informing historical background are also features which are highlighted in this selection of essays; as they are important features, too, of the wider field of contemporary projected-image art. Through detailed analyses of particular examples, as well as through an engagement with existing histories of the projected image, the aim of this book is to develop a framework for the understanding of 'the projected image in contemporary art', which is properly attentive to the specificity of the gallery-space in which it is often found, as well as to the fuller artistic and cultural history with which it often engages. Furthermore we hope that the account offered here will help to begin to develop a new theoretical model for the critical evaluation of projected images.

The phrase 'projected image' used to describe a distinctive category of art first came to widespread public attention in the early years of the twenty-first century, with the show curated by Chrissie Iles at the Whitney Museum of American Art, *Into the Light: The Projected Image in American Art.*[6] Two years later the phrase 'the projected image in contemporary art' was used as the title of a roundtable discussion in the journal *October* (to which Iles was a contributor).[7] My use of the term is intended to acknowledge both these previous publications, as landmarks in the critical history of the type of art under discussion here. Each attempted to articulate for the first time a theory of projected images as a specific category in art, and it is largely with their theorisation that this book sets out to engage.

Whilst, as we have seen, classic works of experimental artist's film – such as Stan Brakhage's *Mothlight*, for example – are often included in contemporary projected-image exhibitions, and are important for the understanding of contemporary projected-image art, it is important, I believe, to acknowledge and begin to theorise the development since the 1960s of a largely separate tradition of projected-image work (using film, video, slide-shows or a variety of other media), made by artists often trained in the painting or sculpture departments of art schools, who often (though not always) make works in other media (whether paintings, sculpture, still photographs, artists' writings, drawings, or photo-and-text pieces), and whose works often develop from and reference the wider history of visual art in general. These artists' works are typically designed to be shown in a gallery and not in a cinema; awareness of which space often importantly structures the work. None of these features is a hard-and-fast rule – and the essays included in this book often encompass the wider history of artists' film, as a necessary part of sketching the wider context for contemporary developments – but together they describe characteristics which are broadly shared by much of the projected-image work currently shown in art galleries and museums in the UK, Western Europe and the USA (which are the main areas for the present study). An alternative phrase might be 'gallery film', which broadly describes the category of works I intend to capture, except that, as I have indicated, these works are not restricted to the specific medium of film.[8] A strength of the term 'projected image', by contrast, is that it helps draw attention to the diversity of the different material technologies of projection which may be employed (16mm film, digital projection, video, slides, etc.); attention to which is often a crucial feature of the ensuing work.[9]

The category of projected-image art also helps to signal, as I have indicated, the distinctness of this type of work from other traditions which might more broadly be called artists' film. To an extent there are connections between contemporary projected-image art and some of the earliest examples of artists' film; in particular, works by 'New Vision' and Surrealist artists including László Moholy-Nagy, Fernand Léger, Marcel Duchamp, and Man Ray. Since these artists had such an impact on the development of twentieth-century art, their films have often been seen by contemporary artists working in projected images, although it is a moot point whether the film works of these historic avant-garde artists are any more important in this respect than their works in other media.

However, projected-image art importantly differs from the history of non-gallery-based independent or experimental filmmaking; a tradition which is also sometimes called 'artists' film', but which includes video (for a history of which the reader cannot do better than turn to the aforementioned book by A. L. Rees). As I have already suggested, artists working with the gallery-based projected image have usually been formed more by developments in the wider history of art than by the rich history of experimental film which, since the 1940s, has been a flourishing subculture in the US and (since the 1960s) in the UK. The distinctiveness of this lineage accounts for the frustration frequently voiced by practitioners and historians of experimental film that projected-image artists currently showing in and acclaimed by institutions such as MoMA in the US or Tate in the UK seem ignorant of the history of artists' film. In fact, the two histories are largely parallel and separate; and whether this is regrettable or not is quite a different matter from the fact that it is so.[10] The history of an artform, unlike the history of scientific discovery, is, after all, not a matter of simple precedent in matters of technique or form, but instead involves questions of reception, influence, and lineage. Quite simply, artists trained for the most part in the painting and sculpture departments of art colleges and exhibiting their works in galleries, where it takes on resonances to the history of the kinds of art typically shown in galleries, belong to a substantially different cultural tradition than experimental filmmakers, despite their shared materials, and despite the overlaps and exchanges which have waxed and waned over the years. It is therefore not a matter of one set of artists – the gallery-based artists – being ignorant of the work of other practitioners in the same artform ('artists' film'). Rather, this book argues, gallery-based artists work, for the most part, in the distinctive form of gallery-based projected images (using a variety of technological bases). How to describe the distinctiveness of this form is an emerging area of scholarship, to which this book aims to contribute.[11]

However, one vital exception must be acknowledged. The two histories, of experimental film on the one hand and of gallery-based, projected-image art on the other, share a common origin (and this fact of a shared ancestor is perhaps at the root of the disappointment sometimes expressed about their subsequent divergence). Although the histories of experimental artists' film and gallery-based projected images have been largely separate in the last thirty years, for a time in the 1970s, with the growth of the 'structural film' in America, they overlapped; and this confluence was foundational for both the traditions of experimental filmmaking and projected-image art which followed. In the late 1960s and early 1970s experimental filmmakers such as Michael Snow and Hollis Frampton shared concerns and ways of working with artist-filmmakers such as Richard Serra, Robert Morris, and Yvonne Rainer. The concerns of the latter group of artists always remained more connected to the other works they made (which were sculptural in the case of Morris or Serra, and connected to dance and performance for Rainer). For these artists, making films was only one and was not the most important of the kinds of art they made, whereas Snow and Frampton were primarily filmmakers and their works contributed fundamentally to the tradition of experimental film which developed in the US and UK over the next decade. Nevertheless 'structural film' was the matrix which enabled the development of both the practice of projected-image art and of experimental filmmaking; and, furthermore, it was crucial in the formulation of a critical framework for both these artforms, as I shall now briefly show.

'Structural film' and the current critical framework

The American film scene of the early 1970s in New York was centred around a key institution, the Anthology Film Archives, founded in 1970, and the critics and filmmakers who were its founders: P. Adams Sitney, Jonas Mekas, Stan Brakhage, and Peter Kubelka. Between 1970 and 1974 it housed a purpose-built cinema designed by Kubelka (in which, famously, the seats had side-wings to prevent any peripheral disturbance distracting the viewer from his or her concentration on the screen), where regular screenings were held which attracted contemporary artists, filmmakers, and critics. However, the purpose of the AFA was not only to show, but also to collect a library of key artists' films and to publish writings contributing to a critical history of the form. Four volumes of essays written and/or edited by Sitney between 1971 and 1978 proved profoundly influential in this project, and the history they outline is still foundational to present-day accounts of the history of artists' film (the basic lineaments of Sitney's history are still visible, for example, in Rees's recent book).[12]

The now-familiar trajectory Sitney outlined began in the 1920s with artists such as the Surrealists in France and the Dadaists in Germany, using film in connection with their wider artistic projects, and moved in the postwar period to the US. Here Sitney charted the growth of an 'underground' film subculture in the 1940s and the development of what he called the 'trance' or 'mytho-poetic' film associated, in different ways, with Maya Deren and Kenneth Anger. This was followed in the 1960s by the development of more rigorously experimental film works which begin to isolate and take apart particular elements of filmic technique, again in connection with wider developments in the art world. It was in connection with this work that Sitney's writings proved most influential, helping to form the development of a critical theory for the artists' film of his own contemporary moment, with his definition of what he called 'structural film'.

Sitney defined structural film as centrally concerned with shape, and often characterised by one or more of the following four features: flicker, fixed-frame filming (i.e. an unmoving or largely unmoving camera), loop printing ('the immediate repetition of shots, exactly and without variation'), and re-photography from the screen.[13] The definition he provided is, however, less useful for the particular, intrinsic features of a film which he listed (since, as he acknowledged, a structural film may have none of them) than for the general approach which he described the structural film as taking, and the external factors he described as conditioning this approach. Two things in particular were crucial here. First, he stressed that structural film was linked to the aesthetic of Minimalism, as this had developed in the wider arts of painting and sculpture during the 1960s. Second, Sitney emphasised that the films of Andy Warhol (made largely between 1962 and 1968) were structural film's most important forerunners.[14] These features of the definition indicate how inextricable experimental film was from gallery-based artistic production at this point, as well as how little it owed to previous developments in the history of film per se.

Sitney's definition of structural film was arguably the direct, though unintentional cause of the divergence between experimental and gallery-based artists' film from this point on. For artists who viewed themselves primarily as filmmakers, Sitney's definition of structural film became a key reference point most importantly because it combined a techniques-based formulation of a new aesthetic with the potential for a critique-based, avant-gardeist political programme for film. This combination proved particularly important in the UK for the strand of experimental filmmaking which led to the formation of the London Film-Makers' Co-operative, where an understanding of Sitney's 'structural film' developed into the more hard-line, more Marxist (and Brechtian) kind of filmmaking renamed 'structural-materialist'.[15] Fundamental to structural-materialist film was the rejection of narrative, illusion and representation; the rejection of which characteristics was sometimes, mistakenly, believed also to have motivated US structural film.

A backlash against structural-materialist film split the experimental-film scene in Britain in the later 1970s, articulated by women filmmakers in particular; many of whom withdrew their work from the 1979 exhibition *Film as Film* at London's Hayward Gallery, in protest at what they saw as its dogmatic and formalist politics, to which the rejection of representation, they believed, was key.[16] The 1980s and 1990s saw the development of a more diverse field of experimental film and video in Britain; and yet structural-materialist film continued to be an important influence, in part because representatives of this tradition held (and continue to hold) teaching posts in UK art colleges. Thus Sitney's original definition of structural film has continued to exert an influence on the development of experimental film, despite the fact that American structural film was always more subtle and various than the British reception of it suggested. Rather than any stipulation prohibiting illusionism or narrative, as we have seen, the sculptural issue of shape was the most prominent feature Sitney described. Similarly, the account given of the work of the 'structural' films of Michael Snow by Annette Michelson, whose writings on the artist were instrumental in bringing Snow to fame amongst experimental filmmakers, were far more cryptic and unexpected than their reputation would suggest.[17]

As for the strand that led from Sitney's definition of structural film to the art world, Sitney's theorisation arguably became so influential on the development of a critical context for gallery-based projected images because of the way it in part arose from and also chimed with arguments being put forward by critics in connection with other forms of art at the time. Sitney's books and anthologies were published in just the same years that (or just a little after) arguments about Minimalism were splitting the old guard of 1960s art criticism (above all, Clement Greenberg and Michael Fried) from the champions of a new, more diversified art scene. The development of a rigorous and intellectually exciting theorisation of Minimalist art became foundational to the careers of a new generation of artists and critics, and to this project was allied a new theorisation of film and video, not only by Sitney but by other writers, including Rosalind Krauss and Annette Michelson. In 1976, Krauss and Michelson (together with Jeremy Gilbert-Rolfe) founded a new journal, *October*, the first issue of which included an essay by Krauss on video and an essay on film by Hollis Frampton.[18]

The consequences of this closeness were twofold, influencing both practice and theory. On the one hand, the 'structural' filmmakers themselves were close to Minimalist artists such as Serra and Morris, whose own sculptures and film works explored similar issues at the time, so the practice called 'structural film', as Sitney pointed out, naturally showed commonalities with the largely sculptural practice of Minimalism. At the level of theory, however, the confluence of the two movements meant that what Sitney was able to isolate as being of importance about structural film, that is, his articulation of a putative critical framework for it, which would explain what could count as the values of such film, was arguably itself influenced by what critics such as Krauss and Michelson had already isolated as important in works of Minimalist art: shape, physical sensation, and phenomenological complexity.

In the American artworld of the 1980s and 1990s, the work of formulating an ongoing critical paradigm for artists' film- and video-work fell largely dormant. Articles on film in the pages of *October* thinned out, and the modernist project for the articulation of a set of values for artists' film was overtaken by an upsurge – largely antithetical to the editors of *October* – of video work which documented performance art, was dedicated to the body and identity issues, or contributed to the burgeoning genre of installation art. The formulation of a critical programme based on the formal features of film and video – as the definition of structural film had been – went into abeyance. There were good reasons for this: the more plural and diversified field of artistic production and criticism which emerged from the overthrow of what became known as 'Greenbergian modernism' in the 1960s – to which the journal *October* had been crucial – resulted in the rise of a more explicitly politically driven and activist-based conception of art to which formal features seemed of less importance.

In this situation the work of analysing and describing artists' film and video fell largely to individual exhibitions and curators, with the consequence that the critical picture of projected-image art was inevitably fractured and multiple. It was not until Chrissie Iles published her aforementioned catalogue for *Into the Light* that a clear critical account comparable to Sitney's emerged, which once again concisely presented both a history of and a framework for the evaluation of projected-image work. Perhaps not surprisingly, the account Iles presented held much in common with Sitney's. Like Sitney, Iles importantly synthesised a critical framework drawn from the writings around Minimalism together with an acute and concise history of artists' film. (Importantly, Iles put artists' film and video into a wider history of art including Duchamp.) The result was a powerful critical framework for evaluating artists' film and video in the gallery, the most salient features of which were the criteria of criticality and resistance to mass commodified culture defined as 'spectacle', which was held to be achieved by features drawn from Minimalism: an emphasis on the physical space of projection; efforts to heighten the viewer's awareness of the projection apparatus; and the critique of popular cinematic codes of representation.

Likewise from Iles's catalogue emerged a powerful theorisation of the gallery space, which she described as a location *between* the 'black box' of the cinema – characterised as seductive, illusion-heavy, promoting viewing as apathetic and passive consumption (in line with the characterisation of cinema presented by generations of critics from the Left, including Siegfried Kracauer and Roland Barthes) – and the 'white cube' of the gallery, which in this account is idealised as the space of critical and alert viewing (this despite Brian O'Doherty's well-known and influential analysis of the ideological machinery of this very space).[19]

Perhaps paradoxically, the practical effect of this return to a critical framework drawn from Minimalism has been to enable the articulation of a renewedly *modernist* set of values against the diversified and vividly 'spectacular' artworld which projected images had done so much to create. This much became obvious when the historical analysis and critical framework presented by Iles were reiterated and reinforced in the roundtable discussion published in *October* in 2003 (to which Iles contributed). The view is articulated by several contributors to this roundtable, and is also echoed in exhibition catalogues and critical writing devoted to artists' film from just before and since then, that the increasing ubiquity of projection in galleries represents a capitulation to political 'spectacle' (in the sense theorised by Guy Debord) and marks a wider condition of image saturation in contemporary culture. More specifically critics cite the widespread abandonment of the monitor and the film projector, as the materially specific machinery of video, on the one hand, and film on the other, in favour of the ceiling-hung digital projector (which is quiet, invisible, and easily imperceptible) as importantly contributing to the spectacular and 'virtualising' effects of this work.[20] Thus, in the shift away from the material specificity and awkwardness of the projection/transmission machinery of each 'medium', deep anxieties are stirred – inherited, it seems, from the modernist critical paradigm laid down so indelibly by Clement Greenberg. Artists who continue to insist on the physical distinctness of 'film', refusing to transfer the films they have shot onto video or other format for digital projection, and who similarly insist on the importance of keeping the projector in the physical space of projection, are few and far between; and have been critically valorised for these decisions. (Tacita Dean is probably the most well-known amongst these artists at the present time, although her concerns are arguably unmodernist.)

The shift to the non-medium-specific term 'projected images', characteristic of curating and critical writing in the 1990s, is a consequence of this material change, and points also to an important aspect of viewing this work. As others have pointed out, 'projection' names both a non-medium-specific mechanism of image-making, encompassing and eliding film and video, and a psychological mechanism of viewing historically treated with mistrust by cultural theorists of the Left.[21] There is thus a political dimension to my deliberate adoption of the term for this book; not only does it acknowledge a common feature of the current state of affairs (that it is mostly correct to call contemporary work neither film nor video, since much of it is shot on film and then transferred to digital media), but it is also intended to reject the critical suspicion of this shift, and to reject the suspicion of projection as a psychological mechanism which also seems so embedded a part of the contemporary framework for interpretation of the projected image. The history of theorising the projected image, as I have outlined it briefly here, despite arising originally from the wish to break away from an increasingly rigid modernism represented for many of the artists and critics of the 1960s by the criticism of Greenberg, seems to have circled back to a version of materially specific modernism which seeks to reject the values – both materially plural and psychologically seduced – represented by the category of 'projected images'. One of the questions which this book seeks to answer is whether it is possible to achieve a rigorous critical theory of the projected image as a category in contemporary art, which is materially attentive and formally specific, but is not exclusionary of popular culture, considerations of identity or rapt and sensuous viewing responses in the way that the modernist critical framework for the projected image, it seems, continues to want to be.

Towards a new theory: 'screen/space'

To summarise, this book arose from the sense that the critical framework outlined above is inadequate to deal with contemporary artists' film and video. The current critical framework has a continuing legacy of modernism embedded within it, which entails neglect of several important things; to which each section of the book is intended as a corrective.

The first section considers 'Histories', and opens with an essay by Noam M. Elcott, examining an early effort to introduce the projected image into the museum, and the kinds of changes to the museum's presentation of time and space which this promised. Taking as case-study the unrealised collaboration between ex-Bauhaus master László Moholy-Nagy and Alexander Dorner, the director of the Hanover Provincial Museum, to create a 'Room of Our Time' (*Raum der Gegenwart*), filled with radically experimental works of photography and film, Elcott shows the ways in which the detailed plans for this room disrupted and re-modelled the kind of progressivist and narratively chronological presentation of displays elsewhere in the museum. Whilst the project remained unrealised, Elcott argues that it provides a fascinating glimpse forward into an alternative future, now past, with the capacity to cast a raking light on the 'mediatised' museums of our present.

The question of the museum and its capacity to present the projected image is taken up by Maxa Zoller, who contributes the second essay in this section. Taking as case-study the festival, *Exprmntl 4* held in 1968 in the Belgian town of Knokke-le-Zout, at which Michael Snow's *Wavelength* (1967) won first prize, Zoller explores the contrasting presentation of experimental film in the environment of this festival, on the one hand, and later, in the 'museum', on the other. At the same time, Zoller recovers a far more 'Expanded' model of so-called 'structural film'; her research showing *Exprmntl 4* to have been a more diverse occasion than the popular conception of it as a structural film festival would suggest. Her retrieval of the widespread use of multi-screen projection and the integration of performance art with films projected there serve the welcome function of re-connecting the history of structural filmmaking to histories of performance and body art. Zoller suggests that a re-approach to such occasions via renewed theoretical attention to the 'festival' opens out a new and more expanded sense of space and time in experimental film of the late 1960s and early 1970s.

The history and legacies of the structural film are the central themes of our third essay in this section, by Kate Mondloch. Focusing on two key films by Michael Snow, which she considers alongside two of Snow's more sculptural film- and video-installations, Mondloch argues that the complexities of his work are are not brought out by dominant interpretations of it as 'structural' (although, as Mondloch acknowledges, Annette Michelson's writing on Snow was always more subtle and nuanced than its popular reception would suggest). Instead, Mondloch argues that Snow's work is exemplary of those elements of 1960s and 1970s practice which do not conform to a Minimalist sculptural paradigm, but which instead engage with play between the physical and an illusionist space of projection.

Our second section is entitled 'Screen', and here three authors develop new approaches to theorising screen-based viewing responses via in-depth analyses of individual works by artists including Gillian Wearing, Salla Tykkä, and Pipilotti Rist. The responses our authors focus on in particular are those which are sensuous, erotic, absorbed, hypnotic, narcissistic and identificatory; responses which have historically been neglected in phenomenologically-based Minimalist frameworks. Each of the three authors, Joanna Lowry, Maria Walsh, and Amelia Jones, suggests new approaches to these previously neglected structures of viewing-response, offering theories of, variously, the viewing chamber as diagnostic, screen spectatorship as entranced and the screen as enfleshed.

In her essay, the first in this section, Joanna Lowry analyses contemporary video portraits by artists including Gillian Wearing, Thomas Struth, Phil Collins, and Sam Taylor-Wood, arguing that these works inherit a 'diagnostic' viewing-position for the spectator from medical photographs of psychiatric patients in the late nineteenth century. Lowry argues for a specific elision between video and still photographs owing to the use of extreme slowed-down speeds which many of these video portraits employ; as well as to the states of pathology which appear as performed for the camera in such works. The passive and yet critical, diagnostic gaze adopted by the spectator on this account falls uneasily into some third space between the 'active, critical' spectator idealised by the avant-garde, and the passive consumer of spectacle theorised by postmodernism's critics. The semi-somnolent state into which viewers lapse in front of these works seems to prompt a sharing of the blankness and anomie exhibited on screen, even while we observe them voyeuristically as 'other'; a fault-line which she argues it is the business of these works to mine and exploit.

The idea of blankness and anomie as not necessarily un-critical viewing positions is taken further by Maria Walsh in her essay; the second in this section. Examining key contemporary films by the Finnish artist Salla Tykkä and the British artist Runa Islam, as well as the older *News from Home* (1976) by Chantal Akerman, Walsh develops an argument linking these works to the work of the pioneering woman filmmaker of the 1940s, Maya Deren. Asking the question 'Does affect have a history in film theory?', Walsh argues that Deren's model of 'trance film' as taken up by these artists unhinges narrative structures and dis-enables the spectator's narrative identifications, but at the same time enables a more intense viewing engagement, via a hypnotised, partial spectatorial identification with the blankness of the filmic apparatus itself; a kind of abstract entrancement. Walsh's argument suggests the idea of a specifically feminine cinematic agency, and her focus on whiteness, whether of the depicted snow in Tykkä's work, or of technological, video-static, or of Deren's solarised film-prints, indicates that Hélène Cixous's notion of 'writing in milk' may be an implicit reference here.

In the final essay in this section, Amelia Jones develops the idea of a specifically female filmic and erotic agency further; arguing that these were differently articulated in feminist practice between the 1960s and the 1990s. In a detailed comparison of an iconic work of feminist film-practice, Carolee Schneemann's *Fuses* (1964–67), with contemporary Swiss artist, Pipilotti Rist's video work, *Pimple Porno* (1992), Jones argues for recognition of a fundamental shift in conceptions of sexual identity and embodiment in this period; using in part Laura Marks's theorisation of the 'skin of the film' to tease out the different material specificities of 16mm film – as used by Schneemann – and the televisual body of Rist's video practice, and exposing their implications.

An important element which emerges from all three essays is the importance of Surrealism, in not only its filmic manifestations but also as a wider movement. Indeed it is evident that Surrealism has become a pervasive influence in contemporary art more widely, so perhaps it is no surprise that it should prove so important for projected-image work; and yet its importance here is quite specific in understanding the challenge which much of this work presents to a resurgently modernist critical paradigm, even as it helps also to re-structure our understanding of our forms of engagement with ordinary visual culture. This form of engagement has long been an object of suspicion; the present book therefore contributes we hope an equally long-overdue analysis of these responses by re-connecting with a wider critical history for the projected image.

The third section is headed 'Space'; which, after 'screen' provides another fundamental element in the structure of the projected image as it is defined here (even though, as we shall see, the essays in this section also work to expand beyond this paradigm). In the first essay in this section, Andrew V. Uroskie develops a re-appraisal of the idea of site-specificity, which to date has been largely familiar as an outgrowth of Minimalist concerns with the physical locatedness of sculpture. In a consideration of the work of Stan Douglas, Uroskie shows how Douglas's work complicates this idea, suggesting that in his work a unitary conception of site gives way to layered literary and imaginative textures of place and displacement which owe much to the example of Robert Smithson; who himself once announced, in what may stand as the epigraph, perhaps, for our entire book, 'after the structural film there is the sprawl of entropy'.[22]

The second essay in the section is my own, which explores the replacement of the 'sculptural' model for artists' film, which, as we have seen, was of such importance to artists of the 1960s and 1970s, with an 'architectural' model in works by women artists since the 1990s. Through a study of selected works by Jane and Louise Wilson, Tacita Dean and Rosalind Nashashibi, and Lucy Skaer, I ally this shift to a re-theorisation of the idea of the apparatus, suggesting that the support supplied by 'architecture' enables for these artists a re-thinking of the materiality of film as a machinery for projecting and housing new forms of filmic desire; in the process returning to the idea of a specifically feminine cinematic agency. Marcel Duchamp's *The Bride Stripped Bare By Her Bachelors, Even* (1915–23), also called the *Large Glass*, emerges as a perhaps unexpected reference point: simultaneously a giant lens and a surface for projective drawing in which to 'net' architectural space it is shown here to supply an unexpectedly fertile model for these artists' re-imagining of the film-machine (and the irony of finding Duchamp's 'celibate machine' a source of 'fertility' for women's film is deliberate).

The final essay is contributed by Christine Ross, and considers the expanded situation for 'projected images' which is supplied by new digital technologies and forms of projection, grouped under the heading of 'augmented reality', or 'AR' art. Taking up the question of how AR art might change our understanding of the critical stakes of projection, Ross sets out to explore how AR might expand our understanding of 'projected image installations' beyond a focus on the image, and towards an altered theorisation of the psychological mechanism and social effects of projection itself. Exploring work by a range of artists including Lincoln Schatz, Rafael Lozano-Hemmer, and Kazuhiko Hachiya, Ross argues that the exploitation of surveillance-based technologies and formats in specific works leads to a form of interactivity that cannot be simply valorised as 'participatory', along the lines of the old, avant-gardeist conception, but which is not simply politically confining either. Instead, Ross argues, AR artworks have the potential to build a form of networked and surveilled community which also permits moderate individual agency and some limited inter-subjectivity. The complexity of the relationship between individual, group, and spectacle, she suggests, needs to be acknowledged and articulated if we are to begin to be able to find ways to describe the new forms of our existence and relationship to others in society today.

The projected image as such is of less importance to the work discussed in Ross's essay than it is elsewhere in this collection; expanding the paradigm of 'projection' as she does beyond the use of either film or video and into the wider reaches of new, not necessarily image-based media. There is a link however, in this expansion, to the flexibility of media discussed in Amelia Jones's essay earlier in the book: the video and film works by Pipilotti Rist and Carolee Schneemann which she discussed there prove robust, as Jones showed, in the transition to digital media and alternative viewing-environments. Such robustness and flexibility is key to much contemporary artists' film, which, like music, is increasingly viewed and shared across the internet; and both Ross's and Jones's essays are attentive to the wider social shifts which underwrite such technological changes and which shape both artists' and viewers' changing sensibilities. Such features are evidence that the context for what I have called here 'projected images' is already changing, and that the re-theorisation of the category may already be necessary. In such a situation, is my insistence on the importance of the gallery space to projected-image art anachronistic?

The essays collected here would suggest not. What emerges from this book is a nuanced view of the museum as a space in flux, but not outmoded: constantly inflected by the other spaces to which it is related by the works on show within it, and by new viewing technologies and the unfamiliar habits of viewing which they bring. After all, many of the works of new media discussed by Christine Ross return to and are shown within the museum; just as the film- and video-works discussed by Amelia Jones may be screened in a gallery or viewed at home, on VHS and DVD. Such migrations are becoming the normal condition of the projected image; yet the museum remains (no doubt for largely commercial reasons; though the interpretive and aesthetic significance of the museum is not negated by that fact) an important integer within this networked situation. At the same time, a knee-jerk rejection of the 'mediatised museum' which results from this traffic between artworld and alternative, domestic and/or commercial spaces is refused by the authors collected here, and instead, in each essay, the museum is located as a space which has at least this semi-utopian function: to house and open for examination a set of dialectical and mutually transformative exchanges between spaces with different socio-economic conditions and histories. (Some of these spaces, indeed, such as the recreated *Raum der Gegenwart*, have grown extinct in the outside world and are preserved in memory-form only in the gallery space.)

As diverse as the essays collected here are, nevertheless considerable coherence emerges from them; and not only in their treatment of the museum. Together the essays in this volume describe a quality of viewing intensity, importantly allied to a new structure of spatial 'interiority' within the screen, which offer a new critical direction in theories of spectatorship. Seduced and entranced, the viewing model described here is nevertheless not uncritical and does not collapse into the sort of infatuated mirror-gaze at pop culture which has dominated critical representations of artists' film especially since the 1990s. Likewise, the work we discuss often excavates and holds to the light modernist formal paradigms and histories, and yet this work is not modernist. Psychic knots and structures of narrative, emotion, nostalgia, affect, colour, projection and displacement – all alien to the modernist paradigm – are key strategies that receive discussion here. It remains an open question what model of politics this constitutes in relation to 'spectacle' – this must be ongoing work to which I hope the reception of this volume will contribute.

Further directions for ongoing work are indicated by the several omissions in the present collection. It was never the intention of this book to be comprehensive; aiming instead, as I have said, to develop, through focused case-studies, a critical and historical framework for contemporary projected-image art. Nevertheless, I regret the failure of this book to treat adequately, for example, dance and performance contexts for the projected-image, monitor-based and multi-screen installations, and the projection of still rather than moving images (in slide-tapes, for example).[23] Most of all I regret that our collection focuses almost exclusively on projected-image work made by Western European, British and American artists. In part this is because the aim of the collection – and the conference which formed its original starting point – was to address the critical framework for the projected-image which developed in British and US contexts; contexts in which, until recently, Western European and Anglo-American artists had tended to predominate. But the outstanding and important work made by numerous non-Western artists (including Shirin Neshat, Kutlug Ataman and Fikrit Atay, amongst others) deserves a place in any full consideration of contemporary projected-image art, and that they do not find it here is an omission which I hope future work will correct

On the question of politics, however, at least one thing is clear. A feature which emerges overall from this collection is the importance of women's practice in contemporary projected-image work, and the potential new models of critical engagement which emerge from attention to this work. I did not set out intending to produce an anthology of criticism devoted to women's practice, but that this has been to an extent the result reflects the particular strength and richness of women's work on the contemporary scene. The emphasis which has emerged here perhaps goes some way to correcting what has been a notable imbalance in previous histories of artists' film which have often relied on male artists' filmmaking to build robust critical paradigms (this is for example apparent in Sitney's account of structural film as well as in the British structuralist-materialist formation). Too often women's film and video has been confined to the 'ghetto' of representational and identity concerns, rather than mined and studied for what formal paradigms might emerge from it. This question has emerged as a particular focus of this book and it is one I am pleased to acknowledge here, where I hope that it, too, may encourage future work.

Notes

1 This book arose from a conference held at the University of Edinburgh in April 2007. Some people who spoke then could not contribute their papers to the present volume; I have expanded the list of speakers' papers with essays commissioned from other authors. I would like to thank in particular Samantha Lackey, who co-organised the conference with me and undertook preliminary editorial revisions of some of the essays presented here, and I would also like to thank all participants, speakers, and audience for their contributions. I gratefully acknowledge the conference funding given by the British Academy, the University of Edinburgh, and the AHRC Centre for the Study of Surrealism and its Legacies. Finally I would like to thank the two anonymous readers for Manchester University Press for their helpful and constructive suggestions on the text.

2 The situation has improved recently, and since the date of our original conference, with the welcome publication of Tanya Leighton (ed.), *Art and the Moving Image: A Critical Reader* (London: Tate Publishing/Afterall, 2008); Stuart Comer (ed.), *Film and Video Art* (London: Tate Publishing, 2009); and Maeve Connolly's *The Place of Artists' Cinema: Space, Site and Screen* (Bristol/Chicago: Intellect Books/University of Chicago Press, 2009), which is the first monograph in English on the kind of contemporary projected-image art discussed here.

3 To a large extent the history of video art forms a separate tradition of its own to the work discussed here, not least because in the early part of its history it was importantly monitor-based. I intend the category of 'projected images' specifically to exclude such monitor-based transmission of video works, though sometimes there is inevitably an overlap. Where, as is often the case nowadays, video works are displayed by digital projection, such work usually belongs to the category I describe here as 'projected images'. For more on the history of video, see Ira Schneider and Beryl Korot (eds), *Video Art: An Anthology* (New York and London: Harcourt Brace Jovanovich, 1976); Doug Hall and Sally Jo Fifer (eds), *Illuminating Video: An Essential Guide to Video Art* (New York: Aperture/Bay Area Video Coalition, 1990); Julia Knight (ed.), *Diverse Practices: A Critical Reader on British Video Art* (Luton: Luton Press/ACE, 1996); Michael Rush, *Video Art* (London: Thames and Hudson, 2003); and Catherine Elwes, *Video Art: A Guided Tour* (London: I. B. Tauris, 2005).

4 A. L. Rees, *A History of Experimental Film and Video* (London: British Film Institute, 1999). A recent conference held at Tate Modern, 'Expanded cinema: activating the space of reception', in April 2008 (to which two of the authors included in the present volume, Noam Elcott and Maxa Zoller, were contributors), was also important in developing and disseminating new scholarship in this area.

5 Each of these works was shown in the exhibition *Close-Up: Proximity and Defamiliarisation in Art, Film and Photography* at the Fruitmarket Gallery in Edinburgh, 24 October 2008–11 January 2009. The descriptions given here are drawn from my review of this show, 'Looking closely', published in *Photography and Culture*, 3:2 (July 2010; Berg Publishers, an imprint of A&C Black Publishers Ltd).

6 Chrissie Iles (ed.), *Into the Light: The Projected Image in American Art, 1964–1977* (New York: Whitney Museum of American Art, 2001). The term 'projected images'

was also used earlier, unusually at the time, as the title for an exhibition in 1974 at the Walker Art Center in Minneapolis; although the category was not used consistently by the contributors, who tended to employ other terms. See Martin Friedman et al., *Projected Images* (Minneapolis: Walker Art Center, 1974). The term has also been used since the early 1980s by James Coleman to describe his own work, which consists of slide projections; although I do not intend any link to this particular usage here. For a theorisation of Coleman's practice, see Rosalind Krauss, '"... And then turn away?"' (1997), reprinted in George Baker (ed.), *James Coleman* (Cambridge, Mass: MIT Press, 2003), pp. 157–83; p. 160.

7 'Roundtable: the projected image in contemporary art', *October*, 104 (Spring 2003), pp. 71–96.

8 For usage of this phrase, see, for example, Catherine Fowler, 'Room for experiment: gallery films and vertical time from Maya Deren to Eija Liisa Ahtila', *Screen*, 45:4 (Winter 2004), pp. 324–43.

9 I believe the term 'projected images' as a categorisation of this work has advantages over 'moving images', which is the term adopted by Leighton in her recent anthology (cited above), because that term in my view too strongly suggests a connection to cinema (via 'moving pictures' or 'the movies'), and because much of projected-image art is still rather than moving, or moves only very slowly. At any rate the fact that it is projected seems more important to its nature than the fact that it may or not be moving. Leighton discusses some of these issues in her *Art and the Moving Image*, p. 11.

10 The separateness of the two forms should of course not be overstated and, as I acknowledge, there have been overlaps and exchanges between the two. I do not mean to argue that the two are entirely isolated from each other, but only that they are relatively separate, and that the concerns of artists working with the projected image have mainly arisen from an art-world context, rather than a context of experimental film.

11 For further, recently published discussion of this point, see Jonathan Walley, 'Modes of film practice in the avant-gardes', in Leighton (ed.), *Art and the Moving Image*, pp. 182–99. A number of (mostly younger) commentators have also recently published essays which argue from a similar principle, of the separateness (to a large extent) and distinctiveness of the tradition of 'gallery film' or, as I am calling it here, projected-image art. See Maeve Connolly, *The Place of Artists' Cinema*, Catherine Fowler, 'Room for experiment', and Chris Dercon, 'Gleaning the future – from the gallery floor', *Vertigo*, 2:2 (2002), pp. 3–5. It is interesting that most of these commentators – whose background is mainly in film studies, rather than art history – emphasise a relationship between projected-image art and mainstream cinema, or even claim that this is of primary importance to the works in question. Whilst this may be the case for individual artists (such as Douglas Gordon, for example), it seems of less importance to others (such as Tacita Dean), and I would contest the claim that a relationship to cinema, rather than the wider history of art, is of defining significance to projected-image art in general.

12 See P. Adams Sitney (ed.), *Film Culture: An Anthology* (London: Secker and Warburg, 1971; originally published in the US by Praeger Publishers Inc, under the title *Film Culture Reader*); P. Adams Sitney, *Visionary Film: The American*

Avant-Garde, 1943–2000 (1974; Oxford/New York: Oxford University Press, 3rd edition, 2002); P. Adams Sitney (ed.), *The Essential Cinema: Essays on Films in the Collection of Anthology Film Archives* (New York: Anthology Film Archives and New York University Press, 1975); P. Adams Sitney (ed.), *The Avant-Garde Film: A Reader of Theory and Criticism* (New York: New York University Press, 1978).

13 Sitney, 'Structural film' (1969), reprinted in Sitney (ed.), *Film Culture: An Anthology*, pp. 326–48; this definition given p. 327.

14 As soon as it was published, Sitney's article attracted protests from practitioners within the Co-op or underground film movement. Peter Kubelka and George Maciunas each wrote to Sitney to argue with his prioritisation of Warhol and to point out that underground filmmakers had formulated key techniques and strategies first. Sitney acknowledged these objections in an addendum to his essay when it was reprinted in his anthology, and he also printed a table by Maciunas showing the filmmaker's revised order of priority. See Sitney, 'Structural film', with table by Maciunas, p. 349.

15 See Peter Gidal, 'Theory and definition of structural/materialist film', *Studio International*, 190:978 (November/December 1975), pp. 189–96; and Gidal (ed.), *Structural Film Anthology* (London: BFI Publishing, 1976).

16 The 1979 Hayward exhibition is discussed further by Maxa Zoller in chapter 2 of the present volume. For further reading on the legacies of this debate within the UK experimental film scene of the 1980s and 1990s, see Nina Danino and Michael Maziere (eds), *The Undercut Reader: Critical Readings in Artists' Film and Video* (London/New York: Wallflower Press, 2002).

17 See Annette Michelson, 'Toward Snow', *Artforum*, 1971, reprinted in P. Adams Sitney (ed.), *The Avant-Garde Film*, pp. 172–83; and Annette Michelson, 'About Snow', *October*, 8 (Spring 1979), pp. 111–25.

18 Indeed the name of the journal itself was taken from a revolutionary film, Sergei Eistenstein's *October* (1927–28). The full list of the first issue's contents, which included a number of essays on film and video, was: Michel Foucault, 'Ceci n'est pas une pipe'; Richard Forman, 'The carrot and the stick'; Nöel Burch, 'To the distant observer' and 'Towards a theory of Japanese film'; Richard Howard, 'The giant on giant-killing'; Rosalind Krauss, 'Video: the aesthetics of narcissism'; Jeremy Gilbert-Rolfe and John Johnson, '*Gravity's Rainbow* and the *Spiral Jetty*'; Jean-Claude Lebenstejn, 'Star', and Hollis Frampton, 'Notes on composing in film'.

19 For negative characterisations of cinema, see Siegfried Kracauer, 'The little shopgirls go to the movies' (1927), reprinted in Kracauer, *The Mass Ornament: Weimar Essays*, trans. and ed. Thomas Y. Levin (Cambridge, Mass.: Harvard University Press, 1995), pp. 291–95; Roland Barthes, 'Upon leaving the movie theatre' (1979), reprinted in Theresa Hak Kyung Cha (ed.), *Apparatus: Cinematographic Apparatus, Selected Writings* (New York: Tanam Press, 1980), pp. 1–4. The kind of politically motivated scepticism towards cinematic enthrallment expressed by Barthes and Kracauer was developed and made more rigorous in the criticism published in the British film journal *Screen* in the 1970s, especially in Laura Mulvey's important essay 'Visual pleasure and narrative cinema' (1975), reprinted in Gerald Mast and Marshall Cohen (eds), *Film Theory and Criticism: Introductory Readings* (New York: Oxford University Press, 1985), pp. 837–48. For analysis of the ideological

coerciveness of the gallery space, on the other hand, see Brian O'Doherty, *Inside the White Cube* (1976; revised and expanded edition, Berkeley, Calif.: University of California Press, 1986).

20 Hal Foster describes a 'rampant virtualism' in much contemporary projected-image work; see 'Roundtable: the projected image in contemporary art', p. 75. On the 'spectacular' effects of artists' abandonment of the monitor see for example, John Ravenal, who in his catalogue essay for a recent exhibition of video art writes that 'Large-scale, high-definition video projection offers the means to make enveloping spectacles of moving light and sound, especially when using multiple simultaneous projections. For many artists, this embrace of a cinematic aesthetic replaces the alternative aspirations of early single-channel video.' The critic Eleanor Heartney, writing in the same catalogue, agrees, arguing that whilst 'early video is a creature of its time, embracing the anti-commodity and anti-institutional ethos, the visual austerity and the conceptual questions about the essence of the medium that permeated the avant-garde art of the 1960s and 1970s', by contrast, 'video installation today seems to have moved toward a position that embraces the museum or gallery as its ideal environment and appears to be less concerned with machines or technology in themselves than with the often spectacular effects they can achieve'. See Ravenal (ed.), *Outer and Inner Space: Pipilotti Rist, Shirin Neshat, Jane and Louise Wilson and the History of Video Art* (Vancouver, BC: University of British Columbia Press, 2002).

21 See Dominique Païni, 'Should we put an end to projection?', trans. Rosalind Krauss, *October*, 110 (Fall 2004), pp. 23–48.

22 Robert Smithson, 'A cinematic atopia' (1971), in Jack Flam (ed.), *Robert Smithson: The Collected Writings* (Berkeley, Calif.: University of California Press, 1996), pp. 138–42.

23 On this latter omission, in particular, see Darsie Alexander, *Slide Show: Art and the Projected Image* (Baltimore, Md.: Baltimore Museum of Art/University Park, Pa.: Penn State University Press/London: Tate Modern, 2005).

Part I
Histories

1

Rooms of our time: László Moholy-Nagy and the stillbirth of multi-media museums[1]

Noam M. Elcott

In his 1926 treatise on the philosophy of film, Rudolf Harms declares that the cinema should 'guarantee the highest degree of bodily detachedness and seek to alleviate the shortcomings of the individual's fixed and local bondedness'.[2] When implemented successfully, cinema is composed of nothing but 'undulating light in spaceless darkness'.[3] Spaceless darkness – the neologism appears to be Harms's – is more than the absence of light; quite the contrary, it is completed only by a luminous projection. As a metonym for the entire cinematic apparatus, spaceless darkness has come to mean the extinction of the bodies of spectators, the dematerialisation of their environment, their extraction from real time and real space, and their unwitting ensnarement within an ideological apparatus beyond their control.[4] Whilst transhistorical accounts – like that of Jean-Louis Baudry – link the cinematic apparatus all the way back to Plato's cave, media archaeologists from Theodor Adorno and Friedrich Kittler to Jonathan Crary and Jörg Brauns have located the consolidation of this *dispositif* in the nineteenth century. This technology and administration of spectatorship, however, was not widely fused with cinematic projection in Europe until the rise of the film palaces of the First World War, that is, just in time for the avant-garde.[5]

Though rarely named as such, spaceless darkness has been the *bête noire* for countless theorists and practitioners of avant-garde art and film, especially since the late 1960s. Where spaceless darkness disembodies, suspends time and space, and subsumes reality within the apparatus, it is often avowed that avant-garde art and film are corporeal, assert real time and space, and expose the working of the apparatus. Where traditional cinema engenders a darkness so immersive as to be spaceless, expanded and avant-garde cinema are understood to activate the space of reception. According to prevailing wisdom, however, this activation is undone by the reconstruction of the 'black box' cinema environment in the contemporary museum. In the new, 'mediatised' museum, it is claimed, individual works are shipwrecked amid the waves of aleatory perception and distraction, lost – as Frederic Jameson has cogently argued – in an unmappable 'space assembling and disassembling itself oneirically around you'. He continues:

> This is not a recovery of the body in any active and independent way, but rather its transformation into a passive and mobile field of 'enregistrement' in which tangible portions of the world are taken up and dropped again in the permanent inconsistency of a mesmerising sensorium.[6]

According to this account, and many others like it, the cinematic *dispositif* exchanges the discipline of the theatre for the less coercive – but no less controlling – black box museum, producing a new brand of passivity and disembodiment, distraction, and spacelessness.

Without losing sight of the constraining effects of the cinematic *dispositif* and the productive dismantling effected by artists, filmmakers, and theorists, I hope to overturn any simple opposition between passive, 'cinematic' immersion and active, avant-garde dismantling. The interwar avant-garde also struggled to activate the space of reception, but rather than see cinema as the problem, they often turned to cinema as the solution. Rather than negate or subvert the cinematic *dispositif*, they worked dialectically to conserve and abolish it at the same time; an intriguing model which I think it is worth retrieving. In service to this aim, I will present a constellation of performances, exhibitions, artworks, and films from roughly the year 1930. The constellation orbits around the 'Room of Our Time' (*Raum der Gegenwart*): an unrealised collaboration between ex-Bauhaus master László Moholy-Nagy and Alexander Dorner, the director of the Hanover Provincial Museum.[7] If it had been brought into effect, this would have been the first permanent museum gallery to exhibit photography, film, and other technological media as the culmination of the history of art. Since it was never realised, the Dorner–Moholy-Nagy collaboration presents us with the opportunity to consider a counterfactual history, which at the same time complicates our understanding of the involvement of the historic avant-gardes with cinema and with the construction of the modern museum. The history of this unrealised collaboration, as I shall reconstruct it here, points not so much towards an archaeology of 'media art', but rather to an archaeology of the interwar imagination of time and space; that is, an account of the rise of a certain, 'mediatised' conception of time and space, constructed through photography, film, and architecture, as these are presented in the museum. To begin with, then, we must turn to an account of the museum in Hanover for which Dorner proposed this project.

Time and space in the museum

The 'Room of Our Time' as a permanent gallery within the Hanover museum was intended to serve as the culmination of Dorner's sweeping survey of the history of art from the Middle Ages to the present: a climactic culmination of the 'modern' positioned as the summation of a teleological trajectory, which would also capture the broader artistic 'will' of its epoch. To explain how this could be, I need first to describe briefly Dorner's museum philosophy and his plan for the existing galleries showing earlier historical material.

When he arrived at the Provincial Museum in Hanover, Dorner inherited a collection largely devoid of contemporary art which was organised not chronologically or geographically but according to donor, and was arranged in symmetrical salon style such that similarly sized paintings were hung in identical positions on opposite sides of a wall.[8] Dorner radically revamped the organisation and presentation of the artworks into a series of so-called 'atmosphere rooms' (*Stimmungsräume*). Quite different from period rooms, the Riegl-inspired 'atmosphere rooms' were meant to provide insight into the artistic will (*Kunstwollen*) of earlier periods. Aloïs Riegl, a turn-of-the-century Viennese curator and art historian, left a legacy of expansive cultural history. Riegl's hermeneutic, adopted by Dorner and many others of his generation, insisted that 'in every period there is only *one* orientation of the *Kunstwollen*'.[9] In 1922 Dorner published an essay in which he developed his own adaptation of Riegl's idea, stressing above all that our understanding of *Kunstwollen* is reliant on our sense of our own present time:

> *Kunstwollen* understood theoretically is a formal, timeless conceptual definition pertaining to general aesthetics and devoid of substance.
> *Kunstwollen* as an epiphany in the present is no more than an intuitively grasped inclination.
> *Kunstwollen* understood historically is the series of the artworks themselves grasped with the concepts of the present [*Gegenwart*].[10]

This final definition is precisely what Dorner attempted to put into practice in the Hanover Provincial Museum.

In the Medieval galleries, walls were painted purple and the ceiling a deep, dark blue in order to transpose the darkness of medieval churches, which lacked luminous interiors. The Renaissance galleries, by contrast, had cool white and grey walls and ceilings which emphasised the cubic character of the room, and picture frames therein, in order to help draw attention to the rise of linear perspective and the attendant conception of painting as a window onto the world. (Not coincidentally, at the same time that Dorner was reconfiguring the galleries in Hanover, Erwin Panofsky was formulating his own Riegl-inspired theory of perspective as symbolic form, that is, perspective as a historically contingent conception of space (*Raumvorstellung*) that emerged as a conception of the world (*Weltvorstellung*).[11]) Further along in the museum, red velvet and gold frames adorned the Baroque galleries as space lost its clear definition. Each gallery was to carry the signature – in particular, the spatial signature – of the art of its time such that the historical vision and the works of art would animate each other in aesthetic reciprocity.

Dorner's faith in the capacity of colour and form to carry the artistic will of an age is arguably a marker of the influence of Riegl on interwar art history. The dubiousness of this programme was identified by Meyer Schapiro already in 1936, as part of his broader critique of the so-called Vienna School. According to Schapiro, the 'broad abstractions and unverifiable subtleties' of Riegl's followers are reminiscent:

> of the practices of contemporary art and art criticism, in which the inventive sensibility creates its own formalised objects, delights in its own 'laws', and enjoys its absolutely private fantasy, justifying this activity as an experimental system of artistic deduction or as an intuitive perception of essences and wholes.[12]

Schapiro's rebuke was addressed toward the scholarship of Hans Sedlmayr and other Riegl devotees, but his critique could be levelled against Dorner's museum design as well. What Dorner lacked in scholarly rigour, however, he made up for in his attunedness to contemporary artistic practice. Indeed, Dorner straddled the worlds of art history, museum curating, and contemporary art – spheres that, at that time, were far less intertwined than they are today. Dorner's application of modernist aesthetics to exhibition design proved the bridge between art history and the contemporary art practice and criticism of which he was a signal champion. Parallel to his appointment as curator and, later, director of the Hanover Provincial Museum, Dorner was the director and then chairman of the Kestnergesellschaft, a private organisation that supported and exhibited contemporary art and literature. Under Dorner's stewardship, the Kestnergesellschaft shifted its focus from figurative Expressionism to abstract Constructivism. Dorner supported artists such as El Lissitzky and Moholy-Nagy through commissions and exhibitions at the Kestnergesellschaft and became the first museum director to purchase a work by Piet Mondrian. He quickly sought means to extend his atmosphere rooms so that they would not only include works of contemporary art, but would also more fully reveal the contemporary 'artistic will'.

In order to extend the museum's evolutionary history of art to the present, Dorner commissioned El Lissitzky to design a final gallery for contemporary abstract painting and sculpture. In the famous Abstract Cabinet, works by Pablo Picasso, Mondrian, Fernand Léger, Moholy-Nagy, Lissitzky, and others, were rigged to mobile casings that could be moved up and down by visitors to reveal further paintings behind. More importantly, solid walls were replaced with a variable white-grey-black lath-system that changed in accordance with the position and movement of the viewer. Thus, the ground behind Lissitzky's *Proun 1C* (1919) would change from white to grey to black, as one moved from left to right before the painting. For Lissitzky, the primary goal was the activation of the viewer.[13] For critics such as Siegfried Giedion, however, the result was a dematerialisation of the physical environment.[14] Whereas cubic or gold frames in the earlier galleries had summoned perspectival space and its upheaval, Dorner did away with frames altogether in the Abstract Cabinet in order to signal the end of paintings as windows onto the world. In Dorner's estimation, the Abstract Cabinet marked a major step forward in his era's conception of space (*Raumvorstellung*): no longer bound to the laws of perspective or the window on the world delineated by the picture frame, abstract painting and Lissitzky's Abstract Cabinet helped inaugurate a space that was multi-perspectival and thus immaterial and transparent, composed of streams of movement and energy.[15] For Dorner, the infinite, dissolving, dematerialising, optical space produced by the Abstract Cabinet corresponded exactly to the works within it, such that – in Maria Gough's penetrating analysis – dematerialisation was the atmosphere of this final atmosphere room.[16]

Dorner situated the initial dissolution of traditional perspective in the Romantic period, that is, as part of a continuous history of painting. After the Abstract Cabinet was completed, however, he became progressively more convinced that the triumph over perspective in the twentieth-century unfolded in dialogue with a new medium: film. Because of film and its introduction of the temporal fourth dimension, Dorner argued, 'It has become necessary to replace the fixed vantage point by a relative, moving one' such that painting was now obligated 'to absorb the illusion of generally mobile space' (a task even more difficult than the transposition of a three-dimensional world into a two-dimensional picture).[17] Successful paintings by Lissitzky, Moholy-Nagy, Lyonel Feininger, and others were composed of 'transparent planes … without massiveness or weight', 'crystal without substance', 'relative vantage point', and 'massless tension'.[18] Dematerialisation was but one facet of a new conception of space tied to the mobility, transparency, weightlessness, immateriality, and multi-perspectivalism of cinematic space, which Dorner hoped to transpose into his museum.

This is where Dorner and Lissitzky parted ways. Like Dorner, Lissitzky praised the 'imaginary space' constructed in abstract films like Viking Eggeling's *Diagonal Symphony*. 'However', and this was Lissitzky's primary criticism, 'the cinema depends on dematerialised surface projection using merely a single facet of our visual faculties'.[19] Like so many avant-garde artists engaged with film, Lissitzky wanted to do away with the two-dimensional surface projection. But unlike Dorner – or, for that matter Giedion and Moholy-Nagy – Lissitzky utterly resisted dematerialisation, disembodiment, and pure opticality, and strove instead toward a paradoxical 'amaterial materiality'.[20] Lissitzky demanded the destruction of walls in order to disrupt contemplative paintings and activate the body of the viewer. Dorner, to the contrary, savoured the shimmering walls as part of a new experience of space governed by simultaneity, multiple perspectives, transparency, and immateriality.

Where Lissitzky saw the dematerialisation and opticality of film as its fatal flaws, Dorner was convinced that those very same qualities pointed the way forward. In light of the immateriality and transparency on offer in cinema, Dorner went so far as to question the longevity of painting as a viable form of spatial experimentation. But because film was still dependent on the camera, with its linear perspective, and was presented frontally, like theatre, Dorner acknowledged that, 'for the time being, painting and film – each with its advantages and disadvantages – run side-by-side after the ideal representation of the new experience of reality'.[21] With Lissitzky's Abstract Cabinet, Dorner felt he had pushed the new conception of space as far as painting would allow; but, in 1930, his museum still lacked the conquests of cinematic space. Upon his visit to the 1930 *Exposition de la société des artistes décorateurs* in the Grand Palais in Paris, Dorner believed he had found a solution.

The *Exposition de la société des artistes décorateurs*, Paris, 1930

For the first time since the Great War, the German Werkbund sent a delegation, led by Walter Gropius, to the annual French design exhibition. Under the rubric of life in a high-rise, Gropius, Herbert Bayer, Marcel Breuer, and Moholy-Nagy each designed rooms. The room designed by Moholy-Nagy, and seen by Dorner in Paris, set the template for the eventual design of the 'Room of Our Time'. Indeed, many of the exhibits in it were the same as those later included in Dorner's plan. As described by Siegfried Giedion, amongst the highly varied elements in Moholy-Nagy's *salle deux* (room two) (figure 1.1) were examples and photographs of modern German lighting; life-size figurines from Oskar Schlemmer's *Triadic Ballet*; a projection room, replete with rows of chairs and walls of Trolite – a trade name for cellulose acetate – which contained 'Deutschland Reportage', a looped slide-show of German industrial design; models of Gropius's Total Theatre and Moholy-Nagy's 1929 production of *The Tales of Hoffmann*; photographs by Lotte Jacobi of Moholy-Nagy's 1929 production of *The Merchant of Berlin* for Erwin Piscator; and, finally, his *Light-Prop for an Electrical Stage*, constructed for the occasion with the help of the architect Stefan Sebök and the AEG theatre department.[22] These would be the very images, objects, and installation techniques which Dorner and Moholy-Nagy subsequently planned to include in the 'Room of Our Time'.[23]

There can be little doubt that it was Moholy-Nagy's extensive engagement with the new media of photographic reproduction and projection that piqued Dorner's interest. In addition, perhaps more subtly influential was the way that the whole installation was rendered under the sign of cinema – as evidenced by Bayer's film-strip-layout of its content for the exhibition catalogue (figure

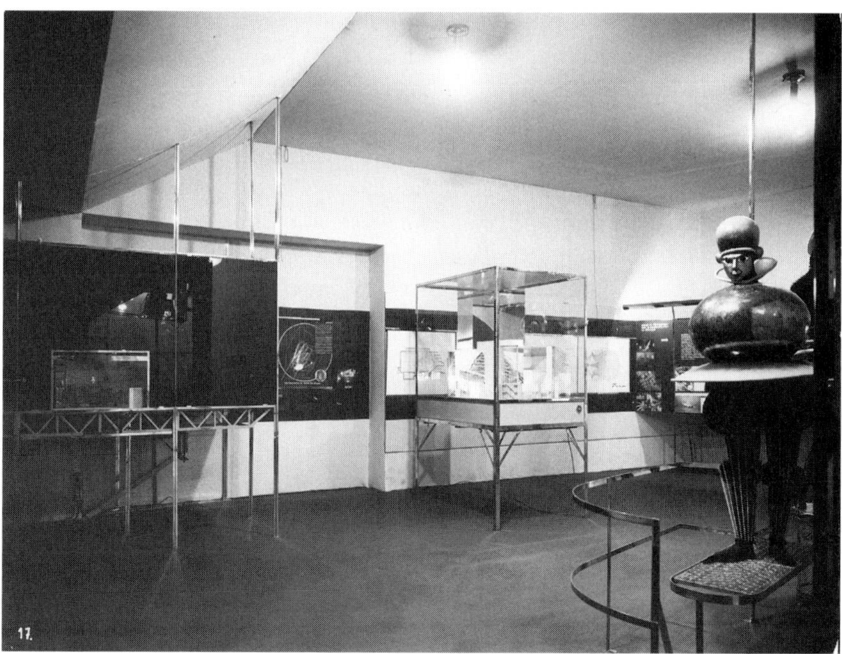

László Moholy-Nagy, *salle deux*, in *Section allemande*, Werkbund Exhibition, Paris, 1930. Installation photograph. © 2010 Artists Rights Society (ARS), New York/VG Bild-Kunst, Bonn. Courtesy of the Bauhaus Archiv, Berlin. 1.1

1.2). What is certain is that Dorner reviewed the exhibition for the *Hannoverscher Anzeiger* and contacted Moholy-Nagy in the hope of obtaining the exhibited objects for the final gallery of his museum. Dorner wanted Moholy-Nagy's *salle deux* to serve as the basis for the integration of photo-murals and theatre designs, light props and film clips, into his museum. He thus entrusted Moholy-Nagy to create the first modern multi-media exhibition space in an art museum. A notable consequence of this is that, even as the Provincial Museum maintained an enviable collection of Old Masters and offered the foremost presentation of recent abstract paintings, its final gallery would have been entirely devoid of unique originals – the logical outcome of Dorner's controversial 1929 Kestnergesellschaft exhibition where he dared amateurs and connoisseurs to distinguish original drawings and watercolours from their technologically fabricated facsimiles.[24]

Dorner contacted manufacturers, corporations, and businesses in an effort to secure materials, objects, and images lent – but not given – to the Paris exhibition, and an engineer named Luderer drew up axonometric plans for the room's museological transposition (figure 1.3). The 'Room of Our Time' was to measure 5.56 by 8.12 metres, with an approximate height of 4 metres.[25]

It would probably have been located in a reconfigured gallery 44, such that a visitor would enter unswervingly from Lissitzky's Abstract Cabinet (gallery 45) and would exit directly into the main cupola.[26] The first impression of the gallery would have been an undulating, transparent wall – a section of the wall employed in the Paris Werkbund exhibition – which would direct viewers' eyes to the right half of the room as it guided their bodies leftward. Thus separated from the outset, body and vision would have been reunited through a series of interactive displays, where a push of the button set in motion film-clips or an endless band of backlit photographs. (Such displays would indeed have helped the body to emerge as a mobile field of 'enregistrement', to return to Jameson's phrase, though we may doubt its professed passivity.) The curved, transparent wall encountered upon entry would have been echoed in the circular, transparent glass plates suspended with wires and used to display sculptural and design objects. By seemingly freeing the room's sole tangible objects from the constraints of gravity, the suspended plates would have helped to produce an atmosphere of lightness.

The remaining elements in the room would largely have been constructed around the display of images and would have followed a near-symmetrical layout. Metre-high photo-murals would have traversed both long walls;

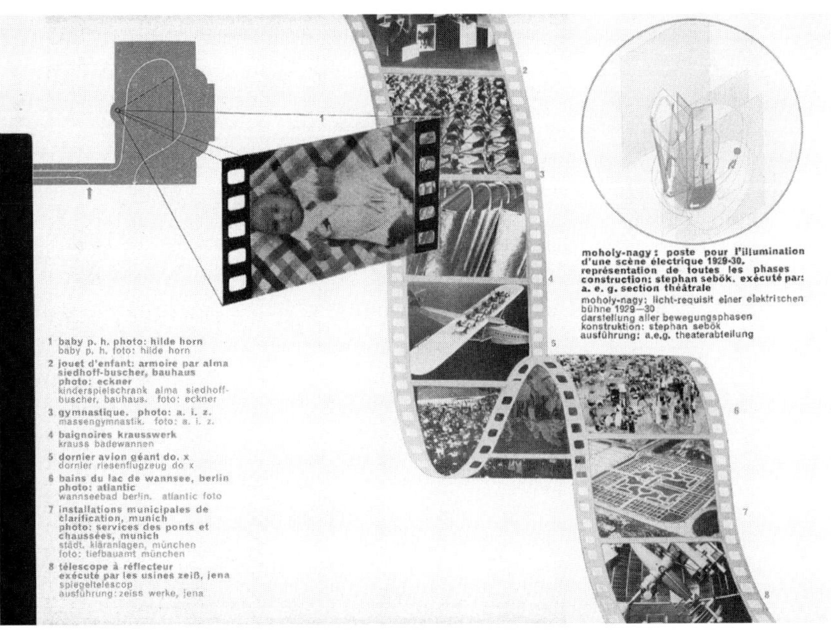

1.2 Herbert Bayer, *Section allemande* catalogue page depicting the content of Moholy-Nagy's *salle deux*, 1930. Courtesy of the Bauhaus Archiv, Berlin.

their content was never fixed but they would probably have been similar to the photographs presented in Paris, which depicted German design and architecture as well as avant-garde theatre. At the near-centre of the room, a black box with two open sides would have housed a central screen on which slides were projected: from the left, showing images of modern transportation and, from the right, snapshots of athletes in action; the two together displaying mechanical and human motion. The corners of the room would have proffered an endless band of backlit photographs; an aluminium poster rack for the display of new typography; vitrines for models, plans, and/or production photographs of theatre; and finally a wall text – written by Dorner and mounted in metal or wood type on nickel wires or wooden laths – would have asked: 'What does history teach us for the present [*Gegenwart*]?'[27] Most important of all, where Moholy-Nagy's *salle deux* in the Paris exhibition had invoked cinema without exhibiting it, the 'Room of Our Time' was to include a pair of black, private viewing consoles at the precise midpoint of the gallery, on the wall opposite the entrance. The literal centrality of cinema in this planned display was essential in focusing and emphasising the centrality of the cinematic theme from amongst the miscellany of objects and images on display.

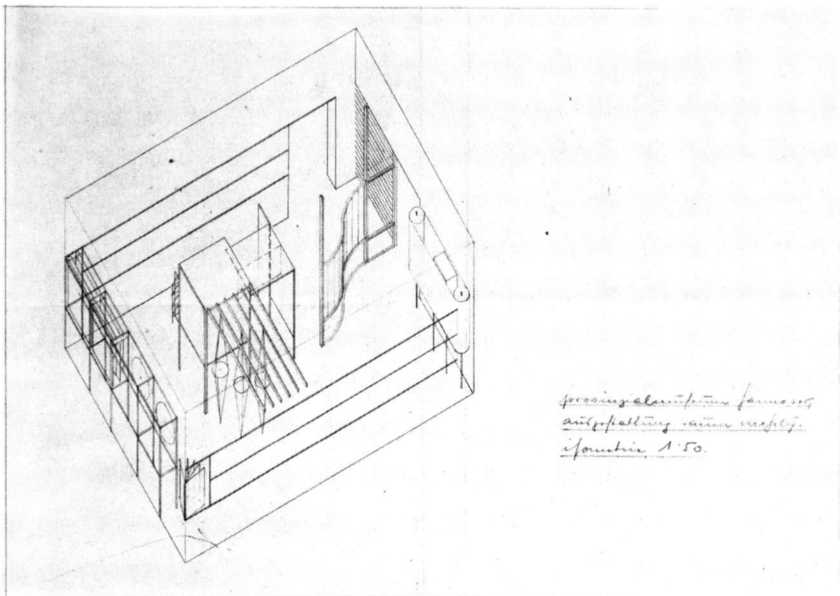

László Moholy-Nagy, *Raum der Gegenwart*, 1930 (isometric drawing by Luderer). © 2010 Artists Rights Society (ARS), New York/VG Bild-Kunst, Bonn. Courtesy of the Sprengel Museum, Hanover. 1.3

Although the precise content of the 'Room of Our Time' cannot be ascertained definitively, three sets of projects loomed especially large in the Paris Werkbund exhibition and deserve sustained attention here: the Total Theatre designed for Piscator by Gropius; theatrical and opera productions by Moholy-Nagy and Piscator; and Schlemmer's *Triadic Ballet*. This constellation of theatre designs – from costumes and lighting to sets and architecture – not only delineates Moholy-Nagy's primary focus in the late 1920s and early 1930s, but hints at the underlying dialectic at play in the 'Room of Our Time'. In order to draw this out I will discuss each of these projects in turn. Above all what they illustrate, as I shall show, is the way in which Moholy-Nagy and other key figures of the interwar avant-garde used film and projected light not only to display images, but also to remake the spatial environment of the theatre.

Like many of his contemporaries, German theatre director Erwin Piscator worked to bridge the gap between stage and auditorium. What set him apart was his attempt to do so through cinematic means. After introducing film into mid-1920s productions like *Trotz alledem!*, Piscator turned to Bauhaus director Walter Gropius to design a total theatre that would place film at the centre of the scenery and the audience in the centre of the film.[28] The result would have allowed for the systematic deployment of three distinct stage types: in the round, like a circus; semi-circular, like a Greek or Roman amphitheatre; and the deep stage, which separates itself off from the audience, turns the sets into surface projections, and leaves the spectator, according to Gropius, 'inactive'.[29] This final incarnation – the so-called *Guckkastenbühne* so despised by the avant-garde – served as the basis for contemporary cinemas. Nevertheless, Piscator and Gropius turned primarily to film to redeem this nearly irredeemable stage. Gropius expressed particular interest in the use of film, projections, and screens in order to replace real theatre props and *coulisses*: 'for in a neutral, dark stage space', Gropius argued, 'one can build with light using abstract or representational light media'.[30] By extending screens between the twelve supporting columns surrounding the audience and synchronising the twelve projectors, so Gropius concluded in a pronouncement quoted across popular and trade presses:

> [the total theatre] can set the entire auditorium – walls and ceiling – within the film … [I]n place of the projection surfaces in use until now, a projection space emerges. The real auditorium, neutralised through the absence of light, becomes, through the power of projected light, a space of illusion, the site of the scenic events themselves.[31]

Gropius envisioned cinema not as a surface projection, but as an illusionistic space 'filled by film'.[32] Screens are multiplied into oblivion, surpassed by an immersive cinematic space.

When Piscator failed to find the necessary funds to erect Gropius's Total Theatre, he turned to Moholy-Nagy to realise a similar vision within the constraints of his more modestly outfitted theatre on Nollendorfplatz. Already in 1925, Moholy-Nagy announced a Theatre of Totality (*Theater der Totalität*).[33] Published alongside essays by Oskar Schlemmer and Farkas Molnár, Moholy-Nagy's text calls for 'mechanical eccentrics' to replace actors, that is, for the optical- or phonetic-mechanical reproduction of thought through films, gramophones, and loudspeakers. To facilitate not only 'surface films' but also 'spatial light displays', the stage in Moholy-Nagy's Theatre of Totality is composed largely of flat surfaces or linear surface demarcations; a full-size screen for rear-projection is enhanced through on-stage walls covered with white canvases or screens that capture and deflect coloured light projections. Moholy-Nagy had no architectural training. His most elaborate sketches for the Theatre of Totality appear more like filmstrips than blueprints. But many of his aspirations anticipate the plans of Gropius, which were elaborated more fully the following year. Moholy-Nagy republished his speculative essay in the *Bauhaus* journal in 1927, as Gropius's more viable Total Theatre came to prominence; and once again in 1929, in the February issue of the German national opera magazine.[34] This final publication coincided with Moholy-Nagy's first realisation of a theatre of totality through the integration of light, film, screens, and space in a production of Jacques Offenbach's *Tales of Hoffmann* for the experimental Kroll Opera in Berlin.

Officially known as the Staatsoper am Platz der Republik, the Kroll Opera – as it was affectionately called by Berliners – existed but four short years: from autumn 1927 until 3 July 1931, the day it was closed due to political, economic, and bureaucratic pressures. During that time, the Kroll Opera assembled some of the most adventurous and stunning opera productions of the interwar period. Under the leadership of conductor Otto Klemperer, the Kroll Opera attracted leading figures from the worlds of music, theatre, art, and criticism: Alexander von Zemlinksy, Gustaf Gründgens, Giorgio de Chirico, Moholy-Nagy, Oskar Schlemmer, Ernst Bloch, and Theodor Adorno conducted, directed, designed, or wrote about groundbreaking performances of Arnold Schoenberg's *Erwartung* and *Glückliche Hand* and Paul Hindemith's *Hin und Zurück* (Klemperer, Curjel, Moholy-Nagy, 1930), as well as radical reinterpretations of opera standards by Mozart, Wagner, and Puccini (including Moholy-Nagy's *Madame Butterfly*).

The Tales of Hoffmann proved to be a veritable light laboratory for Moholy-Nagy, providing spaces and resources otherwise unavailable to him, as he often and bitterly complained. Among his great coups, Moholy-Nagy was able to direct short cinematic sequences for the production and exhibit them in any way he saw fit, and these provided him with his best opportunity to experiment with light creation (*Lichtgestaltung*) through cinematic and other means. The effect these experiments had on the audience is difficult to measure. Bernhard Diebold, among the most distinguished Weimar theatre critics and an early supporter of abstract film, seemed unpersuaded. In his extended review, he repeatedly opposes 'Paris', a metonym for Offenbach and the French reception of German Romanticism, to 'Dessau', the site of the Bauhaus, which Moholy-Nagy had left a year before but with which he was still strongly associated. Where 'Paris' explores the fantastic, 'Dessau', with its love of glass, stands for purity to the point of sterility. Diebold doubts the two can ever merge, even as he acknowledges the audience's tremendous applause and empathises with the artistic desire to find a modern idiom for Romantic fantasy. By the time he arrives at the short film of the evil incarnation of the third act, Dr Miracle, it appears that there can be no synthesis of Romantic music and modernist sets:

> The musician Offenbach lost himself to pathos-filled ecstasy in the attic of a Spitzweg idyll. What is Dessau to do now? In the best case scenario, Dessau constructs an atelier with a glass roof; on a white surface, a film of Dr Mabuse (or Miracle): gigantic devil's eyes blinking, his convulsing ghost-hand snatching at the soul of the dying Antonia. Watch out: close-up! ... But the intimacy? The magic is intrusive. There are very beautiful demons in the details. But in the space as a whole, the singing-soul of this Schubert maiden is orphaned and fades away.[35]

Diebold's sarcasm – 'watch out: close-up!' – belittles the film sequence even as it tries to make sense of it: prismatic exposures become blinking eyes, the hand appears ghostly and trembling. He dismisses the space as mismatched for the Romantic heroine. And yet Diebold is receptive to the otherworldliness of bare space filled with little more than light and shadow. Of the second act he writes that:

> The 'decoration' ['*Dekoration,*' i.e. scenery sets] has nothing to decorate. It need only be 'space.' But a magical space. And rarefied magical air in the stratosphere. Romanticism with its cushioned furniture and drapes was merely a luxurious salon. Here the fairytale cannot be compared to reality. With its immaterial construction-logic, Dessau innocently accommodates the sung irreality of the opera performers. In the no-longer-material [*Nichtmehr-Materiellen*], opera and Dessau meet.[36]

If Diebold had paid closer attention to the 'white surface' on which the Dr Miracle film was projected, he might have found yet another meeting point. For, as was otherwise clear to him, Moholy-Nagy's conception of light creation through film is rooted less in the image than in the environment. The sets – rather than the film images – were Moholy-Nagy's ultimate concern. The musicologist and critic Adolf Weißmann did not fail to notice that the third act of *Hoffmann* 'gives us something new: a construction illuminated diffusely from above, covered in an angular screen.'[37] Weißmann saw more or less the same on-screen images as Diebold – a trembling hand and ghostly face – but realised that the innovation came in the form of a screen. Herein lay Moholy-Nagy's innovation. And yet it was by no means the highpoint of his production.

In the catalogue to the Paris Werkbund exhibition and in the final pages of his 1929 book *From Material to Architecture* – later translated into English as *The New Vision* – Moholy-Nagy reproduces a photograph, taken by Lucia Moholy, of the sets from the first act of *Tales of Hoffmann* (figure 1.4). Visible are subtle steel and canvas modulators of shadow and electric light, which are cast and reflected on the surrounding walls. They are not only screens, but also props for an electrically illuminated stage: a construction whose steel rectangles modulate light and shadows; a form that doubles as a frame through which to see those light and shadow effects. Rather than construct a series of screens for the reception of images – which would function as projection surfaces – Moholy-Nagy identifies this stage set as 'an attempt to create space out of light and shadow'.[38] Even Diebold admits as much: 'the indubitable highpoint of the evening: the first act … The Empire-salon of yore has become a laboratory in white. The entire stage space lies naked before the white horizon upon which vague shadows play.'[39]

Later that year, Piscator entrusted Moholy-Nagy with the costumes, lighting, sets, and films – including several shorts shot for the occasion by

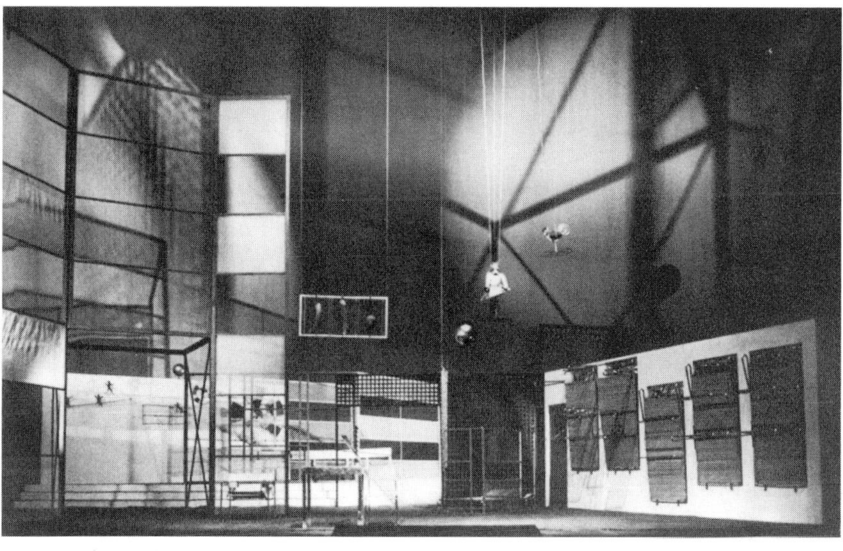

László Moholy-Nagy, *Tales of Hoffmann*, Act I, 1929. Photograph by Lucia Moholy. Courtesy of the Bauhaus Archiv, Berlin. 1.4

Alex Strasser – for his production of Walter Mehring's *The Merchant of Berlin* (*Der Kaufmann von Berlin*). Piscator must have seen an ally in the ex-Bauhaus master's effort to create a total theatre. And, at least in this respect, he could not have been disappointed. The highly charged political content provoked vitriolic attacks from the Right and the Left,[40] but even hostile critics acknowledged that Moholy-Nagy's production 'brings Piscator one step closer to the total theatre toward which he strives'.[41]

But what was the Total Theatre toward which Piscator strove, and what role did film play therein? Piscator later described the unrealised Total Theatre as an architecture infused with technology that would confront the fundamental problem of 'abolishing the distance between stage and auditorium so as to obtain the public's active participation'.[42] In a 1927 article unambiguously titled 'What I want', he declared the need to 'explode the circumscribed space of the proscenium stage and open it to four-dimensional theatre with a living *coulisse*'. 'The living *coulisse*', he continued, is none other than 'film'.[43] In Moholy-Nagy's sets for *The Merchant of Berlin*, that living *coulisse* was pushed from the back and wings of the stage to the front: a transparent scrim onto which film was projected. The result, as Diebold observed in the *Frankfurter Zeitung*, was that 'a wall of shadows that lay at the rear of Plato's cave was forced from the background to the foreground' such that '[t]he fourth wall before the audience – which, until now, was no wall at all – suddenly becomes visible'.[44] In other words, the proscenium or deep stage is exploded and, with it, the distance between stage and audience collapses.

Although commissioned to design a number of theatre and opera productions, Moholy-Nagy was hardly a man of the theatre. And although sympathetic to Leftist causes, Moholy-Nagy's primary public persona in Germany was never political. In contradistinction to Piscator, political theatre is hardly the rubric that best describes his work. In *Das Politische Theater*, Piscator's 1929 overview of his theatre practice and theory, the director highlights the use of the recent past to revolutionise the present.[45] When Moholy-Nagy mused on the same joint production, however, it was as an example of new space-light relations.[46] Moholy-Nagy and Piscator shared primarily an interest in constructing space out of 'steel and screens'.[47] Moholy-Nagy quickly exhibited photographs of his sets for *The Merchant of Berlin* and he slated them for installation in the 'Room of Our Time' – only not under the aegis of political theatre.

'Light-space'

Moholy-Nagy's phrase 'space-light-relations' (*Raumlicht-Relationen*) – a term he introduced in the months leading up to the Paris exhibition – hints at the underlying organising principle of the 'Room of Our Time'. Given Moholy-Nagy's emphasis on creation in light (*Lichtgestaltung*) in the Paris Werkbund exhibition and Dorner's preoccupation with conceptions of space (*Raumvorstellungen*) in the Hanover Provincial Museum, it follows that the atmosphere of this would-be final atmosphere room was conceived under the rubric of space-light or, to adopt Moholy-Nagy's preferred term in the years before and after his collaboration with Dorner, light-space (*Lichtraum*). But what is the definition of light-space and how might it serve as the atmosphere of a gallery or the artistic will of an age?

Moholy-Nagy's writings from the period provide scant evidence. He probably adopted the term from Hans Richter, who employed it extensively to describe the unique space constructed cinematically out of light and time.[48] In his epoch-making treatise, *Painting, Photography, Film* (1925), Moholy-Nagy invokes light-space in order to describe the next task of optical creation: 'to expand the technological horizon of a light-space construction [*Lichtraumgliederung*] hitherto created only with great difficulty'.[49] The fact that Moholy-Nagy quickly – if only temporarily – abandoned the term 'light-space' can be attributed to a petty feud with Richter as well as a certain disappointment in the latter's early abstract films.[50] But he remained committed to practices of light-space – or space-light relations – in his painting, photography, film, sculpture, theatre, and writing. Indeed, the centrality of light-space to the 'Room of Our Time' would find its most striking validation only retrospectively. For the undisputed centrepiece of the gallery was the *Light-Prop for an Electrical Stage*, later and more famously dubbed the *Light-Space Modulator*.

As exhibited in Paris and envisioned for Hanover, the *Light-Prop* bears little resemblance to the kinetic sculpture now exhibited with ever greater frequency. As meticulously enumerated by Moholy-Nagy himself, the *Light-Prop* was to be housed in a 120–centimetre-square box, with a circular opening on one side, flanked by rings of coloured electric light bulbs.[51] The *Light-Prop* was never intended to be viewed as a free-standing kinetic sculpture. Rather, Moholy-Nagy directs the viewer to the light and shadow effects cast on the rear wall of the enclosed box. Should the performance take place in a darkened room, Moholy-Nagy notes parenthetically, the box's rear wall can be removed and the colour and shadow projections can be displayed on a screen of any size.

Even when Moholy-Nagy presented the *Light-Prop* as a kinetic sculpture, it was the light and shadow effects that take precedence. Moholy-Nagy honed this relationship in an extended caption in the 1938 edition of *The New Vision*, the only edition to address and reproduce images of the *Light-Prop*:

> This kinetic sculpture was designed for automatic projection of changing chiaroscuro and luminous effects. It produces a great range of shadow interpenetrations and simultaneously intercepting patterns in a sequence of slow flickering rhythm. The reflecting surfaces of the apparatus are discs made of polished metal slotted with regularly spaced perforations, and sheets of glass, celluloid and screens of different media.[52]

Projection, luminous effects, flickering rhythm, celluloid, screen, media – this is the language of cinema adapted to the realm of sculpture. The overlapping layers, mechanical repetitions, bright reflections, and dark cast shadows of the *Light-Prop* anticipate the use of double exposure, serial repetition, high contrast, and negative footage in Moholy-Nagy's famous film of the *Light-Prop*, namely, *Cinematic Light Display: Black, White, Grey* (*Lichtspiel: schwarz, weiss, grau*). Contrary to received wisdom (implanted in the discourse by the artist himself), Moholy-Nagy's nearly abstract film was not completed until 1932 (and probably was not begun in earnest until 1931) and could not have been included in the 'Room of Our Time', as originally conceived.[53] But the aesthetic kernel of the film lies embryonically in the *Light-Prop*, for in its multiple layers, repetitions, reflections, and shadows, the *Light-Prop* makes over the pro-filmic – that which lies before the camera – according to the dicta of the filmic, that is, the manipulations available only to the cinematic medium. The editors of the Hungarian journal *Korunk* (Our Age) nearly say as much in an editorial note appended to a published lecture (which accompanied a screening of the *Lichtspiel* film), which Moholy-Nagy presented at venues throughout Germany. They write that 'rather than the apparatus, its effects – shadows, superimpositions, and light effects – play the lead in *Lichtspiel: schwarz, weiss, grau*'.[54]

The *Light-Prop for an Electrical Stage* or *Light-Space Modulator*, in other words, is a film projector without film, a realisation of Moholy-Nagy's 1925 petition for an expanded light-space construction. In this context, one might equate the circular openings of the *Light-Prop*'s enclosing box with Moholy-Nagy's mid-1920s circular diagram for poly-cinema (reproduced in *Painting, Photography, Film* in 1925). And there is no question that a vital link exists between these two projects. Yet there is an even more radical proposition that has yet to be considered, namely that the square box functions as a portable movie theatre or expanded cinema. For in the absence of a darkened space, the interior of the box itself must function as the white screens onto which the coloured light-and-shadow play unfold. In this respect, the *Lichtspiel* film proves an instructive model for viewing the *Light-Prop*. Moholy-Nagy films the *Light-Prop* and its shadows from countless angles and uses a wide range of techniques – including double exposure, slow motion, and negative images – but he rarely deviates from the extreme close-up as his preferred shot scale or camera distance. If the film models the proper viewing distance of the *Light-Prop* – if 'the reflection is more beautiful than the original', as Moholy-Nagy ostensibly suggested – then viewers might be interpreted as being encouraged to thrust their heads through the circular aperture and enter the light-space of the *Light-Space Modulator*, to see not the apparatus, but its effects – shadows, superimpositions, and light.[55] This action, further encouraged by the constricted gallery space in the 'Room of Our Time', would enable viewers to abandon their physical environment and enter the box so as to immerse themselves in a realm of light and shadow, colour and movement.

In the lecture and screening he presented in the early 1930s, Moholy-Nagy subsumed the abstract films of Oskar Fischinger, Eggeling, Walter Ruttmann, and Richter – not to mention his own – beneath the rubric of 'spatiality' (*Räumlichkeit*) or a 'culture of space' (*Raumkultur*).[56] But the nature of this 'spatiality' remained as ambiguous as ever. I have argued that 'light-space' is the best term with which to understand the 'spatiality' toward which Moholy-Nagy and others strove. But in order to grasp the culture of space which gave rise to light-space, a second term is required. That term, as should now be obvious, is latent in the first: light-space is nothing if not the precise dialectical counterpart to 'spaceless darkness'. What is more, just as this second term is present dialectically in the first, so too is its physical manifestation present within the 'Room of Our Time'. For immediately opposite the enclosed *Light-Prop* in the design of the 'Room of Our Time' were two similarly circular apertures in which avant-garde films were to be projected at the push of a button. Like the *Light-Prop*, the films in the consoles would be best experienced 'inside' their enclosing: not viewed from a distance and framed by the circular openings, but rather by immersing one's head so as to enclose it within the dark interior. Where the *Light-Prop* illuminates all six surrounding surfaces – doing away with the single surface projection in favour of an immersive cinematic space – the film consoles would enclose a single, luminous screen on which the films of Eggeling, Dziga Vertov, or Sergei Eisenstein would be rear-projected. Where the *Light-Prop* dissolves itself in favour of cinema without film, the immersive darkness of the film consoles would appear to negate space in favour of the projected, filmic image. In short, where the enclosed *Light-Prop* constructs light-space, the diminutively cavernous film consoles would distil spaceless darkness. Neither the peep shows of early cinema nor the multi-screen spaces envisioned elsewhere in the 'Room of Our Time', the film consoles were interwar film palaces writ small.

Just as the 'Room of Our Time' multiplies the potentialities of light-space – from Piscator's scrims and Gropius's architecture to Moholy-Nagy's *Light-Prop* – so too was it designed to engage a multiplicity of spaceless darknesses: not only the spaceless darkness variously appropriated and challenged by the selected avant-garde films, but also – to offer a final example – the theatre of Oskar Schlemmer. Due to space restrictions, the life-size figurines from Schlemmer's *Triadic Ballet* exhibited at the Werkbund exhibition could not be incorporated into the 'Room of Our Time'. But archival evidence makes clear that photographs of the production – also included in the *salle deux* in Paris – would have found their way to Hanover. And there can be no doubt that Schlemmer's ballet would have found particular resonance at the Provincial Museum. For each of the ballet's three acts had its own mood (*Sinn*), highlighted by a strikingly coloured background: first, 'cheerful-burlesque' in lemon-yellow; second, 'festive-solemn' in pink; and, finally, 'mystical-fantastic' in black.[57] The synaesthetic correspondence of colour and meaning was a familiar trope in German avant-garde circles at least since Wassily Kandinsky's paintings, performances, and writings of the early 1910s. But, given Dorner's insistence on colour as the dominant factor in conceptions of space, the inclusion of figurines or photographs from the *Triadic Ballet* would function as a commentary on Dorner's own exhibition techniques.

Schlemmer's conception of theatre begins with the agon between the human organism and the cubic, abstract space of the stage. When the latter conforms to the laws of the former, the result is naturalistic-illusionistic theatre. The inverse – humans revamped according to the dicta of the cubic stage – results in abstract theatre, Schlemmer's theatre.[58] The dancer-human (*Tänzermensch*), according to Schlemmer, obeys the laws of the body and of space. And none of Schlemmer's figures negotiate the boundary between the human body and abstract space more emphatically than 'the abstract one' (*Abstrakte*). Moholy-Nagy's *salle deux* included three life-size figures, all from the final, black scene of the ballet. Similarly, the two photographs from the *Triadic Ballet* included in the Paris exhibition came from the final scene: the first from the so-called wire dance and the second, positioned directly beside the undulating, transparent wall: the *Abstrakte*. Schlemmer likened the figure to a Boschian creation and considered it to be the 'main attraction' of the ballet. Initially slated for the first dance of the final act, the *Abstrakte* ultimately served as its grand finale. Due to the difficulty of navigating the costume, Schlemmer would often perform the role himself. More than any other, this costume is fully integrated into its background. It is, in many respects, metonymic of Schlemmer's larger project. In black-and-white photographic reproduction, the costume's colourful details are lost completely. What remains are a striking right leg (covered in white felt), half of a 'robotic' head, a cylindrical right hand with a white halo, the linear remains of a right arm, and a pronounced breastplate. The rest of the body is clad in black and disappears against the black backdrop (not unlike a subject in Marey's chronophotographs). The result is a figure that literally dances in and out of the spaceless darkness, a *pas de deux* between the human body and abstract space.

Spaceless darkness and the mediatised museum

Unfortunately, there is not space enough in this essay to examine in detail each of the exhibited works. But neither was there space enough to exhibit them properly in the 'Room of Our Time'. Instead – and this is my central argument – the 'Room of Our Time' or *Raum der Gegenwart*, was to be an exhibition space not of different media *works* but of clashing and dialogic contemporary media *spaces* – what might be described as a *Raum der gegenwärtigen Räume*, a room/space of contemporary rooms/spaces. Each of the other galleries in the museum worked to integrate its artistic content into a 'cohesive unity', as a catalogue from the period triumphantly declared.[59] The vehicle for this cohesive integration was a common conception of space. This spatial common denominator is carried over in the 'Room of Our Time'. But it is attained through radically different means. In place of a singular conception of space and an amorphous *Kunstwollen*, all the spaces foregrounded in the 'Room of Our Time' partook in an avant-garde dialectic of different spaces which rose to prominence alongside the cinematic *dispositif*: spaceless darkness and light-space.

This shift – never adopted or even stated explicitly by Dorner or Moholy-Nagy – must be unpacked, even if only schematically, for the implications are manifold. Dorner's Hegelian-Rieglian history of art, apparent in his construction of the rest of the galleries in the Hanover Museum, was turned on its head by the model of space which emerged from the planned 'Room of Our Time' – in deed, if not in word. In Dorner's reading of Riegl, conceptions of space (*Raumvorstellungen*) were the product of a conception of the world (*Weltvorstellung*) or artistic will (*Kunstwollen*). Thus, for example, in various unpublished brochures and lectures, Dorner identifies the German Romantic conception of space as a hybrid condition (*Zwitterzustand*), at once bound to – and struggling to free itself from – traditional Renaissance perspective. Early Romanticism attempted to explode the boundaries of perspective through extreme gaps between foreground and background (*überräumlicher Kontakt*) as well as the incorporation of displaced views into a single coherent image. The result – as evidenced not only in the paintings of Caspar David Friedrich and Erdmann Hummel but also in the panoramas, dioramas, and pleoramas of the period – initiated the breakdown of traditional perspective that would dominate art and visual culture until the end of Expressionism. Similarly, the widespread success of film as a medium can best be explained, according to Dorner, by its ability to satisfy a new conception of space, composed – like abstract art – not through linear perspective so much as immateriality, interpenetration, weightlessness, multi-perspectivalism, and dynamism.[60]

Dorner thus constructed a dialectical history in which art expressed changing rather than timeless ideals, partook in broad conceptions of the world, and advanced along a progressive, evolutionary course. Dorner, like Riegl or Panofsky, preferred not to stipulate that this dialectical change was powered by Hegel's dialectical spirit or *Geist*, but he left little doubt that, in Hegelian fashion, artistic will preceded the multifarious aesthetic expressions of an age, whether painting, music, pleorama, or film. Dorner's 'gigantic novel' of art history betrayed no fissures between the immateriality and dynamism in

Lissitzky's post-perspectival paintings and demonstration rooms, on the one hand, and Moholy-Nagy's dematerialised energy, on the other.[61] Had Dorner completed the 'Room of Our Time', however, his exhibition design would have told a different story.

In the Provincial Museum, Classicism was housed in a greenish-light-grey-blue room. The walls of the Romantic gallery were painted dark-greyish-violet tones. Impressionist paintings were set against a dirty white. In contradistinction to the Medieval, Renaissance, or Baroque rooms, Dorner offers no indication as to how these colours and forms convey the respective conceptions of space.[62] Panoramas, dioramas, and pleoramas are central to Dorner's history of Romantic art, but they are nowhere to be seen in the Romantic gallery. The Romantic conception of space as presented in the museum is an amorphous projection of modernist colour and form rather than a media archaeology of sites and conditions of reception. And yet the seeds of such an archaeology lay buried in Dorner's (verbal) narrative. Jonathan Crary completes the missing argument:

> Forms as seemingly different as Daguerre's Diorama, Wagner's theatre at Bayreuth, the Kaiserpanorama, the Kinetoscope and, of course, cinema as it took shape in the late 1890s are other [in addition to the panorama] key nineteenth-century examples of the image as an autonomous luminous screen of attraction, whose apparitional appeal is an effect of both its uncertain spatial location and its detachment from a broader visual field.[63]

Updated for the interwar period, this list might also include: Trolite rooms for the projection of slides, backlit endless bands for the exhibition of photographs, black and white cubic enclosures with circular openings for the reception of light in motion, a Total Theatre comprised of twelve synchronised projectors and 360 degrees of screens, and a darkened stage which highlights abstract, moving forms against a black backdrop. More than images, the 'Room of Our Time' exhibited and deployed media spaces. (Freed from the constraints of unique originals, Dorner planned to rotate the images regularly in the 'Room of Our Time'.) In this final atmosphere room, historical conceptions of space relayed through landmark paintings and modernist colour and form would have been superseded by technologically constructed spaces and interchangeable images that act on the body of the viewer. Well developed in nineteenth-century sites of attraction, media spaces would finally have arrived in the museum of art.[64]

We begin to see, then, that the embryonic 'Room of Our Time' would have necessitated a conceptual shift, putting pressure on older art-historical models. (And this is, perhaps, one reason why it could not be realised.) The shift from conceptions of space to technologically mediated spaces necessitates a methodological move from *Kunstwollen* to the *dispositif* and from Aloïs

Riegl to Michel Foucault. For Foucault, spatial conceptions and practices are a product of:

> a thoroughly heterogeneous ensemble consisting of discourses, institutions, architectural forms, regulatory decisions, laws, administrative measures, scientific statements, philosophical, moral and philanthropic propositions – in short, the said as much as the unsaid. Such are the elements of the [*dispositif*]. The [*dispositif*] itself is the system of relations that can be established between these elements.[65]

Such a shift is already present nascently in certain texts of the time. Thus, for example, Rudolf Harms's *Philosophie des Films*, published in 1926, often reads like a movie theatre operating manual. Harms is incapable of discussing 'spaceless darkness' or 'the cognitive ego' without also addressing comfortable seating and proper ventilation, sound insulation, and audience decorum. For it is the apparatus that constructs Harms's desired 'cognitive ego'. Dorner, too, was not above 'material needs' like comfortable sofas, seasonal heating, and so forth, but his conception of artistic development certainly hovered above the material constraints of a given era.[66] The heterogeneous ensemble of technologies, laws, architectures, mores, sciences, economies, and geographies that constituted the cinematic *dispositif* in the interwar period proves much firmer ground than an amorphous *Raumvorstellung* in an effort to recover the 'Room of Our Time' as part of a larger network of forces aimed at constructing the subject.

Only in this context does the signal import of spaceless darkness emerge. Spaceless darkness identifies a spectatorial condition in which the subject is disembodied; freed from the constraints of time, space, and gravity; hyper-focused on the luminous, moving image; disengaged from the local environment; isolated in a crowd; in short, immersed in a darkness so pervasive as to annihilate space itself. Thus spaceless darkness captures an essential aspect of modernity and its dominant visual culture. Equally important from the perspective of the interwar avant-garde, the subject position defined by spaceless darkness opens onto a set of formal parameters that can be manipulated, tested, inverted, and untethered from their strict power relations. Thus spaceless darkness – consistent, at least ideally, in each of its instantiations – initiates a seemingly infinite spectrum of light-spaces from glass architecture and theatres of steel and screens to avant-garde films and photographs. These light-spaces partake in the dominant cinematic *dispositif* but deflect its disciplinary forces in what Michel de Certeau, in a different Foucaldian context, has dubbed 'the network of an antidiscipline'.[67] As the culmination of Dorner's pedagogic history of art, the 'Room of Our Time' would have engaged visitors not (only) as passive and mobile field of 'enregistrement' – to return one final time to Jameson's phrase – but also as active participants in the intellectual and aesthetic realisation of myriad light-spaces. Intimated through documentation and implemented through diverse apparatuses, these light-spaces would have presented the power of the cinematic *dispositif* in an environment conducive to critical and historical reflection on the present.

In keeping with its strong proclivity toward Hegelian dialectics, the avant-garde's light-spaces offer a model which it is worthwhile to retrieve, of a dialectical sublation – a simultaneous abolishment and conservation – of the cinematic *dispositif* and its spaceless darkness, rather than a subversion or even *détournement*. Disembodiment, immateriality, weightlessness, and illusion were not conditions to be overcome but experiences to be mobilised toward new ends. This is evident not only in the architecture of Gropius and the divergent theatres of Piscator, Moholy-Nagy, and Schlemmer, but in the 'Room of Our Time' as well. The overall effect of the gallery is perhaps best articulated by Dorner in his later analysis of Herbert Bayer, whose wartime MoMA exhibitions were 'done not with heavy architectural elements of volume but with lights, flat and curved planes, transparent screens, suspended objects, anything that gives an atmosphere of lightness, bodilessness, and hence spacelessness'.[68] Once again: an architecture of steel and screens, disembodied spacelessness, the cinematic *dispositif* – only now not in darkness, but in light. Because light-space, like the 'Room of Our Time', was never fully concretised in the interwar period, it never suffered the fate of other failed avant-garde utopian ambitions. It remains the dialectical counterpart to the cinematic *dispositif*, engaging with – but never succumbing to – its normativising function. Walter Benjamin's discussion of architectural plans reproduced in the first volume of *Kunstwissenschaftliche Forschung*, an anthology of essays by Riegl's followers, applies perfectly well to the light-spaces assembled in the 'Room of Our Time': 'one cannot say that they *re*-produce architecture. They *produce* it in the first place, a production that less often benefits the reality of architectural planning than it does dreams.'[69] And yet the 'Room of Our Time' captured a very material – and, thus, typically modernist – form of dreaming. Neither completed nor utopian, the 'Room of Our Time' marks the stillbirth of the multi-media museum. But in its almost-realised state, it also captures the emergent centrality of mediatised spaces in the avant-garde art, architecture, photography, film, and theatre of the interbellum.

However dynamic, even a dialectic like that of light-space and spaceless darkness ultimately limits the potentialities of alternative aesthetic spaces within or outside the museum. In place of the singular or binary structures of Riegl, Dorner, or even Foucault, I will turn, in conclusion, to Gilles Deleuze, who, in answer to the question 'What is a *dispositif*?', envisions not a monolithic ideological apparatus, but a multi-linear ensemble composed of broken lines always subject to changes in direction. 'Visibility', he writes, 'cannot be traced back to a general source of light which could be said to fall upon pre-existing objects: it is made of lines of light which form variable shapes inseparable from the [*dispositif*] in question'.[70] Spaceless darkness was certainly the dominant *dispositif* of normative, interwar cinema; but it was not a black hole. Enough lines of light escaped to form the manifold practices promised – if unrealised – by the 'Room of Our Time'.

Notes

1 This essay is part of a book-length project on avant-garde photograms, film, and media architectures. I would like to thank Oliver Botar and Tamara Trodd for their meticulous edits and thoughtful suggestions to earlier drafts of this text and Ines Katenhusen for her scholarly generosity. Unless otherwise noted, all translations are mine.

2 Rudolf Harms, *Philosophie des Films* (Leipzig: Felix Meiner, 1926; reprint, 1970), p. 60.

3 Harms, *Philosophie des Films*, p. iii.

4 See, most famously, Jean-Louis Baudry, 'The apparatus: metapsychological approaches to the impression of reality in the cinema' (1975), reprinted in Philip Rosen (ed.), *Narrative, Apparatus, Ideology* (New York: Columbia University Press, 1986).

5 See especially Jörg Brauns, *Schauplätze: Zur Architektur visueller Medien* (Berlin: Kadmos, 2007). I develop the problem of 'spaceless darkness' and cinema architecture at greater length in my forthcoming book.

6 Fredric Jameson, 'Transformations of the image in postmodernity', in Jameson, *The Cultural Turn* (London: Verso, 1998), p. 112.

7 The 'Room of Our Time' has recently been (re)constructed stunningly by Kai-Uwe Hemken and Jakob Gebert, originally as part of the 'Kunst*Licht*Spiele' exhibition at the Kunsthalle in Erfurt (March to May 2009), before travelling to the Bauhaus in Dessau (June to October 2009) and the Schirn-Kunsthalle in Frankfurt (October 2009 to February 2010) and settling permanently in the Van Abbemuseum Eindhoven. See Ulrike Gärtner, Kai-Uwe Hemken, and Kai Uwe Schierz (eds), *KunstLichtSpiele* (Bielefeld: Kerber Verlag, 2009).

8 On the symmetrical salon style hanging, see Mary Anne Staniszewski, *The Power of Display* (Cambridge, Mass: MIT, 1998), pp. 16–17.

9 Aloïs Riegl, 'The main characteristics of the late Roman *Kunstwollen*' (1901), reprinted in Christopher S. Wood (ed.), *The Vienna School Reader* (Cambridge, Mass: MIT, 2003), p. 94.

10 Alexander Dorner, 'Die Erkenntnis des Kunstwollens durch die Kunstgeschichte', *Zeitschrift für Ästhetik und allgemeine Kunstwissenschaft*, 16 (1922), p. 222.

11 Erwin Panofsky, *Perspective as Symbolic Form* (1927), trans. Christopher S. Wood (New York: Zone Books, 1997), p. 34. See also Christopher Wood's introduction, p. 15.

12 Meyer Schapiro, 'The new Viennese school' (1936), reprinted in Wood (ed.), *The Vienna School Reader*, p. 462. See also Wood's brilliant elaboration of this insight in the introduction to the volume.

13 See El Lissitzky, 'Exhibition rooms' (c. 1926), in Sophie Lissitzky-Küppers (ed.), *El Lissitzky: Life, Letters, Texts* (London: Thames & Hudson, 1968).
14 See Siegfried Giedion, 'Lebendiges Museum', *Der Cicerone*, 21:4 (1929).
15 See Alexander Dorner, 'Die neue Raumvorstellung in der bildenden Kunst', *Museum der Gegenwart*, 2:1 (1931).
16 Maria Gough, 'Constructivism disoriented: El Lissitzky's Dresden and Hannover *Demonstrationsräume*', in Nancy Perloff and Brian Reed (eds), *Situating El Lissitzky* (Los Angeles: Getty Research Institute, 2003), pp. 108–9. Gough convincingly argues that Dorner's claim to a correspondence of space and works deviates radically from Lissitzky's own conception of the space. I will point to a second, equally pronounced deviation below.
17 Alexander Dorner, 'Three newly acquired paintings', *Bulletin of the Rhode Island School of Design*, 26:2 (1938), p. 10.
18 Dorner, 'Three newly acquired paintings', pp. 10–11. These phrases describe Lyonel Feininger's painting *The Church of Gelmerode* (1929), acquired by the Museum of the Rhode Island School of Design, where Dorner was recently installed as director.
19 El Lissitzky, 'K. und Pangeometrie', in Carl Einstein and Paul Westheim (eds), *Europa Almanach* (Potsdam: Gustav Kiepenheuer Verlag, 1925; reprint, 1993), p. 111. In one of the final footnotes to his essay on perspective, Panofsky dismisses Lissitzky's claim to imaginary space achieved through, for example, the traces of a glowing piece of coal in motion, as being no less Euclidean than any other space. Panofsky is not as harsh – or, at least, not as convinced of the error – vis-à-vis Lissitzky's claims on the 'intensive' creation of illusory space through juxtaposed colour surfaces in the works of Mondrian and Kasmir Malevich, i.e. the type of abstract works that would eventually hang in the Abstract Cabinet. See Panofsky, *Perspective as Symbolic Form*, pp. 153–54, n. 73.
20 Lissitzky, 'K. und Pangeometrie', p. 113. Dorner, to the contrary, championed unfettered immateriality.
21 Dorner, 'Die neue Raumvorstellung in der bildenden Kunst', p. 37. Cf. Alexander Dorner, 'Considérations sur la signification de l'art abstrait', *Cahiers d'art*, 6 (1931), p. 357.
22 See Siegfried Giedion, 'Der deutsche Werkbund in Paris', *Der Cicerone*, 22:15/16 (1920), pp. 430–31.
23 The precise content of the 'Room of Our Time' cannot be ascertained definitively. In addition to the above-mentioned catalogue, see Monika Flacke-Knoch, *Museumskonzeptionen in der Weimarer Republik. Die Tätigkeit Alexander Dorners im Provinizialmuseum Hannover* (Marburg Jonas Verlag, 1985), pp. 77–99; Sabine Lange, 'Der Raum der Gegenwart von László Moholy-Nagy', in Annette Kruszynski, Dirk Luckow, and Freya Mülhau (eds), *Museum der Gegenwart – Kunst in öffentlichen Sammlungen bis 1937* (Düsseldorf: Kunstsammlung Nordrhein-Westfalen, 1987); Alexander Dorner and László Moholy-Nagy, 'Briefwechsel zwischen Alexander Dorner und Moholy-Nagy', in *Malewitsch-Mondrian: Konstruktion als Konzept. Alexander Dorner Gewidmet* (Ludwigshafen am Rhein: Wilhelm-Hack-Museum, 1977); Joan Ockman, 'The road not taken: Alexander Dorner's way beyond art', in R. E. Somol (ed.), *Autonomy and Ideology* (New York: The Montacceli Press, 1997).

24 The controversy over the exhibition lingered for over a year and led to Dorner's exclusion from the International Museum Association. Erwin Panofsky, among others, weighed in on its implications. See Alexander Dorner, 'Das Lebensrecht des Faksimiles', *Beilage zum hannoverschen Kurier*, 264:65 (1929), and Erwin Panofsky, 'Original und Faksimilereproduktion', *Der Kreis*, 7:3 (1930). I develop this issue in my forthcoming book.

25 For details on the 'Room of Our Time', see Jakob Gebert and Kai-Uwe Hemken, 'Raum der Gegenwart: die Ordnung von Apparaten und Exponaten', in Gärtner, Hemken, and Schierz (eds), *KunstLichtSpiele*, and Flacke-Knoch, *Museumskonzeptionen in der Weimarer Republik*, pp. 77–99. My descriptions of the 'Room of Our Time' are derived from archival research and my direct impressions of the (re) construction as presented in the Bauhaus in Dessau, summer 2009.

26 This proposal was first made by Kai-Uwe Hemken, to whom I am indebted for sharing this research. The proposed gallery configuration is the first to account properly for the dimensions of the 'Room of Our Time' as well as the desired route through the museum.

27 For an elaboration of this thematic, see Ines Katenhusen, 'Alexander Dorners und László Moholy-Nagys "Raum der Gegenwart" im Provinzialmuseum Hannover', in Gärtner, Hemken, and Schierz (eds), *KunstLichtSpiele*.

28 For details regarding Piscator and Gropius's Total Theatre, see Stefan Woll, *Das Totaltheater: ein Projekt von Walter Gropius und Erwin Piscator* (Berlin: Gesellschaft für Theatergeschichte, 1984).

29 Walter Gropius, 'Vom modernen Theaterbaus, unter Berücksichtung des Piscatortheaterneubaus in Berlin', *Die Scene*, 18 (1928), p. 4.

30 Gropius, 'Vom modernen Theaterbaus', p. 5.

31 Gropius, 'Vom modernen Theaterbaus', p. 6.

32 'Piscator baut ein "Totaltheater"', *Berliner Herold*, 1927. See also 'Das Totaltheater von Gropius', *Filmtechnik*, 3:24 (1927).

33 László Moholy-Nagy, 'Theater, Zirkus, Varieté', in *Die Bühne im Bauhaus* (Berlin: Gebr. Mann Verlag, 1925; reprint, 2003).

34 The original essay was republished with minor typographic changes as László Moholy-Nagy, 'Wie soll das Theater der Totalität verwirklicht werden?', *Bauhaus*, 3 (1927). It was excerpted as 'Theater der Totalität', *Blätter der Staatsoper* (February 1929).

35 Bernhard Diebold, 'Opernzauber 1929' (1929), in Hans Curjel (ed.), *Experiment Krolloper, 1927–1931* (München: Prestel-Verlag, 1974), p. 266. Carl Spitzweg was a German Romantic painter; one of his more famous works depicts a poor poet in his derelict attic. Dr Mabuse was the eponymous protagonist of Fritz Lang's 1922 thriller *Dr Mabuse: The Gambler*, from which Moholy-Nagy reproduces a film still in *Painting, Photography, Film*.

36 Diebold, 'Opernzauber 1929'. The music critic Oscar Bie, largely critical of what he considered tyrannical Constructivist formalism, noted that the Venice of Act 2 is 'wholly dematerialised'. Oscar Bie, Untitled (1929), in Curjel (ed.), *Experiment Krolloper, 1927–1931*, p. 262.

37 Adolf Weißmann, 'Ein interessanter Opernabend' (1929), in Curjel (ed.), *Experiment Krolloper, 1927–1931*, p. 260.

38 László Moholy-Nagy, *Von Material zu Architektur* (Berlin: Gebr. Mann Verlag, 1929; reprint, 2001), p. 219. Caption to the photograph.

39 Diebold, 'Opernzauber 1929', p. 265.

40 For criticism from the right, see Johannes W. Harnisch, 'Verhöhntes Volk – gehöhnter Staat', *Berliner Lokal-Anzeiger* (8 September 1929); F. Reuter, 'Walter Mehring: Der Kaufmann von Berlin', *Kölnische Zeitung* (11 September 1929). For criticism of Mehring's anti-Semitism, see Hugo Kubsch, 'Der Kaufmann von Berlin', *Deutsche Tageszeitung* (7 September 1929). Piscator identified two fundamental weaknesses: the absence of the proletariat and the presence of anti-Semitism. See Erwin Piscator, *Das politische Theater* (1929) (Reinbek bei Hamburg: Rowolt Verlag, 1963), pp. 234–43.

41 Manfred Georg, 'Totaltheater der Inflation: Mehrings "Kaufmann von Berlin" bei Piscator', *Tempo* (8 September 1929).

42 Erwin Piscator, '"Totaltheater" (theatre of totality) and "totales theater" (total theatre)', *World Theatre*, 15:1 (1966), p. 5.

43 Erwin Piscator, 'Was ich will', *Berliner Tageblatt* (6 April, 1927).

44 Bernhard Diebold, 'Nie kam die Straße derart aufs Theatre' (1929), *Theatre Heute*, 10 (1979), p. 25. He continues: 'The space is "outside". The Dessau architect [sic] Moholy-Nagy, along with Piscator, invented it this way. It must be invented anew for each new piece. For it is a part of the drama; space has a distinct role: the street belongs to the traffic.'

45 Piscator, *Das politische Theater*, esp. p. 238.

46 László Moholy-Nagy, 'Das Problem des neuen Films: los von der Malerei!', *Bildwart*, 8:4 (1930), p. 152.

47 Piscator, *Das politische Theater*, p. 368.

48 Richter's earliest use of the terms appears to be in 1923. I develop Richter's relationship to *Lichtraum* in my forthcoming book.

49 László Moholy-Nagy, *Malerei, Photographie, Film* (München: Albert Langen, 1925), p. 16; my translation.

50 Richter and Moholy-Nagy's antagonistic relationship appears to have boiled over after Richter referred to Moholy-Nagy as a failed Constructivist who runs after the most fashionable trends. Hans Richter, 'An den Konstruktivismus', *G. Zeitschrift für elementare Gestaltung*, 3 (1924).

51 László Moholy-Nagy, 'Lichtrequisit einer elektrischen Bühne', *Die Form* 5:11/12 (1930).

52 László Moholy-Nagy, *The New Vision* (Mineola, New York: Dover, 1938; reprint, 2005), p. 141. The text, an extended caption, is italicised in the original.

53 Based on Moholy-Nagy's later assertions, the film is regularly dated to 1930. But there is no evidence that the film was completed before 1932, the year it was first screened. The film censor report is dated 4 March 1932, the date of the film's première. The most direct evidence that the film was completed that year lies in an editorial comment inserted into Moholy-Nagy's 1932 essay 'Probleme des neuen Films'. Moholy-Nagy describes the *Light-Prop* and writes that '[m]y plan is now to extend this work into film, not as a reproduction of the machinery and of the light effects, but rather to render it [the *Light-Prop*] cinematically'. The editors then

introduce a parenthetical remark: '(In the meantime, Moholy-Nagy has completed this film with the help of AGFA and AEG. "Lichtspiel schwartz-weiss-grau").' Moholy-Nagy, 'Probleme des neuen Films', *Die Form*, 7:5 (1932), p. 158.

54 Parenthetical editorial note appended to a talk published in Hungarian in *Korunk* and translated as László Moholy-Nagy, 'Neue Filmexperimente' (1933), in Krisztina Passuth (ed.), *Moholy-Nagy* (Weingarten: Kunstverlag Weingarten, 1986), p. 336. *Korunk* was edited at this time by Gábor Gaál.

55 See Sibyl Moholy-Nagy, *Moholy-Nagy: Experiment in Totality* (Cambridge, Mass.: MIT Press, 2nd edition, 1969), pp. 64–66.

56 Moholy-Nagy, 'Neue Filmexperimente', pp. 334–35.

57 See Oskar Schlemmer, 'Mensch und Kunstfigur', in Oskar Schlemmer, László Moholy-Nagy, and Farkas Molnár (eds), *Die Bühne im Bauhaus* (Berlin: Gebr. Mann Verlag, 1925; reprint, 2003), p. 22. See also Dirk Scheper, *Oskar Schlemmer: das triadische Ballett und die Bauhausbühne* (Berlin: Akademie der Künste, 1988), pp. 33–53, and Friederike Zimmermann, *'Mensch und Kunstfigur': Oskar Schlemmers intermediale Programmatik* (Freiburg: Rombach, 2007), pp. 167–88.

58 See Schlemmer, 'Mensch und Kunstfigur'.

59 'Aus dem Vorwort für einen Katalog des Provinzial-Museums' (c. early 1930s), in Henning Rischbieter (ed.), *Die zwanziger Jahre in Hannover* (Hannover: Kunstverein Hannover, 1962). The unsigned entry was either written by Dorner or under his influence; it bears all the traces of his thinking.

60 See, for example, Alexander Dorner, 'Die Grundlagen unserer Raumvorstellung', c. 1933–34, in the Alexander Dorner Papers, Busch-Reisinger Museum.

61 Upon arrival in America, one of Dorner's preferred metaphors for a well-told history of art was the 'gigantic novel'. See, for example, Alexander Dorner, 'My experiences in the Hanover Museum: what can art museums do today?', Alexander Dorner Papers, Busch-Reisinger Museum.

62 See Dorner, 'My experiences in the Hanover Museum', p. 16.

63 Jonathan Crary, 'Géricault, the panorama, and sites of reality in the early nineteenth century', *Grey Room*, 9 (2002), p. 19.

64 In the larger scheme of the Hanover Provincial Museum, Lissitzky's Abstract Cabinet would have functioned not only as 'the transfer station from painting to architecture' – as he famously described the *Proun* abstract painting which hung in the room – but as the transfer station from painting to *media* architecture, that is, from canvases to screens and screen spaces. El Lissitzky and Hans Arp, *Die Kunstismen* (Rolandseck: L. Müller, 1925; reprint, 1990), p. 9.

65 Michel Foucault, 'The confessions of the flesh', in Foucault, *Power/Knowledge: Selected Interviews and Other Writings, 1972–1977*, ed. Colin Gordon (New York: Pantheon Books, 1980), p. 194. Where Riegl introduced the notion of artistic will largely in order to overthrow the supremacy of mechanistic explanation advanced by Gottfried Semper, Foucault's conception of the *dispositif* provides a material approach without forsaking broader explanatory power or a certain 'objective' or 'anonymous' quality (related, in some respects, to what Heinrich Wölfflin famously dubbed 'an art history without names').

66 See, for example, Dorner, 'Was sollen jetzt Kunstmuseen?', 1928, in the Alexander

Dorner Papers, Busch-Reisinger Museum, p. 9.

67 Michel de Certeau, *The Practice of Everyday Life*, trans. Steven Rendall (Berkeley: University of California Press, 1984), p. xv.

68 Alexander Dorner, *The Way Beyond 'Art' – The Work of Herbert Bayer* (New York: Wittenborn, Schultz, 1947), p. 215.

69 Walter Benjamin, 'Rigorous study of art: on the first volume of *Kunstwissenschaftliche Forschung*' (1931/1933), reprinted in Wood (ed.), *The Vienna School Reader*, p. 444.

70 Gilles Deleuze, 'What is a *dispositif*?', in *Michel Foucault: Philosopher* (New York: Harvester Wheatsheaf, 1992), p. 160.

2 'Festival' and 'museum' in modernist film histories[1]

Maxa Zoller

How has the history of artists' film been written? Through an emphasis on what kinds of spaces? In this essay I propose to examine the history of writing about artists' film through a focus on specific case-studies representing different kinds of historical presentation of film and the reception these received. Through my account the canonical place afforded to 'structural' film will be modified and 'Expanded cinema' will be restored to the more significant place it historically occupied. In tandem with this shift, and instrumental for it, the theoretical model of the 'festival' will be used to inflect and change what is currently a museum-centred construction of the history of artists' film. My analysis will thus enter the expanded zone of experimental film projection, which is a space of constant change and experiment.

Unlike traditional artforms such as painting and sculpture, which are solidly rooted within the frame of the post-Enlightenment 'high art' museum, the context of presentation of experimental film is far more heterogeneous: it is 'at home' in mainstream cinemas, in festivals, the film co-op and in the modern art gallery and it can therefore be defined as painterly, sculptural, and environmental. This heterogeneity, whilst it has been critically neglected, is not new: Ludwig Hirschfeld-Mack's 1920s *Reflecting Light Plays*, for instance, were presented as environmental theatre design and as cinematic single screen projections; René Clair's *Entr'acte* (1924), today considered one of the first examples of avant-garde film, was originally shown as part of a Dada ballet performance. Recently, digital technology has introduced a new paradigm shift in film viewing, making films available on the internet on computers, laptops, and mobile phones. This shift, I suggest, makes more urgent a critical return to and recovery of earlier avant-garde paradigms of Expanded cinema.

It is often assumed that time-based media such as film, video, and performance entered the gallery space in the 1960s, when 'institutional critique' challenged the traditional role of the museum. This approach is based on an old-fashioned notion of the avant-garde, which 'conquers the enemy', that is, the institution. This essay seeks to demonstrate conversely that the institution is never a static, unchanging 'enemy' but like art is always in flux, mutating and changing according to wider political and socio-economic shifts. My approach will look at film art as a product of its spatial circumstances, rather than as the autonomous 'brainchild' of an individual filmmaker. Two very different forms of film institution, the festival and the museum, will be examined. First, the 'festival' will be represented by an analysis of the 1967–68 *Exprmntl 4* film festival, which proposed an unorthodox mode of film presentation later named 'Expanded cinema'.[2] Second, the exhibition, *Film als Film: 1910 bis Heute*, which opened at the Cologne Kunstverein in 1977, will be compared to its British version, *Film As Film: Formal Experiment in Film, 1910–1975*, at the Hayward Gallery in 1979, in order to tease out the kind of framework imposed on film by the 'museum'. Finally I will consider the politics of the new, expanded, postmodern museum-space (what Rosalind Krauss has called the 'late capitalist museum').[3] Exploring different modes of film exhibition, this essay will explore the way in which the institutional space affects the mode of film presentation, and by extension the theoretical discourse around art and film.

The film festival: *Exprmntl 4*

After the Second World War there was a general revival of the festival, the international and open nature of which provided an appropriate platform for a society whose hierarchies and values had shifted dramatically. In his 1953 article 'A propos de Cannes', the French film historian and theorist André Bazin emphasised the celebratory and ritualistic aspect of film festivals, the 'Fiestas cinématographiques', which were part of 'the cinematographic calendar like the seasons and public holidays'.[4] Highlighting one of the most important original functions of the festival, the celebration of the seasons, Bazin's text is an indication of the postwar return to the pagan tradition of communal rites. Postwar art consumption was not restricted to an educated class any more, but had become a tool to restore national identity and international relations.

In what follows I will focus on the experimental film festival *Exprmntl*, which was fundamental in the birth of a European underground film scene. The *Exprmntl* festival series developed out of the Festival Mondial du Film et des Beaux Arts, which took place in December 1947 at the Brussels Palais des Beaux Arts. It was an interdisciplinary event and included an avant-garde film programme, an art exhibition, and conferences. This cross-disciplinary approach became a characteristic of the *Exprmntl* festivals; which held a particularly important place in European film culture particularly after the Oberhausen Film Festival blocked the exhibition of radical experimental films in 1967.[5]

1967 was the year of the fourth festival in the series, the now-legendary *Exprmntl 4*, which is often referred to as the birthplace of the European experimental film movement. Although this assumption might be questionable, it cannot be denied that *Exprmntl 4* had a profound impact on the international experimental film scene. Taking place on the brink of the 1968 student revolution, the festival provided European filmmakers with a unique opportunity collectively to explore and challenge the conventions of 'bourgeois' cinema. What made *Exprmntl 4* so exceptional, in addition to its markedly varied and inter-media programme, was the sheer amount of visitors (the festival attracted around 2,000–3,000 people), who within a few days witnessed new and radical standards for experimental film production paving the way for a new European counterculture.

Exprmntl 4 took place between 16 December 1967 and 1 January 1968 in the Belgian seaside resort of Knokke-le-Zout, a 'closed world, completely isolated from the outside', an 'island, a sort of bubble'.[6] While *Exprmntl 4* has often been referred to as a structural film festival, a close look at the film programme reveals that the works were in fact extremely heterogeneous.[7] A few titles suffice to give an impression of the festival's diversity. The programme included, amongst others: Stephen Dwoskin's *Soliloquy* (1967), Paul Sharits's *Piece Mandela/End War* (1966), Ernst Schmidt's *Bodybuilding* (1965), Wilhelm and Birgit Hein's *S&W* (1967), Patrick Hella's *Les Caméleons* (1967), Werner Nekes's *Schwarzhuhnbraunhuhnschwarzhuhnweisshuhnrothuhnweiss oder put-put* (1967), David McNeil's *Week-end* (1967), Roland Lethem's *Les Souffrances d'un Oeuf Meurtri* (1967), Lutz Mommartz's *Selbstschüsse* (1967), Robert Nelson's *Grateful Dead* (1967), Martial Raysse's *Portrait Electro-Machin-Chose* (1967), George Kuchar's *Color Me Shameless* (1967), Klaus Schönherr's *Thaler's Meier's, Sadkowsky's Life in the Evening* (1967), Martin Scorsese's *The Big Shave* (1967), Gregory J. Markopoulos's *The Illiac Passion* (1967), Antonio De Bernardi and Paolo Menzio's *Il Mostro Verde* (1967), and Michael Snow's *Wavelength* (1967), which won the first prize.

The fact that Snow's *Wavelength* won first prize at this festival, and that it shortly afterwards received unusually sustained critical attention from influential American film critics Annette Michelson and P. Adams Sitney, has tended to skew perception of the festival itself as predominantly an event showcasing 'structural' film.[8] In fact, as the list I have given above indicates, and as I shall go on to show, *Exprmntl 4* was a far more diverse affair, and the model it represents, of the nature of artists' film as radically experimental, in dialogue with a range of artistic models rather than in search of any filmic 'specificity', supports an understanding of the festival which is far from the modernist critical paradigm.

Exprmntl 4 was also a magnet for political demonstrations. The French art magazine *Beaux Arts* painted a vivid picture of the festival. It described the filmmakers' 'seizure' of the foyer:

> They were dressed in animal skins and enormous greatcoats, with an indispensable cascade of watch chains and necklaces falling down their chests. They had just-out-of-bed hair, a frogged jacket and black glasses 'à la Mozart' … and, on top of it all, the air of those who want to impress at any rate but cannot be impressed anymore … They have taken over this poor casino, the meeting place of Belgian bourgeoisie, a palace of luxury and wealth, and made it their domain – that is, a domain of crazy people. One could see them everywhere: camping on the stairs, lying around on the carpet, distracting themselves at the bar.[9]

According to the scholar Xavier Garcia Bardon, the German student group SDS (Sozialistischer Deutscher Studentenverbund) was also a main source of political demonstrations (figure 2.1). The SDS included members of the future terrorist group, RAF (Rote Armee Faktion), one of whom was Holger Meins, who attended the festival together with the political filmmaker Harun Farocki.[10] The spontaneous demonstrations, anti-US posters, and leaflets of the SDS became as much part of the festival as the screenings and performances. (Sample slogans included 'Every metre of film showing a naked ass out of the metropoles keeps silence about a burned body in Vietnam!', 'Pas de realité sans

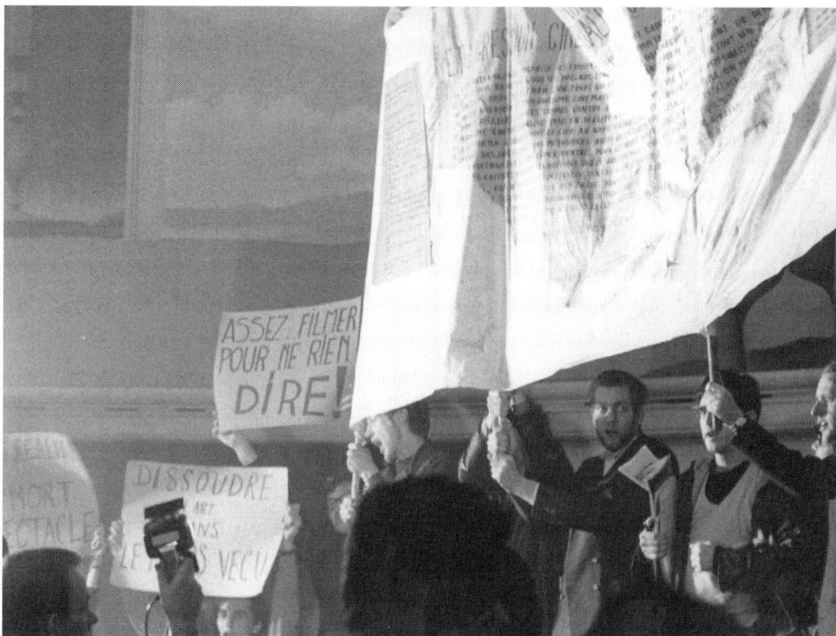

2.1 Demonstration of German students (SDS) at *Exprmntl 4*, 1967–68. Photograph by Virginia Leirens. © Fondation Henri Storck. Courtesy of Cinémathèque Royale de Belgique.

la mort du Spectacle!' (No reality without the death of the spectacle!)). During the screening of Wolfgang Ramsbott's *Der weisse Hopfengarten* (1966), several SDS members went on stage and paraded in front of the audience miming Vietnam soldiers. An alleged torture scene in Koji Wakamatsu's *The Embryo* (1966) was interrupted by forty SDS activists, who built a human pyramid in front of the screen (figure 2.2).[11]

At *Exprmntl 4* politics and the breach of sexual taboos went hand in hand. There were several performances involving nudity, which led to numerous arrests, such as *Mascheroen*, a provocative theatre piece by Hugo Claus.[12] Another popular 'happening' was performed by the French 'father' of performance Jean-Jaques Lebel, who organised a beauty contest in front of the festival selection jury members. Pointing the finger at the committee's conservative notion of beauty, the 'Miss Experimentation' presented a '*defilé*' of naked filmmakers and artists, including Yoko Ono. This 'atmosphère bouillonnante' was described accurately by Lebel, who noted that 'we felt that something was burning and we did everything [we could] to make it explode, without knowing what it was, intuitively'.[13] *Exprmntl 4* was a symptom of the approaching student revolution, a 'rehearsal for the year 1968', according to the Austrian filmmaker Hans Scheugl.[14]

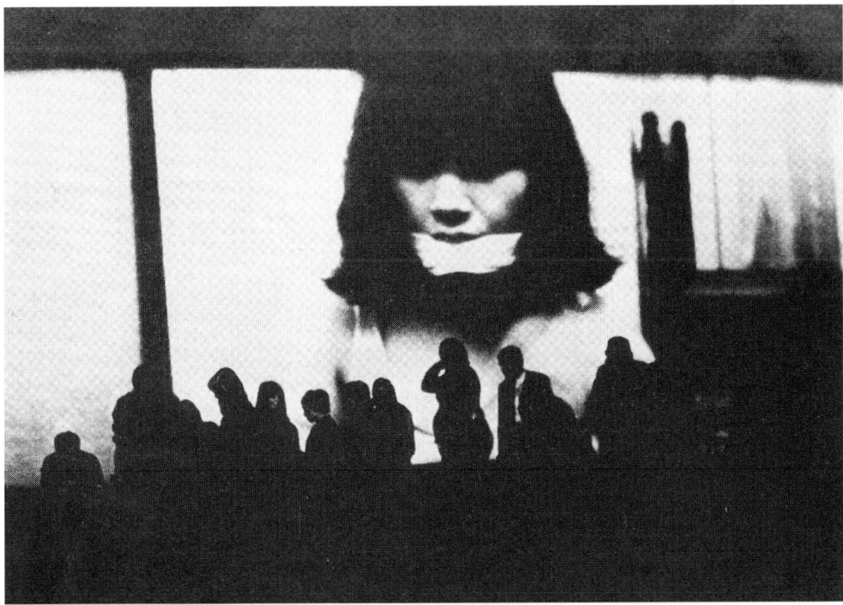

2.2 German students (SDS) boycott the screening of Koji Wakamatsu's *The Embryo* (1966) at *Exprmntl 4*, 1967–68. Photograph by Virginia Leirens. © Fondation Henri Storck. Courtesy of Cinémathèque Royale de Belgique.

Demonstrations, happenings, and a generally very open atmosphere at *Exprmntl* transformed the casino into what we might call an 'all arts space'. In a newspaper review, the German filmmaker Wim Wenders described the atmosphere:

> The 'festivaliers' literally occupied the foyer, spreading their furs. One produces music of the spheres by means of a metal spring, which he has stretched over a glass basin. Another rubs the strings of a guitar with a bracelet. Now and then some go to the cinema. Enough space has been left in front of the first row so that followers of a close-to-the-ground life-style can spread their furs.[15]

Wenders's eyewitness report illustrates that the festival grew out of the cinema space and spread into the entire casino, and even beyond the casino building.[16] Essentially, there were two spaces of action: the theatre and the foyer entrance. The theatre served as a cinema, the official space of film presentation 'en competition'.[17] Here, the dominant mode of presentation was the single screen projection.[18] The performances and Expanded cinema events took place in the festival foyer, which was an open, flexible, and spontaneous platform for 'hors competition' works. The grand round foyer was slightly lowered into the ground, resembling an amphitheatre, and was located centrally in the building. The first-floor balustrade served as 'balcony seats' with a good view onto the foyer. One of the most popular events in the foyer was the *Movie Movie*, which, despite its name, was a gigantic balloon-like inflatable PVC structure, developed by Theo Botschuijver, Jeffrey Shaw, and Sean Wellesley-Hiller of the Eventstructure Research Group. Part art, part entertainment, the *Movie Movie* became a multifunctional sculpture. Scheugl described it as 'a giant plastic balloon, which was divided by a white floor, on which naked bodies moved as if on waves and onto which slides were projected'.[19] The *Movie Movie* also served as projection screen for Jonathan Latham's abstract, colourful animation film *Speak* (1962).

Another popular event in the foyer was Wim van der Linden's 1967 film performance *Hawaiian Lullaby*. It began with the screening of a long list of tongue-in-cheek opening credits and then opened up to a full-moon seaside scene. Finally, a topless female performer started to dance in front of the screen, thus combining live performance with what it seems appropriate to call the filmic 'event'.[20] Another event which combined live performance with film and which took place in the foyer was the performance *Black Bag Piece* by the Fluxus artist Yoko Ono, which consisted of the artist lying in a plastic bag for several hours, while, next to this performance, Ono presented her 1966 *Film No. 4*, which was a humorous take on the idea of the nude. The film shows a close-up of naked walking bottoms. The lines and creases of the individual behinds divide the film frame into four, neat square sections. The foyer space was thus an open, flexible, heterogeneous space where Expanded cinema experiments blended into political manifestations and vice versa.

This demonstrates the interdependence of the space of exhibition and the mode of film presentation. While the single-screen 'en competition' films were presented in the theatre space, the foyer enabled a new form of experimental film practice, one that was spatial, sculptural, spontaneous, performative, and participatory. Most importantly, the film apparatus became part of the film event. The screen turned into an active space (for example, as in the inflatable screen of *Movie Movie* or the silver foil of Verdonk's *The New Electric Cinema*), and the projector became part of the projection (as in Ono's *Film No. 1*). The direct and physical encounter with the apparatus broke down the barrier between work of art and audience. The resultant participatory and sensory aesthetic was symptomatic of an emerging interaction between the technological apparatus and the body in the arts. This 'activist', 'involved' body was incorporated into a media environment in the open space of the foyer.[21]

Thus it can be argued that the experimental film festival *Exprmntl 4* was nurtured by a much broader culture-scape than previously presumed. One of the reasons for the recurrent misreading of this event, I suggest, is the lack of a rigorous theorisation of the festival itself as a type of exhibition space. Unlike the museum or the cinema, the history of the film festival has not yet been examined theoretically. To explore this issue in detail would exceed the frame of this essay; however, steps towards a theorisation of the festival may be taken by drawing on remarks by Michel Foucault. Foucault has described the museum as a modern encyclopedia, where static objects represent the idea of time as 'eternal'. Contrary to the museum, he suggests, the 'festival' represents the idea of the '*chronique*', the 'temporal'. He notes that:

> Opposite these heterotopias that are linked to the accumulation of time, there are those linked, on the contrary, to time in its most flowing, transitory, precarious aspect, to time in the mode of the festival [*fête*]. These heterotopias are not oriented toward the eternal, they are rather absolutely temporal [*chroniques*]. Such, for example, are the fairgrounds, these marvellous empty sites on the outskirts of cities that teem once or twice a year with stands, displays, heteroclite objects, wrestlers, snake-women, fortune-tellers, and so forth.[22]

We have seen the intermittent and 'teeming' temporal character of the festival as described here instantiated in my discussion of *Exprmntl 4*. What these specific temporal and spatial conditions mean for the display of artists' film and video in the museum I shall now go on to show.

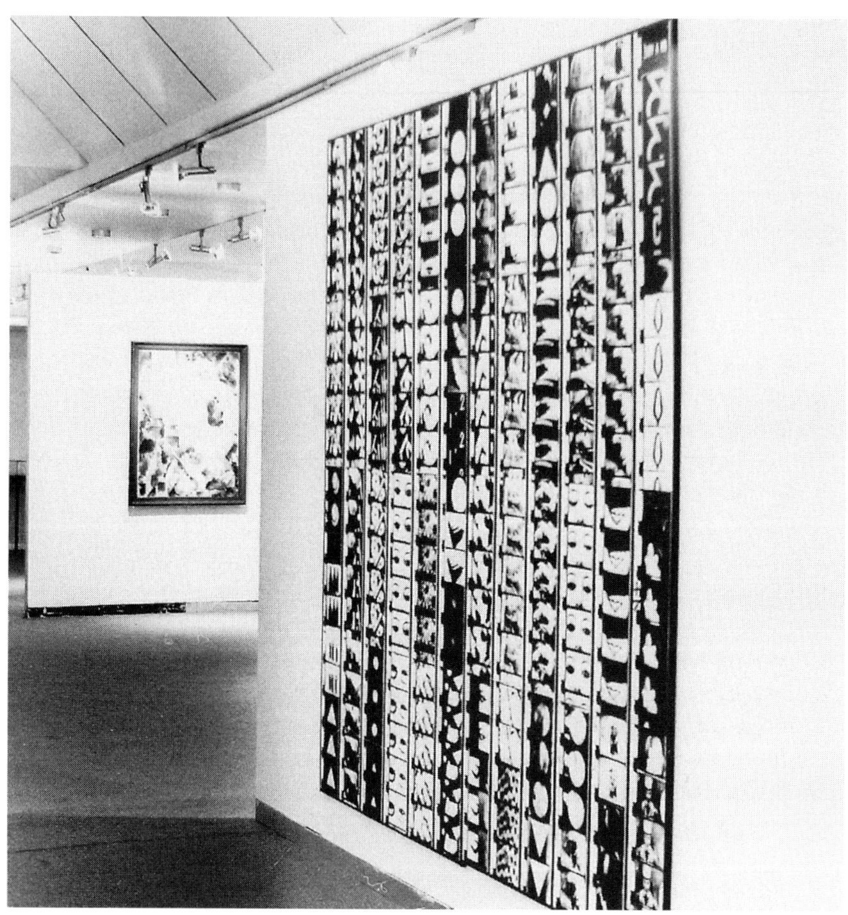

2.3 Installation photograph of *Film als Film: 1910 bis Heute*, Cologne Kunstverein, 1977, showing Fernand Léger and Dudley Murphy's *Ballet Mécanique* (1924) presented in enlarged film stills. © Rainer Hoeft. Courtesy of Historisches Stadtarchiv Köln, reference number 1686 and 1386.

The modernist film exhibition: *Film als Film: 1910 bis Heute*, Cologne, 1977

The 1970s were marked by an increasingly scholarly approach to experimental film history; a number of groundbreaking books, publications, conferences, and exhibitions emphasised and spread the 'academicisation' of film, which also included a major increase in teaching the film canon in art schools. One of the most, if not *the* most ambitious experimental film exhibition was *Film als Film*, which was curated by the German filmmaker Birgit Hein and Wulf Herzogenrath, then director of the Cologne Kunstverein, where the exhibition took place between 25 November 1977 and 15 January 1978.[23] This exhibition was a unique attempt to present a survey of the history of experimental film from its beginning in the early twentieth century to the 1970s. Discursively, *Film als Film*, operated on a primarily didactic level. Following the path set down previously by the writings of primarily British, American, and German-speaking academics, filmmakers, and researchers, the exhibition drew a clear historical lineage from formal European experiments of the 1920s through postwar, West Coast American and European structural film and concluded with the Expanded cinema movement.[24] Excluding the Surrealist film and other not strictly 'formal' movements (such as the 1930s documentary film movement), it represented an essentially modernist avant-garde canon, which focused on Greenbergian concepts of medium self-reflexivity, 'essentialism', and abstraction. The idea of an 'evolution' was set within a frame of logical progression, whereby each style successively led to the next.

My purpose in this essay, however, is to challenge the idea thus established in *Film als Film* of experimental film history as a 'tidy' historical trajectory. While my discussion of *Exprmntl 4* has demonstrated that the concept of a clear-cut and 'pure' modernist film practice in the 1960s is a problematic, if not flawed generalisation, *Film als Film* was one of the original sources of this view of that decade. The exhibition offered a fixed system of aesthetic influences, national styles, and a 'convenient' periodisation ('the 1920s, the 1960s', etc.). While the effort of the curators of *Film als Film* should not be underestimated (as the first major survey exhibition in Europe *Film als Film* made available an unprecedented amount of important film works), the exhibition presented a highly stylised version of the experimental film canon.

From a curatorial point of view, *Film als Film* had to surmount a major challenge. It was the first large-scale exhibition to grapple with the problem of how to present film in the museum, especially since the technical and spatial limitations of the Cologne Kunstverein could not accommodate simultaneous projections of the films. A solution was found by presenting a series of photographs of still film frames. In the first part of the exhibition, which focused on the abstract avant-garde experiments of the 1920s, Viking Eggeling's *Diagonalsymphonie* (1924), Fernand Léger's and Dudley Murphy's *Ballet Mécanique* (1924), and Man Ray's Dada films including his *Retour à la Raison* (1923), as well as the *Emak Bakia* (1927) were presented in the form of photographically enlarged, black-and-white film frame sequences attached to panels which covered large parts of the gallery walls (figure 2.3). This part of the exhibition also presented drawings and sketches, artists' books, small sculptures, and a few paintings by Man Ray, Walter Ruttmann, Marcel Duchamp, and a number of Bauhaus artists. The prewar avant-garde section was followed by a display of drawings and photographs of the graphic and psychedelic experiments from 1940s American West Coast artists, such as the Whitney Brothers, Jordan Belson, and Harry Smith.

Advancing further into the postwar period, the exhibition's mode of presentation changed. The final part of the show presented Expanded cinema works, participatory film installations, and film sculptures, such as Andy Warhol's 1964 *Kiss*, which consisted of enlarged film-frames pressed between thick sheets of Plexiglas. Another highlight was Paul Sharits's 'free-floating' celluloid sculpture: three thin Plexiglas panels of his 1968 flicker film *N.O.T.H.I.N.G.* were suspended in the middle of the gallery, so visitors were able to walk around the 'film', experiencing it 'three-dimensionally'. The Austrian filmmaker Kurt Kren presented enlarged frames of his 1960 film *48 Köpfe aus dem Szondi Test* together with the original photographs of the Szondi Test, whilst in a separate room, Valie Export and Peter Weibel showed their 1969 installation *Das Magische Auge* (The Magical Eye), and props of their well-known 1968 performance *Tapp- und Tastkino*.[25] In a separate room, Taka Imura presented *1 Second and* ∞ (1975), a double-loop film installation, which was running throughout the exhibition period.

Whilst these sculptural forms of presentation might seem to propose a physicalised, expanded model of film consonant with the kind of Expanded cinema practices I earlier analysed in my account of the film festival *Exprmntl 4*, I want to argue by contrast that it in fact, in part perhaps inadvertently, but in part deliberately, imposed a modernist, medium-specific construction of the filmic work. My argument here hinges on the use made by the exhibition's curators of blown-up, framed, and wall-mounted film-*stills*, a technique which in effect reduced film to its material 'essence' in the still, photographic image. Thus, instead of showing experimental film in its original format, that is the collectively received, projected sound-film, film had to be literally 'stopped' and 'framed' in order to 'fit' into the museum. The problem with *Film als Film* was that it did not *present*, but *re*presented film. Unlike other film exhibitions such as the 1974 *Projected Images* at the Walker Art Center curated by Martin Friedman, or the 1976 *Expanded Cinema Festival* at the Institute for Contemporary Art in London, which presented original film installations in the gallery space, *Film als Film*'s inability to present film in its authentic format led to the *re*presentation of film through stills.

One of the exhibition's original curators, Birgit Hein, claims that *Film als Film* was the first exhibition to use the technique of frame enlargements. In an interview with me, she has described the frames at *Film als Film* as merely a 'didactic help'.[26] This statement, however, requires further investigation. The first use of frame enlargements can be found in art journals of the 1920s, such as *G*, *De Stijl*, and *Form*. Werner Graeff, for instance, published individual frames of his film *Filmpartitur* in *De Stijl* in 1923. Theo van Doesburg's seminal article 'Film as pure form' featured frame-by-frame reproductions of Léger's *Ballet Mécanique*, Richter's *Filmstudie*, Eggeling's *Diagonalsymphonie*, and Moholy-Nagy's *Mirakel (Hoffmanns Erzählungen)*. One of the first film exhibitions to present frame enlargements was the 1929 *Film und Foto Ausstellung* (*FiFo*). El Lissitzky and his wife Sophie Lissitzky-Küppers, who were in charge of the Soviet section of the exhibition, presented enlarged stills of well-known Soviet films. Also, Henri Langlois's various film exhibitions at the Musée d'Art Moderne and the Musée du Cinéma used large photographic stills.[27] However, the frame enlargements at *Film als Film* operated in a different way. While Langlois's large-scale stills presented a certain film scene, for example, *Film als Film* enlarged entire filmstrips in order to disclose to the viewer the mechanism of film technology, the perceptual illusionism of the 'persistence of vision', or, as Hein simply put it, 'so that you could see the movement'. The one-by-one frame sequences were an illustration of film's inherent structure. The consequence of this, I want to argue, is that the panels did not only serve pedagogic purposes but instead contributed to developing a modernist idea of filmic medium-specificity.

Thus, while *Film als Film* made underground film accessible to a wider audience, it also deprived the audience of the original experience of the work, limiting it to photographic reproductions. The films themselves as moving images had to be 'imagined'. By my use of this phrase I mean to suggest a deliberate parallel with the notion of the 'imaginary art work', an idea which was first coined in André Malraux's 1947 essay '*Le Musée imaginaire*'.[28] In this groundbreaking text, Malraux, then the culture minister of postwar France, argued that the photographic reproducibility of works of art made possible their virtual and simultaneous presence in the spectator's mind. This mental space, for Malraux, was the imaginary museum or, as the English translation has it, a 'museum without walls'. *Film als Film* created such an imaginary museum; the numerous photographic reproductions of the film frames gave the visitor an idea of the original artwork. However, while Malraux's imaginary museum was born out of a utopian belief in the progressive potential of photography, the 'imaginary films' at *Film als Film* only presented a makeshift solution to the problem of the film exhibition.[29] These frame enlargement panels presented *pre-selected* and *partial* 'imaginary films'. This form of displacement of film from the cinema, the underground festival, and the film co-operative into the taxonomic system of the museum only *pretended* to enable access to the works of art. Paradoxically, the attempt to present the very 'essence' of the medium denied the visitor access to it.

Furthermore, *Film als Film* preserved the historical functions of the museum to preserve the national cultural heritage and to educate its audience. The show paralleled the museum's imperative to display its art objects to the visitor in such a way as to produce (a constructed system of) 'knowledge'. In this vein, *Film als Film* replaced disorder with order, effacing any disruptive counter-developments in film's history, such as Surrealism and Conceptualism. This display was rooted in the museum's *systematic* approach to culture.

Experimental film history was compartmentalised, categorised, and classified. It was *included* in the field of formalism and *excluded* from practices of figuration and narration.

The exhibition also presented drawings, objects, and props in glass frames or inside vitrines, but these placed film within the 'do-not-touch' elitism of the museum. Thus, whereas for the avant-garde cultural theorist Walter Benjamin, for example, the feature film was a 'medium of the masses', an essentially democratic medium, which could be controlled from 'bottom-up' rather than from 'top-down', the exhibition *Film als Film* reversed this theory by presenting film within the framework of the modern art museum, which propagated the idea of the unique work of art.[30] In isolating the film medium from the influence of popular culture, and denying corporate control over it, the exhibition sought to give film political, social, and cultural autonomy. However, we might easily think instead that the mode of presentation for *Film als Film*, in fact *re-fetishised* film, returning it to a discourse of commodification. The exhibition re-inscribed an 'aura' around film through the presentation of film as a singular, unique work of art. It displaced experimental film from the underground, inserting it into the 'high art' valuation process of the museum system.

The postmodern film exhibition: *Film as Film: Formal Experiment in Film, 1910–1975*, Hayward Gallery, 1979

My third case-study, *Film as Film: Formal Experiment in Film 1910–1975*, was the re-presentation of the Cologne show which was installed at the Hayward Gallery from 3 May to 17 June 1979 (figure 2.4). The exhibition was curated by the film historian and Arts Council member David Curtis, together with Richard Francis, curator at the Hayward Gallery, and was supported by a special committee, which included Simon Field, Philip Drummond, Malcolm Le Grice, Birgit Hein, and the film historian A. L. Rees.[31] It was accompanied by an importantly revised version of the catalogue which had accompanied the Cologne exhibition.[32]

The Hayward exhibition layout was so different that *Film as Film* could easily have been mistaken for another show. While the Cologne exhibition was marked by a distanced, historical approach to experimental film, the British curators transformed the entire museum space into a cinematic 'black box' and replaced the scientific style of the Cologne exhibition with a more flexible, cross-referential and playful mode of presentation. This was made possible by a new and exceptional exhibition design: by means of the latest high-tech technology, the entire gallery was darkened and several large screens were suspended from the gallery ceiling. This enabled the continuous projection of films, a vital contrast to the Cologne show. Fischinger's *Kreise*, for example,

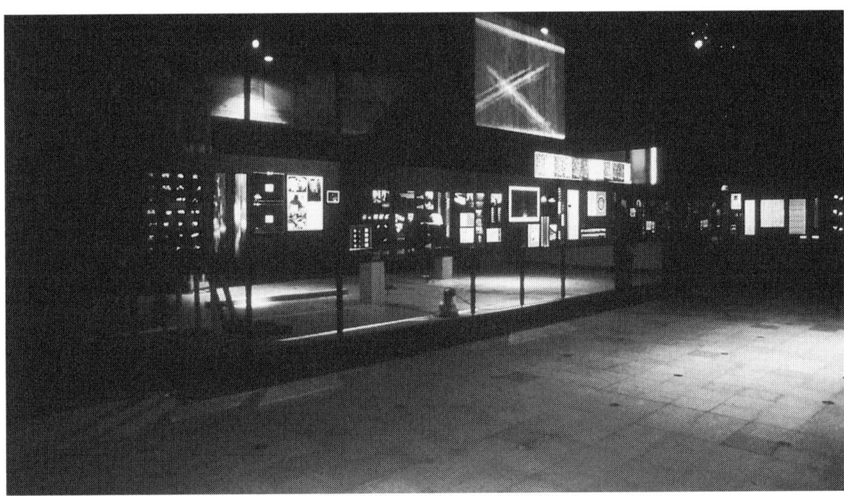

Installation photograph of *Film as Film: Formal Experiment in Film, 1910–1975*, Hayward Gallery, London, 1979, showing large mirror. Courtesy of Arts Council Archive, reference ACGB/56/34. 2.4

'towered' above the 1930s section and a large film projection of Landow's *Film in Which There Appear Edge Lettering, Sprocket Holes, Dirt Particles, Etc.* (1966) was suspended at the centre of the exhibition space, so that it could be seen from any vantage point. Individual sharp spotlights highlighted the objects, glass cases, and photo panels.[33] This exceptional exhibition design enabled the viewer to engage simultaneously with the film projections as well as the objects on display.

These new forms of display sought to accommodate the specificity of the medium within the museum context. It created a new 'hybrid' exhibition format, replacing the scientific, encyclopedic, and information-based style of the Kunstverein version with a more playful 'fairground-like' display. The darkness of the space provided a new form of 'atmospheric' art experience and allowed for a less didactic, more sensual encounter with the works of art.

However, the response to *Film as Film* was much more critical. Most importantly, the exhibition was openly criticised by the most influential group of British women filmmakers. Annabel Nicolson, Felicity Sparrow, Jane Clarke, Jeanette Iljon, Lis Rhodes, Mary Pat Leece, Pat Murphy, and Susan Stein refused to take part in a 'closed art exhibition', which denied 'the ideological implications inherent in the pursuit of an academic dream, the uncomplicated pattern where everything fits'.[34] By leaving one space in the exhibition completely empty, they pointed to the lack of institutional support for women artists and expressed their frustration with the exhibition's exclusively 'male', 'abstract', and formal approach to experimental film. Arguing the case for

Maya Deren and Germaine Dulac, who were included in the exhibition, the protesters claimed these works were 'seen only in relation to the articulation of abstract/formal film'.[35] They proposed to alternatively 're-locate [Deren's and Dulac's] work within the context of their own concerns, giving it a complexity and fullness that the FAF [Film As Film] exhibition denied'.[36]

The women's protest was symptomatic of a paradigm shift in the late 1970s. The discourse of structural film, associated first with US critic P. Adams Sitney but taken up by British filmmakers including Peter Gidal and Malcolm Le Grice, represented a formalist engagement with the film medium which could no longer be sustained within the post-Fordian, post-civil rights, feminist era. Well aware of this shift Le Grice addressed the problem in the catalogue. The political undertone of the catalogue, which in comparison to the German book, presented a more conceptual, less didactic, and encyclopedic approach, was particularly stressed in Le Grice's essay 'The history we need', which started with the words 'The underlying thesis of a historical construction not only affects the ordering of facts but also the articulation of what constitutes the facts themselves.'[37] Le Grice continued that:

> At a more fundamental level, the underlying assumption that a practice would seek autonomy is problematic … Unfortunately the rhetoric of this enterprise has tended to reflect an essentialism – pure painting, pure film – to encourage tautologies like painting is painting, film is film and to become attached to phenomenalism in a way which assumes a kind of unmediated direct response leading to expressions like: 'the work is just itself, an object'. However, this is more an issue of faulty theorisation than faulty practice. In effect, the attempt to determine the intrinsics of a medium is always in one sense or another a relativist and historically placed activity … The technological development of the material and machinery is a pre-requisite, but the form which this technology takes is already enmeshed with historical pre-conditions of its social function and psychological determinants.[38]

Thus the unease and dissatisfaction with the overly modernist, formal, and autonomous construction of film which by this point was associated with the labels 'structural' and 'structuralist-materialist' film, and which was expressed by those women filmmakers who pulled their works out of the Hayward show, were also visible within the organisers' own statements about the show. It is important to bear in mind that the British version of the exhibition took place in 1979, three years after *Film als Film* first opened at the Cologne Kunstverein. These two crucial years were marked by an increasing interest in and ensitivity to issues of identity, history, representational politics, figuration, and narration.[39] The first signs of a shift from modernism to postmodernism were clearly visible and impossible to ignore.

This shift not only concerned the arts, but also the institutional identity of the museum. Neither precisely conventional 'museum' nor festival, the projected-image installation in the 'late capitalist museum' as evidenced by the 'vaudeville-like', spectacular presentation of *Film as Film* was arguably also an indication of this change. That is, despite the commitment of the organisers to a broadly modernist, structural programme for experimental film, in retrospect it seems clear that the introduction of film into the museum context as seen in the exhibitions *Film als Film*, and particularly *Film as Film*, was a key element in the institutional shift of the late 1970s described by Benjamin Buchloh, when the 'culture industry' was 'successfully transferred to the cultural institutions of the bourgeois public sphere'.[40] On the brink of postmodernism, the 'high brow' connoisseurship-based educational museum gradually became part of a 'people-friendly' entertainment 'culture industry'. Writing in 1984 the theorist Fredric Jameson had similarly observed that postmodernism demanded 'the dissolution of the autonomous sphere of culture', in which culture expanded 'throughout the social realm, to the point at which everything in our social life – from economic value and state power to practices and to the very structure of the psyche itself – can be said to become "cultural" in some original and as yet untheorised sense'.[41] Directly referring to Jameson's text the art historian Rosalind Krauss in her turn has distinguished between the 'pre-industrial' and the 'industrial' museum, claiming that 'the industrialised museum will have much more in common with other industrialised areas of leisure – Disneyland say – than it will with the older, preindustrial museum'.[42] She argues that 'the industrialised museum has a need for the technologised subject, the subject in search not of affect but of intensities, the subject who experiences its fragmentation as euphoria, the subject whose field of experience is no longer history, but space itself'.[43]

Published in 1990, Krauss's text is indicative of a crisis of the museum in relationship to the ever-growing incorporation of art into the circulation of capital at the end of the 1980s. It is my argument that the Hayward 'fairground' exhibition format signals this shift. With its multi-screen projection design *Film as Film* enabled a new spatial and temporal simultaneity, which was poles apart from the German exhibition, as it was also from the experimental film 'festival' represented here by *Exprmntl 4*. This was indeed something criticised at the time, for example by the British filmmaker William Raban, who referred to the London exhibition as 'a designer's show', an 'Expo look' with 'projector towers cascading images on four walls at once, and spotlights and backlit graphic displays'.[44] It can be argued that *Film as Film* shifted curatorial emphasis from a historical display of experimental film to a virtual experience of space, which as we have seen in the passage quoted above, is one of the main characteristics of Krauss's 'industrialised museum'.

Thus the history of the display of projected images shows the way in which a hybrid exhibition model developed, which both contributed to, and itself participated in, a radically changed experience of time and space in the wider culture. As the cultural critic Raymond Williams anticipated in 1974, the 'televisual flow' was to become a 'new cultural form'.[45] This new form manifested itself in a number of cultural spaces throughout the 1980s. The theorist Anne E. Kaplan observed this new 'regime of vision' in Music TeleVision (MTV), for example. According to Kaplan, MTV generates a 'kind of decentredness' representing an 'adolescent subjectivity', which 'mimics the cultural formation of contemporary teenagers appearing to live in a timeless but implicitly "futurised" present'.[46] For Anne Friedberg the 'flow' is apparent in the 'spectatorial flânerie' of the video recorder, as well as the 1980s boom of shopping malls and the mushrooming of megaplex cinemas.[47] She argues that 'the shopping mall propagates a form of subjectivity that is directly analogous to the subjectivity produced by cinematic spectatorship. And conversely, the cinematic apparatus, now arrayed in mall megaplexes [and at home in the VCR] is a machine that functions much like the consumer space of the shopping mall.'[48]

The explosion of large multiple film projections in the mid-1990s was an important part of these cultural changes. The hyperspace of the industrialised mega-museum of the millennium, such as Guggenheim Bilbao and Tate Modern, reflect a new age, where virtual space demands a redefinition of physical space. The institution's ability to constantly mutate in order to accommodate new regimes of vision makes possible an interdependence between the new museum and the projected image. Film is a spatial medium, because it is responsive to these institutional spaces, as has been shown in this essay, and its study requires an in-depth analysis of the spatial conditions of the context of presentation, an aspect that is generally missing from experimental film theory.

Notes

1 It would have been impossible to write this essay, which is based on my PhD research, without the help of Jean-Paul Dorchain, head of Centre de Documentation of the Cinémathèque Royale in Brussels and Xavier Garcia Bardon, whose publication in Revue Belge du Cinéma and generous offer to share his expertise opened up a new path in my research. Dimitri Balachoff was kind enough to answer my questions about the *Exprmntl* festivals and I would like to thank him for his time and memories.

2 The term 'Expanded cinema' developed out of the 'expanded arts' movement; see George Maciunas (ed.), 'Expanded arts', special issue, *Film Culture*, 1966. It is unclear who coined the term 'Expanded cinema' first. One of the earliest uses is by Sheldon Renan in his book *An Introduction to the American Underground Film* (New York: E. P. Dutton & Co., 1967).

3 Rosalind Krauss, 'The cultural logic of the late capitalist museum', *October*, 54 (Fall

1990), p. 12. Krauss's concept of the late capitalist museum is based on Fredric Jameson's important essay 'Postmodernism, or the cultural logic of late capitalism', first published in *New Left Review* in 1984, republished in Fredric Jameson, *Postmodernism or the Cultural Logic of Late Capitalism* (Durham: Duke University Press, 1990).

4 'Avant Venise qui annonce l'automne, Cannes inaugure au printemps l'une des deux grandes migrations cinématographiques'. André Bazin, 'A propos de Cannes', *Cahiers du Cinéma*, 22 (April 1953), p. 5 (my translation).

5 In 1954 the Oberhausen Short Film Festival was founded, which up until the late 1960s was the most important film festival for young filmmakers in Europe. However, after the publication of the infamous 'Oberhausen Manifesto' in 1962, the festival entered a crisis and new film funding regulations were introduced in the mid-1960s. As a consequence the 1967 festival rejected many entries by the younger radical filmmakers. This generated a complete restructuring of the experimental festival scene, as a result of which the Belgian film and arts festival *Exprmntl* took over the unique position amongst European film festivals which Oberhausen had previously held.

6 'A closed world', from Xavier Garcia Bardon, 'Exprmntl: festival hors normes: Knokke 1963, 1967, 1974', *Revue Belge du Cinema*, 43 (December 2002), p. 35; 'an island', from statement by Roland Lethem in Anne Head (ed.), *A True Love for Cinema: Jacques Ledoux: Curator of the Royal Film Archive and Film Museum of Belgium, 1948–1988* (The Hague: University Press Rotterdam, 1988), p. 45.

7 See for example the remarks by Rosalind Krauss in her book *A Voyage on the North Sea: Art in the Age of the Post-Medium Condition* (London: Thames and Hudson, 2000), where she writes that the type of 'structuralist film being made in the late 1960s in the context of Anthology Film Archives [was] shown annually at the Experimental Film Festival at Knokke-le-Zoute', and notes further that the founder of this festival was Jacques Ledoux, who 'was the head of the Royal Film Archives in Brussels, which functioned as a repository of the same type of cinematic repertory privileged by Anthology Film Archives', whose members she has earlier described as 'committed modernists'. See Krauss, *A Voyage on the North Sea*, p. 43, n. 46; p. 24.

8 See Annette Michelson, 'Toward Snow: part 1', *Artforum*, 9:19 (June 1971), pp. 30–37; P. Adams Sitney, 'Structural film', *Film Culture*, 47 (Summer 1969), p. 4.

9 'Vetus de peaux de bêtes et d'énormes houppelandes, l'indispensable cascade de breloques et de colliers tombant sur la poitrine, les cheveux en bataille, la veste à brandebourgs et les lunettes noires 'à la Mozart' … avec, en plus, l'air de ceux qui veulent étonner à tout prix, mais que plus rien n'étonne … Ils se sont empires de ce pauvre Casino, lieu de rendez-vous de la bourgoisie belge, palais de luxe et de richesse. Il en ont fait leur domaine. Entendez un domaine de cinglés. On les voyait partout: campant sur les marches, paressant sur la moquette, se distrayant au bar.' Christine Gobron, 'Les carnets d'une festivalienne: une aventure psychédélique chez les hippies', in *Beaux Arts*, 1189 (13 January 1968), p. 15, quoted in Bardon, 'Exprmntl: festival hors Normes', p. 37 (my translation).

10 Holger Meins died in the Stuttgart Stammhein prison by self-induced starvation on hunger strike in 1974. He had been arrested as a member of the German

underground terrorist group RAF in 1972. Harun Farocki is a German filmmaker and visual artist working in Berlin.

11 For more details see the photographic documentation in Bardon, 'Exprmntl: festival hors normes', pp. 50–51.

12 Bardon, 'Exprmntl: festival hors normes', p. 48.

13 Bardon, 'Exprmntl: festival hors normes', pp. 47–53, quoted in Jean-Jacques Lebel, 'Temoignage Jean Jacques Lebel – peintre, poète, cinéaste, plasticien français', in Guy Jungblut, Patrick Leboutte, and Dominique Païni (eds), *Une Encyclopédie des Cinémas de Belgique* (Paris: Musée d'Art Moderne de la Ville de Paris, 1990), p. 160.

14 Hans Scheugl, *Erweiteres Kino: Die Wiener Filme der 60er Jahre* (Vienna: Triton Verlag, 2002), p. 88.

15 'Die Festivaliers haben das Foyer buchstäblich besetzt, sie haben ihre Felle ausgebreitet, einer erzeugt mit einer Sprungfeder, die er über ein Glasbecken gespannt hat, Sphärenmusik, ein anderer reibt Saiten einer Gitarre mit einem Armreif. Manche gehen dann und wann ins Kino. Vor den ersten Reihen hat man genügend Platz gelassen, damit auch dort die Anhänger der bodennahen Lebensweise ihre Felle ausbreiten können.' Wenders, 'title' (1968), in Scheugl, *Erweiteres Kino*, p. 88. Thanks to Andrew Webber for advice on this translation.

16 Films which had been rejected by the jury were shown in a café. See Bardon, 'Exprmntl: festival hors normes', p. 89.

17 'En competition' films were part of the competition programme, whereas the 'hors competition' films were screened outside the official programme.

18 There were, however, exceptions, such as the double screen projections *Il Mostro Verde* (1967) by the Italians Paolo Menzio and Antonino De Bernardi, and Vanderbeek's *A Dam Rib Bed* (1964). Piero Heliczer's *Joan of Arc* (1967), which was probably the only film performance in the competition, combined film projection with poetry reading.

19 'Auf einen riesigen Plastikballon, der durch einen weissen Boden unterteilt war, auf dem sich Nackte wie über Wellen bewegten, wurden Filme und Dias projeziert.' Scheugl, *Erweiteres Kino*, p. 91 (my translation).

20 Scheugl, *Erweiteres Kino*, p. 91. See also Bardon, 'Exprmntl: festival hors normes', p. 45.

21 Amelia Jones, *Body Art: Performing the Subject* (Minneapolis: University of Minnesota Press, 1989), p. 12.

22 Michel Foucault, 'Of other spaces', in Nicholas Mirzoeff (ed.), *The Visual Culture Reader* (London: Routledge), 1998, p. 233. 'Of other spaces' was originally given as a lecture at the Paris Cercle d'études architecturales on 14 March 1967.

23 *Film als Film* toured to different German art institutions, such as the Berlin Academy, the Folkwang Museum in Essen, and the Stuttgart Kunstverein. The Folkwang Museum was the only major German museum with a permanent collection to show *Film als Film*. The other institutions were smaller non-profit organisations (*Kunstverein*). See Birgit Hein and Wulf Herzogenrath (eds), *Film als Film: 1910 bis Heute: Vom Animationsfilm der Zwanziger Jahre zum Filmenvironment der Siebziger Jahre* (Köln: Kölnischer Kunstverein/Stuttgart: Hatje Cantz Verlag, 1978).

24 See for example David Curtis, *Experimental Cinema: A Fifty Year Evolution* (London: Studio Vista, 1971); Birgit Hein, *Film im Underground: Von seinen Anfängen bis*

zum Unabhängigen Kino (Munich: Ullstein, 1971); P. Adams Sitney, *Visionary Film: The American Avant-Garde 1943–1978* (New York: Oxford University Press, 1974); Peter Gidal, *Structural Film Anthology* (London: British Film Institute, 1976) and Malcolm Le Grice, *Abstract Film and Beyond* (London: Studio Vista, 1977).

25 Export displayed the wooden box, which had been strapped around her naked torso as a kind of 'physical evidence' of this event. *Tapp- und Tastkino* had been performed in a Munich shopping street in 1968 during the international filmmakers' meeting 'Europ'. Valie Export carried a box with two holes around her naked torso while Weibel invited the passers-by to 'touch and feel' the performer's breasts 'directly, instead of only imaginarily'. This highly provocative performance became a milestone in experimental film history.

26 Birgit Hein interviewed by Maxa Zoller, Hochschule der Bildenden Künste, Braunschweig, 7 July 2005 (my translation).

27 The French film curator Henri Langlois founded the French Cinémathèque in Paris in 1936. In 1972, the ambitious collector opened the Musée du Cinema in the heart of Paris. While the Cinémathèque was restricted to film screenings, the museum allowed Langlois to display his vast collection of props, posters, costumes, technical devices, and film frames. The Musée du Cinema was unique since it was the first museum to present the history of film not only through film screenings but also through object-based installations. Over 2,000 square metres, Langlois arranged chronological 'scenographies' of the history of cinema from the beginnings of photography up to recent developments. Langlois also curated major shows such as *60 Years of Cinema* at the Paris Musée d'Art Moderne in 1955, and a Méliès exhibition at the Musée des Arts Décoratifs in 1962.

28 André Malraux, *Museum Without Walls* (London: Secker & Warburg, 1967).

29 Birgit Hein, interviewed by Maxa Zoller, Hochschule der Bildenden Künste, Braunschweig, 7 July 2005.

30 Walter Benjamin, 'The work of art in the age of its technological reproducibility (third version)' (1939), in *Walter Benjamin: Selected Writings*, vol. 4, trans. Edmund Jephcott and others, eds Howard Eiland and Michael W. Jennings (Cambridge, Mass.: The Belknap Press of Harvard University Press, 2003), pp. 251–83.

31 The filmmakers Peter Gidal, Annabel Nicolson, and Lis Rhodes left the committee due to disagreements. The original committee members are listed on p. 2 of the catalogue, details of which are given below.

32 Birgit Hein and Wulf Herzogenrath (eds), *Film as Film: Formal Experiment in Film, 1910–1975* (London: Hayward Gallery/London: Arts Council of Great Britain, 1979).

33 David Curtis remarked that the spotlights, which generated a precise beam onto the works of art, had just come on the market. David Curtis interviewed by Maxa Zoller, British Artists' Film and Video Study Collection, Central Saint Martins School of Art and Design, London, 31 March 2005.

34 Annabel Nicolson, Felicity Sparrow, Jane Clarke, Jeanette Iljon, Lis Rhodes, Mary Pat Leece, Pat Murphy, and Susan Stein, 'Woman and the formal film', in Hein and Herzogenrath (eds), *Film as Film*, p. 118.

35 Nicolson et al, 'Woman and the formal film', in Hein and Herzogenrath (eds), *Film as Film*, p. 119.

36 Draft letter from female filmmakers, unsigned and undated, Arts Council Archive, File F, Box 2 ACGB 56/34.
37 Le Grice, 'The history we need', in *Film as Film,* p. 113.
38 Le Grice, 'The history we need', in *Film as Film,* p. 113.
39 Michael Snow's *Rameau's Nephew* (1974) and Malcolm Le Grice's *Blackbird Descending (Tense Alignment)* (1977) can be seen as a 'return to narrative'. For a critical discussion of the relationship between structuralist-materialist film and narrative, see Mick Eaton, 'The avant-garde and narrative: two SEFT/London Filmmakers' Co-op day schools', *Screen*, 19:2 (Summer 1978), pp. 129–35.
40 Benjamin Buchloh, 'Introduction', in his *Neo-Avantgarde and Culture Industry* (Cambridge, Mass.: MIT Press, 2000).
41 Jameson, 'Postmodernism, or the cultural logic of late capitalism', p. 226.
42 Krauss, 'The cultural logic of the late capitalist museum', p. 12.
43 Krauss, 'The cultural logic of the late capitalist museum', p. 17.
44 William Raban, 'Talk: *Film as Film* at the Hayward', *Filmmakers Europe,* 15 (1979).
45 Raymond Williams, *Television: Technology and Cultural Form* (London: Routledge, 1974), p. 86.
46 Anne E. Kaplan, *Rocking Around the Clock: Music Television, Modernism and Consumer Culture* (London/New York: Methuen, 1987), p. 29.
47 Anne Friedberg, *Window Shopping: Cinema and the Postmodern* (Berkeley, Calif.: University of California Press, 1993), p. 120.
48 Friedberg, *Window Shopping*, p. 120.

3 The matter of illusionism: Michael Snow's screen/space

Kate Mondloch

> I do think that my work 'is more radical than that', and why I think that is related to my attempt to make the work a 'now', 'materialist', yes a 'modernist' experience *as well as* to have and to direct the references *elsewhere* of representation, 'away' and back to you and the work itself. (Michael Snow, 'A letter to Thierry de Duve'[1])

Art critic and historian Michael Fried's groundbreaking 1967 essay 'Art and objecthood' is best known as a studied rejection of Minimalism, or, as Fried preferred to call it, 'literalist' art. Fried recognised that this new genre, inasmuch as it compelled a durational viewing experience akin to theatre, undermined both the medium-specificity and the presumed instantaneousness of reception foundational to the Greenbergian/Friedian account of modernism. The impact of Fried's discerning analysis upon contemporary art history and criticism is incontestable. For the purposes of the present study, however, a little-remarked-upon footnote in this otherwise exhaustively analysed article is especially revelatory. In it, Fried speculates that a close reading of the 'phenomenology of the cinema' would reveal how film manages to escape the degraded relational quality that he believed was endemic to literalist art. 'Exactly how the movies escape theatre is a beautiful question', Fried muses. He goes on to suggest that theatricality is not realised in cinema because, among other reasons, 'the screen is not experienced as a kind of object existing, so to speak, in a specific physical relation to us'.[2]

Fried's appreciation of a divide between the cinematic experience and that of Minimalist sculpture was soon to be overthrown by the expanded field of art and film practices that emerged in the late 1960s and 1970s. In the range of overlapping screen-reliant art practices variously known as structural film, expanded cinema, film environments, projected image installation and so on, the seemingly discrete boundaries between cinema and sculpture were deliberately and provocatively muddied. Chipping away at the medium-specific boundaries of formalist modernism, artists as diverse as Dan Graham, Joan Jonas, Paul Sharits, Valie Export, Bruce Nauman, Peter Campus, and, my chief focus here, Michael Snow, created evocative sculptures in which the screen, defying Fried's analysis, is indeed 'experienced as a kind of object existing … in a specific physical relation to us'. Even before the inception of most film and video installations, then, Fried had instinctively recognised that the screen would be a threat to stable modernist categories should its conventionally overlooked objecthood be exposed (a threat he was keen to avoid). Working in the wake of Minimalism, these artists did just that: they invited viewers to understand the screen – as well as the site and experience of screening – as material.

This essay is concerned with the critical reception of what I call screen-reliant installation art – a genre of screen-based sculptural and experiential art works in the late 1960s and 1970s in which the cinematic process and the screen itself emerge as objects of investigation: media objects and their viewing regimes are literally and figuratively put on display in these environmental art works. Michael Snow's experimental films and sculptural installations were especially pivotal to the period's debates surrounding the theory and production of avant-garde art and film, even as they were esteemed for sometimes dramatically varying reasons; the critical reception of the Canadian's seminal film and video works in the late 1960s and early 1970s, both installation and non-installation variants, thus constitutes the central case study here. While Snow's conventionally exhibited experimental films are nearly always considered separately from his film and video installations, this essay reveals what we can learn from considering them side-by-side. This comparative approach allows us to appreciate how screen-reliant installation was initially defined, framed and critiqued in relationship to variant cinematic practices (including experimental film), and promotes a richer understanding of both genres.

Four celebrated artworks organise the following analysis: two experimental films (both commonly described as structural films) – *Wavelength* (1966–67) and *La Région Centrale* (1971) – and two installations – *De La* (1971) and *Two Sides to Every Story* (1974). Because the critical reception of all of Snow's film and video work between 1967 and 1975 is largely circumscribed by his so-called structural films, a detailed appraisal of these films and their critical context is a necessary preliminary for understanding the peculiar reception of the artist's installations.

In a seeming paradox, art-historical references to *Wavelength* and *La Région Centrale* far outnumber those made to Snow's more obviously 'sculptural' installation works. As we shall see in what follows, it is arguably the complex status of the screen, and the viewer's relationship to it, that accounts for this lacuna. Screen-reliant installations such as Snow's reveal that the screen is a curiously ambivalent object – simultaneously a material object and a virtual window; it is altogether an object which, when deployed in spatialised sculptural configurations, resists facile categorisation. This essay proposes that the hybrid status of screen-based environmental artworks – positioned as they are midway between the cinematic and the sculptural – strained dominant critical models of the era, the critical prescriptions and political preoccupations of which proved to be unsuitable for addressing the particular critical interventions of this distinctive mode of art practice.

The problem of film as film

Wavelength is a deceptively simple film which consists of a forty-five-minute-long tracking shot that travels unhurriedly across the length of Snow's studio. The camera proceeds toward a pair of uncovered windows on the opposite side of the room, ultimately finishing with a close-up shot of a black-and-white photograph of choppy water perched between the windowpanes. Several incidental, quasi-narrative events occur as the recording device ambles along – the camera's coloured lenses and shots occasionally change, unidentified characters enter, a murder is discussed, time passes – but each of these brief events and objects are gone as soon as the camera moves past them, seemingly fixated on its relentless march toward the opposite wall. The visual activity is accompanied by a soundtrack that includes ambient city noise, human voices, scattered rainfall, and, perhaps most memorably, a gradually increasing sine wave tone, the eventual shrillness of which inexorably impacts one's experience of the film.

Snow produced *La Région Centrale* just four years later. In this film, a remote patch of Canadian wilderness is subjected to the gaze of a self-operating camera machine that methodically rotates to document the rustic landscape from every conceivable direction. The resulting spiralling footage, both agreeably hypnotic and nauseating in turn, whirls and twists at varying speeds to reveal a 360–degree panoramic landscape from the perspective of the automated recording device. Significantly, the film never depicts the camera/eye itself. 'The centre of the central region is like a black hole', confirms critic and art historian Thierry de Duve; 'the eye of the machinery sees everything but itself'.[3] (In fact, it was only after verifying that no other film camera could avoid inadvertently capturing itself in the panoramic footage at some point that Snow had *La Région Centrale*'s camera custom-built.) As in *Wavelength*, the recording apparatus proves curiously present in its very absence. In both works, the recording process and tools of production inescapably become part of the content of the films themselves.

These two experimental media works are oft-cited exemplars of structural film – renowned for what Annette Michelson called their 'intransigent autonomy' and for the way in which they draw attention to their own internal shape or structure.[4] Prominent American film critic P. Adams Sitney first coined the term structural film in 1969 to describe a new tendency in North

American experimental filmmaking exemplified by the works of Snow, Tony Conrad, George Landow, Ernie Gehr, Hollis Frampton, Joyce Wieland, and Paul Sharits.[5] Applying a strictly formalist mode of criticism, he contended that their films, and *Wavelength* in particular (*La Région Centrale* had not been created at the time of Sitney's essay), constituted 'cinematic propositions in a rigorously ordered form': 'the *shape* of the whole film is predetermined and simplified', Sitney contended, 'and it is that shape that is the primal impression of the film … what content it has is minimal and subsidiary to the outline'.[6]

From the perspective of art history, *Wavelength* is deemed to be remarkable not only for revealing its internal shape (similar to advanced painting of the period), but also for self-reflexively demonstrating its process – concerns that would shortly dominate advanced sculptural practice as well, in works by artists such as Lynda Benglis, Eva Hesse, Robert Morris, and Richard Serra. Art and film critic Annette Michelson's 1971 analysis of the film's critical intervention is typical of the work's vaunted status within the discipline: *Wavelength* is an allegory of phenomenological experience, one that redefines 'filmic space as that of action'.[7] Indeed, from Michelson's writing on Paul Sharits and Michael Snow, to Benjamin Buchloh's and Rosalind Krauss's theorisations of Richard Serra's films, the phenomenological and anti-illusionist interpretation of this sort of North American media art production is well established.[8] And yet, despite the long-standing and enthusiastic embrace of Snow's experimental films by art and film critics alike – Sitney effused in 1976 that '[*Wavelength*] had an impact … incomparable to any other avant-garde film in my memory'; de Duve deemed *La Région Centrale* to be nothing short of a 'masterwork' in 1995 – the underlying criteria employed in the initial reception of Snow's screen-based works were in fact multiple and complex.[9]

An ambitious survey exhibition held at the Cologne Kunstverein in 1977, the British staging of which, *Film as Film: Formal Experiment in Film*, was held at London's Hayward Gallery in 1979, provides an instructive starting point in evaluating the reception of Snow's work within the context of structural film.[10] Motivated at least in part by the desire to grant historical legitimacy to recent developments in contemporary European film art, the exhibition aspired to outline a trajectory of works such as Snow's that 'move beyond' conventional illusionist representation to investigate the very idea of film itself. Curators Birgit Hein and Wulf Herzogenrath emphasised a perceived distinction between more conventional filmic works, on the one hand, and a film 'art' practice (what Hein and Herzogenrath referred to as a 'modernist' sensibility in film) on the other. Significantly, the term 'formal' here is understood to concern the entire cinematic apparatus, including materials and issues of process: formal film served as a catch-all term to encompass a range of filmic works otherwise labelled by the overlapping genres of structural film, expanded cinema, experimental film, and so on.[11] Snow's films were considered to be foundational to contemporary developments and were central to both the exhibition and its catalogue.

The catalogue's essays by prominent film artists and critics Hein, Peter Weibel, and Malcolm Le Grice all place a special emphasis on film works produced since the mid-1960s. Hein's essay on structural film argued that the strictly formalist criteria proposed by Sitney in 1969 – understood to be an adaptation of Greenbergian formalist modernist criticism – are inadequate when dealing with the complexity of experimental film works created since the mid-1960s.[12] While *Film as Film* appreciated certain formal innovations in the works featured in the exhibition, these writers explicitly emphasised what they argued was a decisive shift to examining the representational codes of cinema (a project aided in the British context by the influence of the journal *Screen*, and the growth in radical criticism of mainstream film). In short, these works were celebrated for their alleged interest in rejecting and disrupting conventional media forms and viewing techniques.

Film as Film's implicit, and at times explicit, argument aligning the viewer's participatory experience with a progressive political project was indebted to the work of the two most influential critics associated with British experimental film, Le Grice and Peter Gidal.[13] Both filmmaker-critics championed film works that strove to foreground their material conditions and expose their own ideological workings; this self-reflexive operation was assumed to inevitably produce active, empowered spectators categorically distinct from the passive viewers associated with illusionist cinema. Repeatedly cited in the introduction to *Film as Film*, Gidal defined this sort of artistic production as structural-materialist film: works in which 'the in/film (not in/frame) and film/viewer material relations, and the relations of the film's structure, are primary'.[14] Snow, Malcolm Le Grice, Kurt Kren, Peter Kubelka, Peter Frampton, and Paul Sharits were considered to be representative figures working in this vein. Gidal articulated the political stakes of film art with an uncompromising zeal: artists using film must constantly work to 'disrupt' the cinematic apparatus, specifically the illusory 'referentialism' of mainstream cinema that, according to Gidal, necessarily prohibits any critical awareness on the part of its viewers. Consequently, to use film in any conventional way (be it via narrative content or illusionist representation) is to be inescapably complicit with dominant ideology. Even if the critic's admiration for Snow's experimental films appears to be somewhat misguided, insofar as both *La Région Centrale* and *Wavelength* arguably employ narrative components and/or illusionist content, the larger predicament is that Gidal's appropriation of Snow's work under the narrow mantle of structural-materialist film was so successful that it effectively set the terms for much of the critical reception of the artist's larger practice.[15]

Gidal's and Le Grice's aspirations for a politically engaged film art practice must be understood in relationship to both film apparatus theory, as developed by scholars such as Jean-Louis Baudry and Christian Metz, who sought to define cinema as an 'institutional apparatus' consisting of a programmed relationship between the film, projector, screen, and spectator – and Peter Wollen's well-known theorisation of divergent filmic avant-gardes.[16] Their arguments about film's materialist properties are especially evocative in light of the Friedian anti-objecthood argument outlined at the outset of this essay. First articulated in his landmark essay 'The two avant-gardes' (1975) and later refined in '"Ontology" and "materialism" in film' (1976), Wollen's profoundly influential model proposed the existence of two distinct and coexisting filmic avant-gardes in the 1960s and 1970s: a formalist avant-garde associated with the Co-op movement, predominantly emerging from North America, and especially associated with structural filmmakers like Snow, and an overtly 'political' avant-garde, which Wollen identified as being a distinctly European phenomenon, informed by Brechtian models and associated with filmmakers such as Jean-Luc Godard.[17] While Wollen was ultimately concerned with encouraging the development of a film practice that might be able to incorporate and borrow from both models, he explicitly criticised what he perceived to be the 'unnecessarily' strong ties between the Co-op movement and the art world and art theory. Put simply, Wollen blamed the application of Greenbergian criteria for modernist painting to the very different medium of film for what he judged to be the extreme 'purism' and 'essentialism' of structural film.[18]

Wollen's 1976 article struck down the rationale of 'formal' film even more directly, which, in turn, further complicated the reception of Snow's work.[19] Wollen argued that structuralist filmmakers and critics such as Gidal radically misunderstood two key concepts. First, the notion of film's ontology (by proposing that film is exclusively concerned with formal issues) and, second, they misapprehended the critical value of 'materialism': in what amounted to a misappropriation of post-Brechtian aesthetics, structural-materialist film collapsed an emphasis on materiality and filmic materials (anti-illusionism broadly conceived) with the critical gesture of political materialism (in the specific post-Brechtian sense).[20] In the case of Snow, Wollen's profoundly influential critique of structural-materialist film had unfortunate collateral effects, especially given the artist's paradigmatic status for Gidal's and Le Grice's theorisation of the art form. Film scholar Bart Testa aptly identifies the problem in a retrospective account of Snow's early films: '[If] Gidal narrowly interpreted Snow to make him a materialist filmmaker; Wollen's enormously influential critique of Gidal, a fortiori, made Snow an inadequate one.'[21] The critical reception of structural-materialist film coloured analysis of Snow's experimental films and, by extension, his film installations. (It is symptomatic that neither Gidal nor Wollen directly engaged with Snow's installations, which presumably would have complicated their arguments.)

The matter of projection

Annette Michelson, writing within a North American context, was in many ways the most successful at suitably locating Snow's oeuvre within the expanded context of both film and art discourses in the 1960s and 1970s. In her second essay on Snow, published in *October* magazine in 1979, she developed the phenomenological account she had earlier given of his work by pointing out how the artist and filmmaker productively undercut the predominant 'retreat into sculptural materiality' of much contemporary art since the 'crisis of painting' in the 1960s by probing the 'play between the real and virtual image'.[22] In her discussion of Snow's films in particular, she aptly called attention to their clever extension of key Duchampian gestures, such as those pioneered in *The Large Glass* (1915–23), including the introduction of temporality into pictorial space and the deconstruction of the notion of framing.

Nevertheless, Michelson's sketch of the general development of avant-garde film in the 1960s and 1970s concluded that Snow and others retained a distinctly retrograde emphasis (especially vis-à-vis their peers in the fine arts). Even if so-called structural films invited the possibility of an analytic, cognitive mode of experimental film viewing, argued Michelson, such works still maintained an unwelcome insistence upon an idealist primacy of vision. Revealingly, the shortcoming the critic associated with *Wavelength* is related to the role of the screen-based apparatus, albeit with a new point of emphasis. Michelson explained: *Wavelength* 'appeared as a celebration of the "apparatus" and a confirmation of the status of the subject'. 'By restoring and remapping the space of perspective construction, [Snow] re-established its centre, that place which is the space of the transcendental subject'.[23] *La Région Centrale*, too, fell to the same critique because, in Michelson's view at least, the spectator ultimately identifies with the camera, which neatly reconfirms the subject at the centre of vision.[24]

Even when the screen-based apparatus is not literally present, then, its role was paramount in critical discourses surrounding this type of filmic production. However useful the terms of these materialist critiques may be in certain contexts, they had the unfortunate effect of obscuring the specific characteristics and critical interventions of film and video works when these were configured as specifically sculptural environments. As we shall see in the case-studies of two of Snow's media installations, *De La* and *Two Sides to Every Story*, the screen shifts from being the apex of the viewer's 'cone' of vision (centring the viewer as in perspectival painting) to being a conceptual and literal point of emphasis which the viewer moves *around* (something closer to Minimalist sculpture). Even while the apparatus is central in these sculptures, it does not 'fix' the viewer in place. The material concerns that implicitly adhere to the screen-reliant apparatus in Snow's experimental films (and which so confounded his many, differently allied critics) are actualised in his environmental artworks. In Snow's installations, the self-reflexive engagement with materiality is potentially critical, but it has been obfuscated by the convoluted in-fighting within the dominant critical discourses that surround structural film in general.

It is widely known that a rigorous circularity of key themes and concepts characterises Snow's otherwise remarkably diverse oeuvre; it is unsurprising, then, that many of the ideas tested in the aforementioned films resurface in his installations. *De La* (figure 3.1) is a deliberate reworking of key concepts and materials pioneered in *La Région Centrale* – indeed, the earlier work's custom-made, remote-controlled camera was literally re-sited in the gallery space, and retrofitted with a closed-circuit video camera and four monitors. Unlike *La Région Centrale*, however, the technological apparatus is presented as part of a sculptural environment consisting of the camera-machine, four video monitors, and the exhibition space itself. In contrast to the cinematic mode of reception of experimental film such as *La Région Centrale* – illuminated images projected for a fixed duration in a darkened theatre to stationary

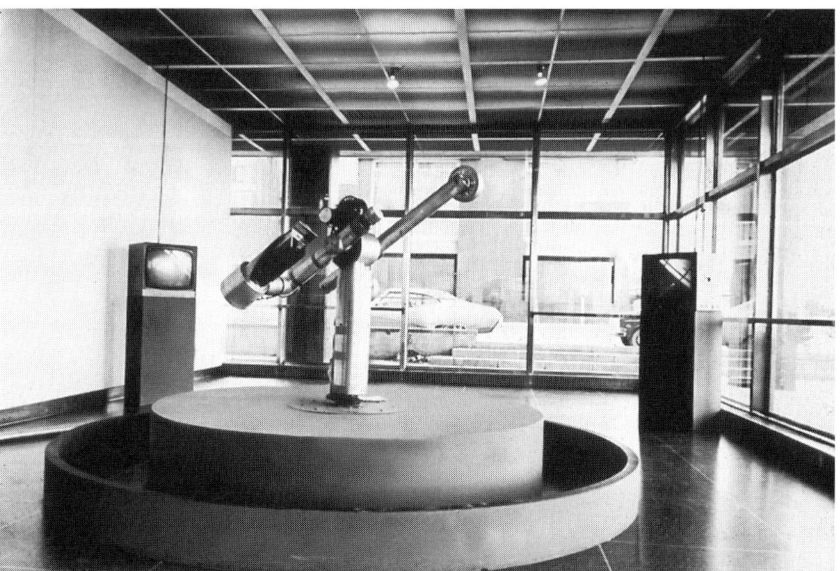

3.1 Michael Snow, *De La*, 1971. Aluminium and steel mechanical sculpture with electronic controls, television camera, and four video monitors. © Michael Snow. Courtesy of Michael Snow.

observers – *De La* (like *Two Sides to Every Story*) is a sculptural media work created for the specific institutional context of the art gallery: it is meant to unfold in time and space and to be experienced by ambulatory viewers.

A curious transformation takes place when Snow allows the actual recording/projecting machine to assume centre stage. While it previously functioned as the invisible, conceptual centre of vision, the aluminium and steel contraption is now palpably and objectively present – an object among other objects, most notably the four video screens mounted on nearly human-sized black pedestals that are positioned in equidistant relations throughout the room. In its sculptural iteration, the camera comprehensively records and documents not an isolated sector of countryside in Quebec, but rather the art exhibition space and its viewers. Although the technological apparatus is unavoidably apparent, it is in no way the primary emphasis of the work. It is only by negotiating the objective presence of the camera and monitors, while also carefully attending to the screen-based virtual imagery, that viewers can make sense of the piece.

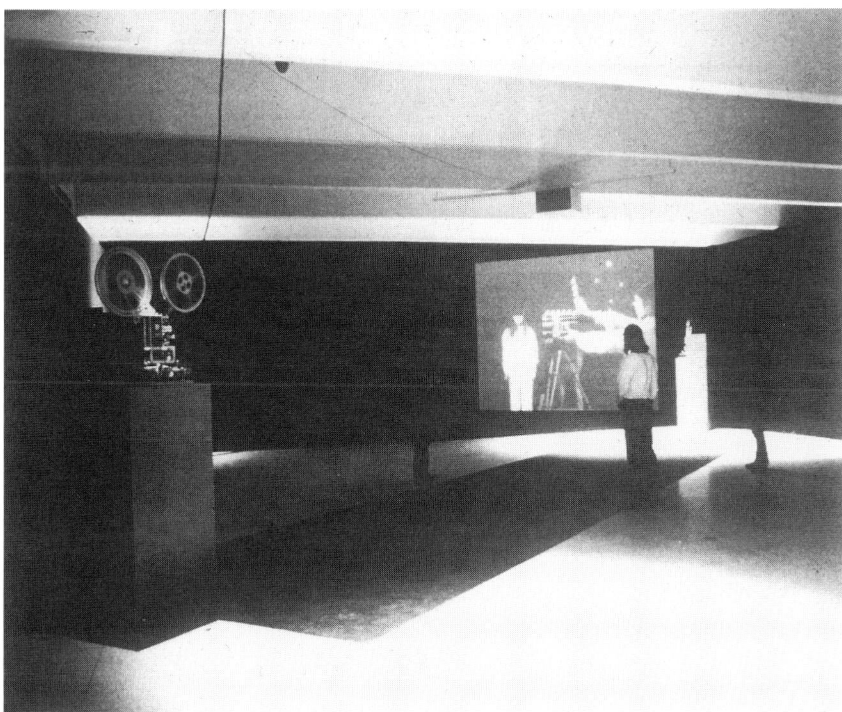

Michael Snow, *Two Sides to Every Story*, 1974. Two synchronised 16mm films, colour, sound, 8 minutes, projected continuously onto both sides of an aluminium screen. Installation view from the exhibition, *Projected Images*, at the Walker Art Museum, Minneapolis, 1974. © Michael Snow. Courtesy of Michael Snow. 3.2

Screen-based surveillance and feedback perform a critical function here.[25] The revolving camera plays back everything within its field of vision, including the work's viewers themselves, who are unexpectedly made part of the screen-based environment. This charged correlation activates the space between the viewer, the camera, and the screens so that the spectator's embodied and phenomenological experience with the spatialised and temporal media objects is central to the work's meaning. Moreover, the way in which viewers are doubled in the representational screen space makes them hyper-aware of their position in the actual gallery space. Viewers are asked to engage in a sort of spectatorial doubleness: to be in two places at once – the real gallery space and the virtual screen space – and, further, to understand the screen as simultaneously an object and a virtual window. *De La*'s hybrid spectatorship, even more than that of the cinematically-presented *La Région Centrale* or *Wavelength*, complicates simplistic readings of Snow's work as either purely formal or as exclusively concerned with materialist interventions.

Snow created his next installation, *Two Sides to Every Story*, in 1974 (figure 3.2). Again, the screen and the recording/projecting apparatus are foregrounded as physical objects: this time twin ceiling-mounted projectors simultaneously churn out two separate but related eight-minute narratives onto opposite sides of a wafer-thin projection surface suspended in the middle of the gallery space. Snow created the film by shooting a scene concurrently from two sides, which has the effect of capturing not only the profilmic events, but also the camera, crew, and the director himself. Screening two opposing perspectives in tandem, *Two Sides to Every Story* transposes the entire filming process and space of production to the space of exhibition. (If *Wavelength* formulates its process of production as subject matter, *Two Sides to Every Story* takes it one step further and collapsed the production process with that of the work's exhibition/reception.)

The storyline itself is fairly rudimentary: Snow, seated on the side of one of the cameramen, directs a young woman to perform various actions that largely revolve around the creation and destruction of a plastic sheet/screen in the centre of the room; throughout this process, the artist periodically asks the cameramen to cover one camera lens at a time with coloured sheets. Depending on which side one is currently viewing, and which cameraman carried out the action, the director's requests – 'now, light blue lens' – may be visually confirmed or disrupted. To experience the piece fully, viewers must perambulate around the projection surface and explore the screen-based spatial environment from both sides. In other words, they must concentrate on the virtual, 'deep' spaces of the on-screen narrative while also contending with the screen as a material object, moving through the exhibition space to scrutinise the work from both sides of its emphatically flat surface.

Two Sides to Every Story was first shown in Minneapolis at the Walker Art

Gallery's 1974 exhibition, *Projected Images*, alongside moving image installations by Campus, Sharits, Rockne Krebs, Ted Victoria, and Robert Whitman. One of the first exhibitions of its kind, this show therefore offers a useful entry point to evaluate the early critical reception of film and video installation. While the various authors contributing to the *Projected Images* catalogue could not settle on any single appropriate label to describe the new kind of work showcased in the exhibition – interestingly, the term 'projected images' was not favoured by any of the writers, despite its use in the show's title – they are united by their emphasis on what they identify as a sculptural or environmental quality to the works, a concern with process, and the spectator's alleged transformation into an active 'participant'. Assessing Whitman's *American Moon* (1960), for example, critic Barbara Rose describes how the multimedia performance 'surrounded and enveloped the spectators', turning viewers into participants 'intimately connected to the performance'.[26]

Curator Martin Friedman emphasises how the artists represented in the Walker exhibition 'conceive of film and video images essentially in environmental terms', which sets them apart from media artists who compose under 'standard technological projection conventions'. The sculptural projected-image works by Snow and others are described as being 'as concerned with the changing spatial and psychological relationships between observer and image as with the character of the image itself'.[27] The curator's proposal to understand these environmental media artworks in opposition to 'conventional' uses of film and video is emblematic of the point of view of the majority of the exhibition's commentators. Michelson, for instance, notes that Paul Sharits's installation 'location' *SYNCHRONOUSOUNDTRACKS* (1973) disrupts normative cinematic viewing (including, presumably, that of structural film) in its overt concern with definitions of space and time and in the permission it grants spectators to move about freely.[28]

Critic Regina Cornwell's catalogue essay on *Two Sides to Every Story* explicitly pointed to the role of the screen in creating a newly spatialised viewing environment and a participatory experience for the spectator. Cornwell observed the way in which 'within traditional film viewing the screen is part of a wall and thus part of the architecture. The film screen becomes a "window to the world" so that we may lose ourselves in it.' In installations such as Snow's, on the contrary, the screen is employed in such a way as to create viewers 'conscious of the space of the event more than merely as a window'. Because of this, argued Cornwell, the spectator 'now becomes a participant', a newly activated viewer.[29] The latter point is important to emphasise. Cornwell's argument, implicit here and throughout the exhibition and its catalogue, is that environmental or installation media works, by calling attention to the 'projective situation', automatically rendered their spectators engaged participants and, just as proposed by the European theorists associated with *Film as Film*, she assumed that this condition is necessarily a progressive critical intervention.

It is here – at the crossroads of the critical legacy of Minimalism's phenomenological approach, Postminimalism's explorations of process and institutional critique, and the ideological critiques of film/media theory – that Snow's screen-reliant work can illuminate the discussion about gallery-based media art in the 1960s and 1970s in new ways. As we have seen through the example of Snow's artistic production, it is reductive to classify these works as simply 'film about film', or to position them as some kind of materialist-formalist intervention against the 'bad ideal' of conventional cinema, including its illusionistic appeals. Cornwell's 1978 comments on Snow's oeuvre in *Film Reader* are particularly instructive; she noted that his film-based works share with Minimalism a 'concern with the object, immediate presence, holistic and dehierarchised structure, and distancing'. Unlike Minimal art, however, Snow's pieces deliberately and unapologetically retain 'a representational image'.[30] Although written specifically in regard to *Wavelength*, this powerful observation applies broadly to all of Snow's media works examined here. The potential radicality of this doubleness, however, is a concept Cornwell leaves undeveloped.

In both *De La* and *Two Sides to Every Story*, the screen-based apparatus and the conditions of viewing and screening emerge as material. However, instead of expunging illusionist, virtual space, as dominant critical models would suggest (including the models advanced on the strength of the artist's structuralist films), Snow's installations persistently present illusionism and material reality as coterminous. Indeed, this is largely true for both his experimental films and screen-based installations; for his experimental films this revelation occurs at the level of content, however, whereas for the installations the media apparatus is manifestly, physically present in the exhibition space. In the installation works *De La* and *Two Sides to Every Story*, the viewing experience is simultaneously material (the viewer's phenomenological engagement with actual objects in real time and space) and immaterial (the viewer's metaphorical projection into virtual times and spaces). Spectators are asked to 'see double': not only are there 'two sides to every story', but also the screen itself is both an object and a window at the same time.

Snow's work stubbornly resists critical models of the era that tended either to foreground the phenomenological experience of the spectator in the space of projection, or to theorise this type of production as exclusively determining, ideological, and materialist. Instead, as we have seen, Snow's screen-reliant installations, which are widely representative of the critical ambitions of a range of art and media practitioners in the era, are material and immaterial, object and illusion; they are not so much a critique of illusionism in favour of materiality – a focus on the space in front of the screen at the expense of the virtual space behind it – as an analysis of the inevitable interconnection of both. Succinctly put, Snow's concern with anti-illusionism and materiality is unvaryingly tempered by his consistent use of the screen as a site of illusion and projection: while Fried's formalist modernism censured the deployment of the cinema screen as a literalist object, Snow is representative of a range of artists who created evocative screen-based works that defied the terms of this criticism by holding objecthood and illusionism in tandem.

Looking back on this period in a 1996 essay, Le Grice discerns an emphasis on screen-based experimentation and confirms that 'the language or discourse of cinema is fundamentally altered – philosophically and in the social/cultural arena – by emerging forms which first establish the screen as surface then reverse the symbolic space from behind to before the screen.'[31] Although Le Grice recognises the pivotal role of the screen in these works, his formulation is incomplete. Screen-reliant installations such as Snow's grapple with (at least) three screen spaces simultaneously: the space behind the screen, the space before the screen, and, finally, the spatial presence of the screen object itself.

The ambivalent objecthood and slippery materiality of the range of screen-reliant spaces in works such as Snow's fundamentally exceeded extant theorisations of avant-garde film and art in the 1960s and 1970s. Even now, the task of theorising the place of the material apparatus is difficult, but it is made especially urgent by the proliferation of media installations since the 1990s. Echoing the terms of Wollen's argument about 'materialist' film some twenty years later, film historian and critic Dominique Païni condemns the propensity of contemporary artists to foreground the projective apparatus as a kind of shorthand for criticality: these works, he argues, 'need, for their meaning, the visibility of the machine that projects them.'[32] Païni singles out Snow's *Two Sides to Every Story* as exceptional in this regard. Snow focuses his intervention not on the apparatus per se, argues the critic, but on the screen: 'It is the screen, essentially the screen, more than an abstract filmic material, which is Snow's burden.' This is a categorically different mode of emphasis, explains Païni, because the screen is, after all, 'nothing but the surface of an apparatus … a fleeting impression.'[33] As we have seen, it is indeed the peculiar status of the screen which, however obscured, has been embedded in the critical discourses surrounding film and video installations since their inception in the mid-1960s.

Inasmuch as reductive binary assessments of cinema versus sculpture, immateriality versus materiality, and illusionism versus anti-illusionism prove to be untenable in assessing Snow's artistic production, it suggests that critics and historians should develop a more nuanced approach to understanding screen-reliant installation art in general – both historic and contemporary variants. In this way, we can better appreciate the truly transformative aspects of the cross-pollination between art and cinema which, while initiated during the flowering of critical art practices in the 1960s and 1970s, remain core concerns of artistic production in the present.

Notes

1 Michael Snow, 'A letter to Thierry de Duve', *Parachute*, 78 (1995), p. 63.
2 Michael Fried, 'Art and objecthood', *Artforum*, 5 (June 1967), p. 23, n. 16.
3 Thierry de Duve, 'Michael Snow: the deictics of experience, and beyond', *Parachute*, 78 (1995), p. 34.
4 Annette Michelson, 'Film and the radical aspiration' (1966), reprinted in P. Adams Sitney (ed.), *Film Culture Reader* (New York: Praeger Publishers, 1970), pp. 404–21; p. 419.
5 In spite of the name Sitney coined to describe it, North American 'structural film' has nothing to do with structuralism as a philosophy (Sitney apparently chose the label to denote the way in which the work's 'structure' is determined in advance). 'There is a cinema of structure, wherein the shape of the whole film is predetermined and simplified, and it is that shape that is the primal impression of the film … the structural film insists on its shape and what content it has is minimal and subsidiary to the outline'. P. Adams Sitney, 'Structural film' (1969), reprinted in Sitney (ed.), *Film Culture Reader*, pp. 326–48. Foreshadowing the confusion to come in regard to descriptive terms for film art, Sitney's coda to the 1970 printing of his essay includes reference to the 'distinguished sculptors' (he mentions Richard Serra, Bruce Nauman, Robert Morris, and Hollis Frampton) currently developing a type of film art practice that Sitney confirmed could not be adequately understood within the framework of structural film. See also Sitney, *Visionary Film: The American Avant-Garde* (New York: Oxford University Press, 1974).
6 Sitney, 'Structural Film', p. 327.
7 Annette Michelson, 'Toward Snow', *Artforum*, 9:19 (June 1971), pp. 30–37. Michelson had hinted at this as early as the 1966 essay from which I have already quoted, when she observed that: 'These films, in their intransigent autonomy, make an almost wholly plastic use of reference and allusion, by no means excluding extra plastic resonances, but animated by a sense of structure as progress-in-time so absolute and compelling that very little else has room or time enough in which to "happen"'. Michelson, 'Film and the radical aspiration', p. 419.
8 See for example Benjamin Buchloh, 'Sculpture and process in Richard Serra's films', in *Richard Serra: Works '66–'77* (Tubingen: Kunsthalle, 1978); Rosalind Krauss, 'Richard Serra: sculpture', in *Richard Serra: Sculpture* (New York: Museum of Modern Art, 1986); Annette Michelson, 'Paul Sharits and the critique of illusionism: an introduction', *Film Culture* (1978), pp. 83–88, and Michelson 'Toward Snow'.
9 P. Adams Sitney, 'Michael Snow: in a room with a camera', *Soho Weekly*, 19 (February 1976), p. 16; cited in Bart Testa, 'An axiomatic cinema: Michael Snow's films', in Jim Shedden (ed.), *The Michael Snow Project: Presence and Absence: The Film of Michael Snow 1956–1991* (Toronto: Art Gallery of Ontario/Knopf, 1995), p. 12; and Thierry de Duve, 'Michael Snow: the deictics of experience, and beyond'.
10 The exhibition first opened at the Cologne Kunstverein in 1977 and travelled to the Hayward Gallery in London in 1979. See the original German exhibition catalogue, Birgit Hein and Wulf Herzogenrath (eds), *Film als Film: 1910 bis Heute: Vom Animationsfilm der Zwanziger Jahre zum Filmenvironment der Siebziger Jahre* (Köln: Kölnischer Kunstverein; Stuttgart: Hatje Cantz Verlag, 1978), and

the revised English catalogue, Birgit Hein and Wulf Herzogenrath (eds), *Film as Film: Formal Experiment in Film, 1910–1975* (London: Hayward Gallery/London: Arts Council of Great Britain, 1979). For an informative account of the interesting differences between the two exhibitions, see the essay by Maxa Zoller which is published as chapter 2 of the present volume. While the historical purview of the exhibition technically spanned from 1910–75, it strongly emphasised developments since the mid-1960s. Essays featured in the English version of the catalogue which were devoted to this era include Peter Weibel's 'The Viennese formal film', Malcolm Le Grice's 'The history we need', and Birgit Hein's 'The structural film'. (Although space constraints prevent me from assessing it here, the multi-authored essay 'Woman and the formal film', by Annabel Nicolson, Felicity Sparrow, Jane Clarke, Jeanette Iljon, Lis Rhodes, Mary Pat Leece, Pat Murphy, and Susan Stein, which was also published in the English version of the catalogue, is an especially fascinating and useful historical document for understanding the critical discourse around experimental film art.)

11 The notion of 'formal film' is reminiscent of the terminology employed by prominent British filmmaker and critic Malcolm Le Grice, amongst others. Le Grice's definition of 'formal film' refers to film that investigates its own material qualities, where, significantly, 'material' is understood to include issues of process (including projection, duration, and the 'psycho-physical'). See Le Grice, *Abstract Film and Beyond* (Cambridge, Mass.: MIT Press, 1977).

12 Birgit Hein, 'The structural film', in Hein and Herzogenrath (eds), *Film as Film*, pp. 93–106.

13 At the time of the exhibition, in 1979, both Le Grice and Gidal were primarily associated with the pivotal London Film-makers' Co-op that Le Grice established in the late 1960s. Key texts included Gidal, 'Theory and definition of structural/materialist film', *Studio International*, 189/190 (December 1975), pp. 189–96, and Le Grice, *Abstract Film and Beyond.*

14 Peter Gidal, 'Theory and definition of structural/materialist film', pp. 189–96. See also Gidal's *Materialist Film* (London: Routledge, 1989).

15 In fact, Gidal's preferred exemplars among Snow's films were *La Région Centrale* and especially <-> (also known as *Back and Forth*) (1969). His support of *Wavelength* was, owing to its undeniable insistence upon narrative components, much more equivocal.

16 See Christian Metz's seminal 1975 essay 'The imaginary signifier': 'The cinematic institution is not just the cinema industry … it is also the mental machinery – another industry – which spectators "accustomed to the cinema" have internalised historically and which has adapted them to the consumption of films … The institution is outside us and inside us, indistinctly collective and intimate, sociological and psychoanalytic.' Christian Metz, 'The imaginary signifier: psychoanalysis and the cinema', in Metz, *The Imaginary Signifier: Psychoanalysis and the Cinema*, trans. Celia Britton, Annwyl Williams, and Ben Brewster (Bloomington, Ind.: Indiana University Press, 1982), p. 7. In addition to Metz's essay, key texts on apparatus theory include: Jean-Louis Baudry, 'The apparatus: metapsychological approaches to the impression of reality in cinema', *Communications*, 23 (1975), and 'Ideological effects of the basic cinematographic apparatus', *Cinéthique* no. 7–8 (1970), both

reprinted in translation in Philip Rosen (ed.), *Narrative, Apparatus, Ideology: A Film Theory Reader* (New York: Columbia University Press, 1986).

17 Although the debt is not openly acknowledged, much of Wollen's argument is prefigured in Annette Michelson's 1966 essay 'Film and the radical aspiration', in which she had already identified a split between formal and political aspects of radical or revolutionary efforts in film production since the 1920s. It is also important to note that Wollen uses the term 'Co-op movement' loosely to refer not only to the activity of the London Film-makers' Co-op but also to related movements emerging in North America (especially structural film). See Peter Wollen, 'The two avant-gardes', *Studio International*, 190:978 (November/December, 1975), pp. 171–75. Wollen's essay has figured prominently in discussions of the intersections between art and film since its publication in the mid-1970s. David James's *Allegories of Cinema* (Princeton: Princeton University Press, 1989), for example, responds to and expands upon Wollen's model by applying his theorisation to the context of 1960s experimental film in North America.

18 Once again, Wollen's critique effectively collapsed North American structural film (including Snow) with Gidal's and Le Grice's quite distinct theorisation of structural-materialist film.

19 Bart Testa evaluates Le Grice and Gidal's problematic application of structuralist theory in verifying Snow's presumed relationship to structural-materialist film in 'An axiomatic cinema: Michael Snow's films'.

20 Writing in 1977, Le Grice's clarification of the theoretical argument behind his position outlined in *Film as Film*'s catalogue can be seen at least in part as a response to Wollen's influential critique. Le Grice proposes that 'the political questions of formal cinema center, not on the issue of political content in the films, but on the political implications of the film's language, conventions and structure'. 'Most importantly', he continues, 'formal cinema centers on the mode of perception and conception which is available to the *viewer* of the film. Form *determines* the mode of response in the audience'. Le Grice, *Abstract Film and Beyond*, pp. 87, 152. Emphasis added.

21 Testa, 'An axiomatic cinema: Michael Snow's films', p. 29.

22 Annette Michelson, 'About Snow', *October*, 8 (Spring 1979), p. 113.

23 It is in those terms, argued Michelson, 'that we may begin to comprehend the profound effect [*Wavelength*] had upon the broadest spectrum of viewers – especially upon those for whom previous assaults on the spatiotemporality of dominant cinema had obscured the subject's role and place'. 'About Snow', p. 118.

24 De Duve directly challenges this interpretation of Snow's films in a retrospective analysis of the artist's early work. See de Duve, 'Michael Snow: the deictics of experience, and beyond', p. 34.

25 In fact, *De La*, along with better-known works such as Frank Gillette and Ira Schneider's *Wipe Cycle* (1969), Bruce Nauman's video corridors, and Dan Graham's video and mirror environments, marks one of the earliest uses of real-time closed-circuit video technology in an art gallery.

26 Barbara Rose, 'Considering Robert Whitman', in Martin Friedman et al., *Projected Images: Peter Campus, Rockne Krebs, Paul Sharits, Michael Snow, Ted Victoria, Robert Whitman* (Minneapolis: Walker Art Center, 1974), p. 41.

27 Martin Friedman, 'The floating picture plane', in Friedman et al., *Projected Images*, p. 6.
28 Michelson in Friedman et al., *Projected Images*, p. 21.
29 All quotations are from Regina Cornwell, 'Michael Snow', in Friedman et al., *Projected Images*, pp. 26, 31.
30 Cornwell, 'Hitting on "a lot of near Mrs"', *Film Reader*, 3 (1978), p. 241.
31 Le Grice, 'Mapping in multispace: expanded cinema to virtuality', in Sabine Breitweiser (ed.), *White Cube/Black Box Skulpturensammlung: Video Installation Film: Werkschau Valie Export und Gordon Matta-Clark* (Vienna: Generali Foundation, 1996), p. 267.
32 Dominique Païni, 'Should we put an end to projection?', *October*, 110 (Fall 2004), p. 32.
33 Païni, 'Should we put an end to projection?', p. 44.

Part II
Screen

Projecting symptoms 4

Joanna Lowry

In *The Visible and the Invisible* Maurice Merleau-Ponty struggled with the development of a theory of vision that would take into account our embodiment, describing the 'chiasmatic' relationship between the viewer and the world, an intertwining through which the world is brought into a kind of visibility. What he felt needed to be put into question and seen as problematic was how the viewer came to be seen as separate from the world – how the visual ever became positioned as something other, something differentiated and separate from the spectator. Stephen Melville sums up the central issue thus:

> Vision is the place where our continuity with the world conceals itself, the place where we mistake our contact for distance, imagining that seeing is a substitute for, rather than a mode of, touching – and it is this anaesthesia, this senselessness, at the heart of transparency that demands our acknowledgement and pushes our dealings with the visual beyond recognition.[1]

Recent studies theorising the history of the visual have made us more aware of its provisionality, and of the extent to which our relationship to the presumed transparency of vision is in fact the product of complex historical conditions and cultural formations. Melville's comments draw our attention particularly to the way in which the very definition of 'the visual' is predicated upon the construction of a distance between the spectator and the world – a distance that is maintained through the work of culture and through the work of technology. Photographic technologies have provided one key cultural mechanism for defining the place of the visual and positioning it in relationship to us. In representing the subject they also define the site of the subject's visibility, the place at which he or she can be seen. They cut through the world; interrupt it, producing difference and distance, and projecting these onto the surface of the paper or the screen. They produce a differentiated space of the visible within which the subject and the spectator are made aware of their otherness and their distance from each other.

In this essay I explore some of the ways in which contemporary video installations have plotted that relationship between the subject and the spectator, and the implications that these developments have for the way in which we understand subjectivity as a cultural construction. I argue that through these practices the self that is projected onto these screens is invariably seen as a potentially hysterical self, peculiarly fragile and troubled. We tend, when confronted with these works, to read the signs of the subject's behaviour clinically – as though they were symptoms of a hidden trauma. One way of understanding this phenomenon is to plot its origins in the early relationship established between photography and mental illness in the nineteenth century. My argument is that the peculiar ambivalence between the clinical and the theatrical that was established in some of these images, linked as it was to ideas about the evidential power of the photographic image itself, established a powerful discursive space that is still being actively articulated in the gallery today. The works that I describe each deploy this discursive space in slightly different ways, but all involve a specific negotiation of the relationship between the spectator and the subject through the way in which they are physically installed, and all of them in some sense construct that relationship as diagnostic, with the subject exhibiting their symptoms to a clinical gaze.

The studio and the clinic

The development of the concept of mental illness in the nineteenth century involved a constellation of ideas around the body as the physical site of observable symptoms, the performance of which could be captured by both photography and film. This construction of a diagnostic apparatus was connected to a production of the hysterical subject through encouraging the patient to perform their symptoms.[2] It is possible to trace the historical congruence that emerged between the clinic or consulting room and the photographic studio from that period into the present day. The relationship between the development of photographic technologies and the representation of mental illness has been well documented by a number of writers, notably Sander Gilman, Allan Sekula, David Green, Jessica Evans, Suren Lalvani, and Georges Didi-Huberman.[3] Central to all these studies was a recognition that photographic technology provided an unprecedented opportunity for the cultural construction of the body as a set of visible signs that appeared to satisfy a positivist desire for visual evidence of hidden mental or emotional states. Drawing on a dominantly Foucauldian perspective, these writers emphasised the role played by these technologies in classifying, monitoring, and essentially producing mental illness as an object of knowledge.

What also emerged in these studies, however, was the observation that in the nineteenth century there was a recurrent concern with the potentially destabilising function of the notion of performance. How could one determine whether the symptomatic behaviour being expressed by the subject was involuntary or performed, and if it was performed, then could it be seen as an authentic expression of an inner state or not? These debates, which circulated in the medical and scientific journals of the time, intimated evidence of a mismatch between the positivist ontology embedded in the scientific reception of these technologies and the popular, performative appropriation of portrait photography as a site for playing with identity and social roles.

Three examples of the photographic documentation of hysterical illness in particular spring to mind, each of which offers some insight into the phenomenon with which we are concerned: the photographs of the insane taken by Dr Hugh Diamond at the Surrey County Lunatic Asylum in the 1850s, the set of photographs taken by Oscar Rejlander in 1877 to illustrate Darwin's study of the expressions of the emotions in man, and the photographs of female hysterics taken by Albert Londe for the French psychiatrist Jean-Martin Charcot at the Salpêtrière Hospital for the Insane in Paris at the end of the nineteenth century.

Hugh Diamond, the resident superintendent of the Female Department of the Surrey County Lunatic Asylum in the 1850s, was responsible for the collection of a large archive of photographs of the patients. Sander Gilman has pointed out that these images were being produced at a time when there was a real shift happening in our understanding of the relationship between mind and body.[4] Early mechanistic relationships between a notion of mental pathology and its physical expression were being supplanted by more complex ones and the photography of the insane appeared to offer a neutral diagnostic space for the analysis of this. In a paper that Diamond read before the Royal Society in 1856, 'On the application of photography in the physiognomic and mental phenomena of insanity', a series of interesting observations about the photographic image may be discerned.

Firstly Diamond claimed that the photograph spoke for itself – it was objectively accurate. It seemed, therefore, in the terms of the positivistic framework within which scientific forms of photography were understood at that time, to offer a neutral, dispassionate representation of the symptoms of the patient. Secondly, he suggested, its archival capacity meant that it offered the potential for the cataloguing of a psychopathology. Thirdly, perhaps most interestingly, he observed that it offered the potential to reveal to patients themselves a representation of their own pathological state. Photography, then, might not only play a part in the diagnosis of a pathology, but might also produce that reflexive moment of self-recognition that could be part of the cure. Gilman describes how Diamond's contemporary, the psychiatrist John Connolly, also noted in response to Diamond's photographs that there was something peculiar to the photographic representation of the expression which could not be replicated through traditional forms of representation: photography, he noted, could capture the after-effect of the impression of a recent muscular agitation, the 'singular expression arising from morbid movements of the mind'.[5]

Anticipating Walter Benjamin's notion of the optical unconscious, Diamond intimated that the camera, disinterestedly mechanical, could usurp our expectations by revealing things we did not know about ourselves – aspects of our behaviour that we would not, otherwise, have been able to see. It is easy to see in such an approach the convergence of a set of ideas about the mind, as a hidden space to be revealed through the interpretation of symptoms played out on the surface of the body and the idea of photography as a privileged screen upon which those symptoms might be projected. It becomes evident that the concept of facial and bodily expression as a special kind of primarily symptomatic sign is supported and sustained by elements of the photographic sign – the indexical, the archival, the mechanistic, the contingent, and the reflexive.

Charles Darwin, writing his book on the *Expression of the Emotions in Man and Animals* in 1871, made extensive use of photographs of the insane to illustrate his examples.[6] It was, he claimed, the insane who suffered the strongest emotions, and who gave uncontrolled vent to them. Darwin encountered a number of interesting problems, however, in his analysis of these photographic images. Sander Gilman has plotted the ambiguity in Darwin's approach to the photographic image, at one point insisting on the veracity of the clinical image – and utilising it precisely because it seemed to indicate verifiable evidence of the emotional states with which he was concerned – and at another point employing the well-known photographer Oscar Rejlander to make photographs of actors posing to represent the emotions. Gilman argues that towards the end of his study Darwin became increasingly sceptical about the veracity of the photographic image and the difficulty of distinguishing within it between the authentic and the performed.[7]

The very same issues concerning the relationship between authenticity and performance were central to the discussions around photography that were taking place at the Salpêtrière Hospital for the Insane in Paris between 1876 and 1888.[8] The principal psychiatrist, Charcot, was celebrated for his investigation of hysteria. Every Tuesday he would hold public audiences at which he would lecture about his patients to the assorted congregation of doctors, students, and general public, bringing them along to act out their hysterical symptoms in public. Through hypnosis he was able both to suppress their symptoms and encourage them to replay their maniacal behaviour to order. He also collected a huge archive of photographs of the patients, which he used to illustrate his emerging classification of hysterical symptoms. One of the most interesting aspects of this practice is the shift that is registered in Charcot's work from a use of photography that was essentially classificatory into one that was diagnostic and which indeed ultimately involved the use of photography to actually produce a set of hysterical symptoms.[9]

It is clear, furthermore, that there were a number of interesting parallels between the theatre of the asylum and the popular theatre. Many of the gestures and expressions of the women bore close resemblance to the stylised melodramatic gestures of contemporary actors. Indeed, one of the great concerns at the heart of Charcot's work was the issue of performance. How could he be sure that the women's symptoms were authentic and that they weren't simulating them? The concern was intensified by the popular belief that one of the key qualities of the hysteric was her tendency towards theatrical performance and dramatic effect. On the one hand, Charcot believed that the photograph was a disinterested scientific tool, allowing for the cataloguing and classification of a number of psychiatric diseases, and indeed allowing for a level of scrutiny of the subject that might expose any artifice or deception. On the other hand, he was complicit in the construction of a photographic theatre that actively incited the reproduction of a symptomatology.

These examples drawn from the nineteenth century are significant because they reveal the emergence of an uncertainty in our relationship to photographically based images that has remained with us ever since. Whilst photography offered an unprecedented objective recording of the physical presence of a person, its invention coincided with the development of complex models of the self and the psyche that rendered such recordings unreliable. This paradox was played out through the convergence of a clinical and a photographic gaze, linked to the diagnostic interrogation of the performance of the self.

Whilst, therefore, the rules for constructing a neutralised scientific space of observation might be elaborate and considered, they also had a tendency to be imperfect and difficult to maintain and control. One of the cultural legacies of this history is, I would argue, a continuing uncertainty in our understanding of the relationship of the performing subject to the image, and also a pervasive ambiguity in our understanding of the kind of performance space represented by the camera. This space is one that often shifts uncertainly between being a theatre and a clinic, a workshop, and a laboratory. If there is a backdrop curtain in a photographic image, then its function can be twofold, both to set a scene and to screen it off. In either case, however, we are considering, as a result of the gradual embedding of these pictorial conventions, a peculiar convergence within photographic technologies themselves of visual discourses concerned with understanding the psychological state of the subject. It is possible to think, therefore, about photography as constituting a particular type of cultural site for the production of the self. It is a site that can be thought of as bounded by a distinctive relationship between the surface of the print as a place on which the identity of the subject is inscribed, and the confined, hybrid space within which that identity is performed for us. It has become established as a concentrated source of knowledge about the psychological state of the subject – a space in which every gesture or expression is to be read as a symptom.

The discursive convergence between theatre and clinic has had a powerful influence on the development of contemporary variations on the theme of the portrait, particularly in the realm of video art, where, since the early experiments of performance artists in the 1960s and 1970s the self is often portrayed on screen as a hysterical subject on the verge of breakdown: weeping, shouting, laughing, confessing, and always in extremis. The figure of the performance artist that dominates this particular moment in history is an agonistic subject performing to the camera in his or her studio, subjecting the body to humiliating feats of endurance or narcissistically interrogating his or her own image and confessing his or her own abjection. Artists such as Vito Acconci, Marina Abramovic, and Bruce Nauman all played a role in establishing the site of video performance as one in which the very basis of the psychic integrity of the person could be routinely subjected to stress, interrogation, and degradation. The video recording of a performance, with its rough, real-time presence became a vehicle of the construction of a discursive space that sought to link concepts of authenticity (registered by the recording itself) and performativity, the space of performance being established as one in which the self might be effectively dismantled.

In these scenarios the psychological subject that emerged was often presented as deeply unstable. Artists engaged in the monotonous repetition of acts or words for hours on end, talking to themselves through the camera, masturbating or hitting themselves, or reproducing some banal activity: Marina Abramovic brushing her hair with increasing violence, or Vito Acconci thrusting his fist in and out of his mouth, so repeatedly and intensely that it eventually became an act of violent self-abuse. The performance to camera rapidly became established, almost by default, as the site of a kind of psychic working through of a trauma, a privileged site for acting out the limits of what it means to be a person. Recorded by the camera, the bare studio spaces in which these activities took place were at once a theatre and a laboratory. In this space all of the wider connotations of identity were stripped away and the subject was exposed to a more acute scrutiny. From the spectator's position, beyond the fourth wall, the performers were examined with a kind of dispassionate dissociation. The assumption that lies behind these practices is that this space, marked out by the narrow margin between the blank studio wall and the screen, is a space within which the fragility of the psyche can be fully tested and revealed.

It is clear here that there are similarities between the development of photography as a space for the performance of unstable psychologies in the nineteenth century and the emergence of the video screen as a site for the performance of hysterical behaviour in the latter half of the twentieth century. Notwithstanding the differences between the two technologies and the different debates about medium-specificity engendered by each of them, I would argue that they both share a common formation, each of them founded, in the early years of their production, as technologies for the performance of the self. These two means of visual reproduction, video and photography, have thus become established in contemporary practice as apparatuses for the production of subjectivity and are thereby linked to a psychic economy that is intrinsically fragile. This is an economy in which the subject, whether posing for a photographic portrait, or performing on the screen, is invariably on the brink of dissolution, is always potentially hysterical.

The experiments of the early performance artists of the 1960s were replayed in a new form in the 1990s in work by artists such as Gillian Wearing and Sam Taylor-Wood who also deployed the use of real-time recording in a quasi-clinical setting to explore notions of psychic instability. Wearing's classic *Confess All On Video. Don't Worry You Will Be In Disguise. Intrigued? Call Gillian* (1994), which features long monologues by masked individuals telling their terrible secrets, was perhaps the most well-known work among many of that period which deployed the confessional discourse of the clinical/therapeutic context as a space of revelation. Wearing's work was always reflexive in its use of medium: the comical masks worn by her subjects, whilst offering them the security of anonymity, also cocked a snook at the camera's ability to show the truth, and posed the fundamental question of how we read any face. In her other work, too, Wearing constantly drew attention to the complicity of the medium in the performance of self, using strategies such as playing tapes backwards or re-dubbing voices over actors' bodies.

Taylor-Wood exploited the ambivalence of performance and hysteria and paid actors to act out the extremes of emotion. In *Method in Madness* (1994) she employed a method actor to act out a gradual emotional breakdown to the camera; in a series called *Crying Men* (2002) she photographed a number of celebrity figures in tears. The ambivalence of the performed emotion was also explored in extremis by Bill Viola, whose portraits of actors performing a variety of exaggerated emotions, from joy to despair, were replayed in slow motion whilst framed as traditional portraits on the wall in the ensemble installation of *The Passions* (2003). The state-of-the-art, mesmerising clarity of these recordings provided a foil to the deconstructive power of the technology, which was, in effect, looking for the chinks in the performance, yet revealing it as a seamless whole. Through their use of both actors and ordinary people, these artists interrogated the ontology of performance. But what is also clear is that video art became the site of a peculiar visibility of the body under stress.

If video was established in the 1970s as perhaps the most significant site for the performance of the instability of the self, in more recent years this phenomenon has been intensified by the emergence of the large screen as a site for its projection. The large-scale projected image of the subject under stress has helped to consolidate the gallery as a place where we engage in a kind of diagnosis of the contemporary subject. The technology of video 'projection' intensifies focus on 'projection' as a psychological mechanism which implicates the viewer. Thus, the new apparatus of video (large-screen, digital projection) has increasingly emerged as a privileged cultural site for the definition of modern subjectivity. Stripped of all external contextual references, and subjected to the rigidity of the video artist's stipulations, clinically interrogated by the lens, our frailty and perversity is exposed at that very moment at which the video camera starts recording.

Projections, symptoms, and therapy

Perhaps perversely, it is in the new form of large-screen video projection that the technologies of photography and video have become most closely interrelated, for it is in this space of installation that the kinds of spectatorship each demands are most closely allied. The use of extreme, slowed-down temporality which accompanies many artists' use of video projection – including Sam Taylor-Wood, Bill Viola, and, famously, Douglas Gordon – confirms this convergence between the still and moving image. Works by these artists produce a video time that tends either towards stasis, repetition, and the loop, or alternatively towards an extended sense of presentness that is experienced as actually *resistant* to time. The diagnostic gaze that we have inherited from photography's historical complicity in the nineteenth-century preoccupation with physiognomy as an indicator of social or mental pathology is implicit in the way we address images in this space.

In 1995, for a work called *Hysterical*, the artist Douglas Gordon acquired some original film footage of two doctors subduing a hysterical woman (figure 4.1). The film was originally made in 1908 by the Italian filmmaker Roberto Omegna, in collaboration with the neurologist Camillo Negro. The woman, presumably a patient, is masked. As she falls into a hysterical fit the two doctors attempt to control her. In the ensuing sequence, as she is forced into submission on the hospital bed, a seemingly brutal struggle ensues. Gordon looped the footage, projecting it onto two slightly misaligned screens, each showing the same sequence, but each slowed down at a slightly different rate so that it was impossible to see the whole at once, or to make sense of the space between the two scenes. There was always something happening on the other screen, something that the spectator might catch out of the corner of his or her eye, something that was evading the gaze. Through the explicit handling and manipulation of film footage the artist was able to disrupt its relationship to the history of film and relocate it in the domain of the psyche, subjecting it to a set of rules that were not unlike those of Freud's dream work – revision, repetition, condensation. The repeated film became an obsessive object in its own right, capable of generating its own relationship to the

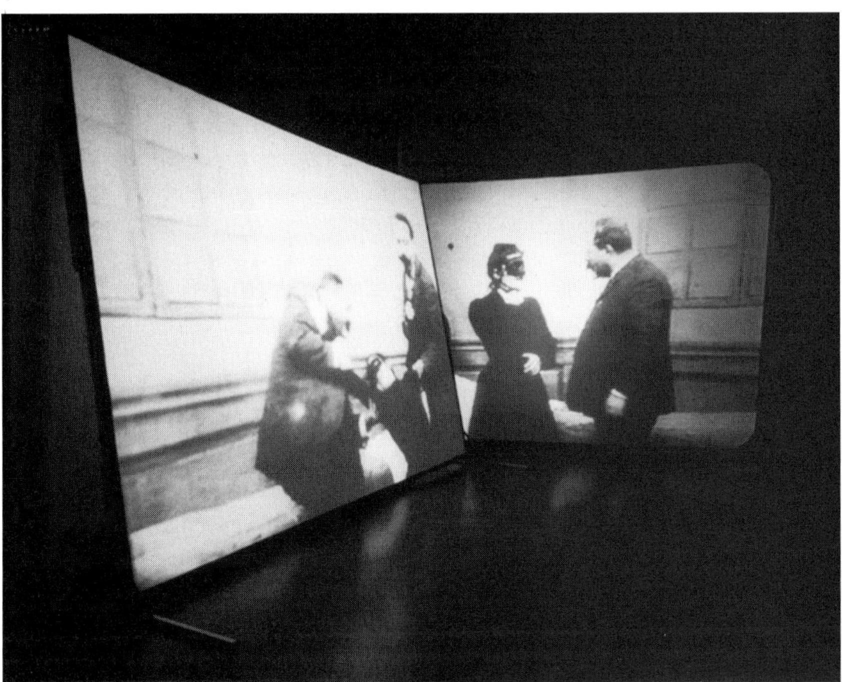

Douglas Gordon, *Hysterical*, 1994–95. Video installation, dimensions variable, black-and-white, silent, 3 minutes. © Douglas Gordon. Courtesy of Gagosian Gallery. 4.1

spectator's desire. Looped time will always put into question the authenticity of the original moment. As the scene is repeatedly replayed the gap between the original moment and the performance expands. In the extraordinary, desperate struggle of the three bodies, the violence becomes less urgent, more like a dance, and as time slows down the long wait between the frames seems to offer the final clue to the origin of the event, to the difference between the 'as it happened' and the 'as we see it now'. Gordon's two screens are strategies of interruption; the spectator cannot immerse him- or herself in this scene; it is always in a state of deferral.

This work deliberately leaves unanswered, and therefore paradoxically emphasises, a set of questions around the screen, the spectator and the representation of hysteria. In the curiously neutralised mise-en-scène of the clinic, with only the blanked-out window and the hospital bed as clues to the origin of the footage, the relationship between the theatrical and the experimental becomes ambiguous and a cultural convergence between the two is effected. The repetition of the looped film reiterates both the process of repetition that is central to theatrical performance and the repetitiveness of the scientific experimental process. Without any contextualisation of the film fragment we are unable to understand why the patient is hysterical, nor the seeming brutality of the medical team, but what is established is the potential complicity of film as a medium in the representation of hysteria. The film documents the hysterical fit, but it also reproduces the repetitive conditions of the symptom through its own processes of repetition. Furthermore the interior space within which the scene takes place is confirmed as a space bounded by the performance of the symptom, its diagnosis, and its management; as a space which we might think of as a clinic, with the spectator taking on a detached and diagnostic gaze. Furthermore, through the objectification of the film itself on the two screens, placed in the centre of the gallery as sculptural objects, the installation draws our attention to the close relationship between the material surface of the film as a medium and the clinical theatre of representations played out upon it.

This convergence between film as a medium, the diagnostic gaze, and a theatre of hysteria was also the subject of another work of the same period, made by Gillian Wearing. From 1997–99, for a work called *Drunk*, the artist worked with a group of itinerant alcoholics (figures 4.2 and 4.3). She set up an improvised theatre in the street, and a white backdrop was hung up against a wall to designate the studio. Over a number of weeks Wearing had befriended a group of alcoholic street drinkers and this became their space of performance.

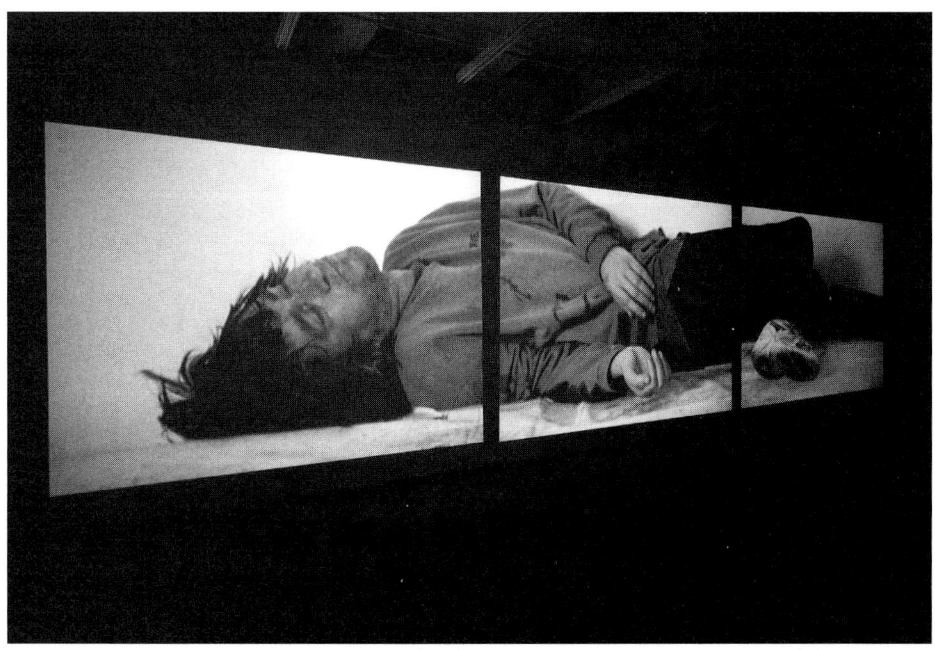

4.2 Gillian Wearing, *Drunk*, 1999. Three-channel video for projection, black-and-white, sound, 23 minutes. Courtesy of Maureen Paley, London.

Her recording of their drunken dissolution was then projected life-size on three interconnected screens, as a triptych. Totally decontextualising the action, the white rectangle of the improvised screen constructed a space of performance for the drunken subjects being represented. For the spectator it was a space of clinical scrutiny, a space that would clarify and intensify our reading of the behaviour taking place within its frame. The white monochrome background that was the boundary line of the performance operated as a parody of the neutralised space of scientific investigation, both spectacularising but also alienating the spectator from the performers. It was painful and, some critics have claimed, perhaps disturbingly unethical, to watch these inebriated figures perform their drunkenness on the screen, their bodies out of control, their emotions veering between a pathological alienation and extreme explosions of anger and grief.[10] This was the spectacle of what happens to the body when the mind loses control, yet in this context it was difficult for the spectator to discern where authenticity ended and performance began. It was only the final fall into comatose unconsciousness that confirmed a kind of truth.

Both of these works of art employ subtle conventions to position the spectator in a slightly deflected relation to the troubling scene that is being enacted. Through the devices of splitting the screen, or, in Gordon's case, dupli-

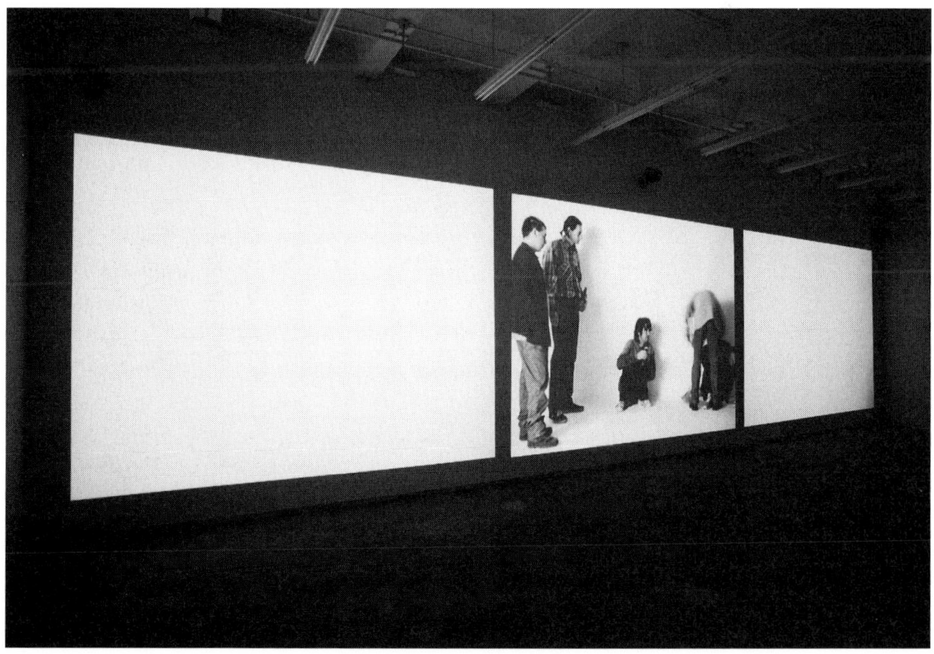

Gillian Wearing, *Drunk*, 1999. Three-channel video for projection, black-and-white, sound, 23 minutes. Courtesy of Maureen Paley, London. 4.3

cating it, the position of the observer is displaced from any direct engagement with the participants in the scene. The spectator is, through this deflection, positioned so that he or she cannot identify with the subject, but must instead observe them. In each case he or she is confronted with the spectacle of a clinical theatre and is thereby situated in a place from which the subject's behaviour demands not to be engaged with or responded to, but instead to be read as a set of symptoms, signs of some invisible and unarticulated trauma. Both these works use the quasi-clinical heritage of photographic technologies to define the individual subject as inherently unstable and hysterical, and to establish the screen of video projection as a site for the display and performance of their symptoms. The medium of video projection has thus become, in a very material way, associated with a particular way of understanding what it is to be a person in contemporary society.

However, developments in the way in which video portraits have been installed in recent years have given their relationship with the spectator an added complexity. The size and scale of these projections and their architectural presence situate them in a very different domain from that of work displayed on a monitor. And the emphasis on a confrontation with the face itself means that the spectator's relationship to the subject is of a very different kind from that represented by the two works described above. In both cases the spectator could be a detached observer of hysterical behaviour, whereas in these works the subject is larger than life and in a sense confronts the spectator, requiring of them, in some obscure and indefinable way, that they read their signs. Between 1996 and 2003 Thomas Struth recorded a series of large-scale video portraits that were to be projected onto hanging screens. These were displayed like spectral presences around the huge museum space, the apparatus of projection subtly concealed. There was an archival structure underpinning the work, arguably borrowed from the example of still photographer August Sander's early twentieth-century portraits of subjects classified by profession: Struth's subjects included a number of distinct bourgeois social types, including an architect, a student, an art dealer, Struth's godson, a little girl … The subjects were not selected for their individuality but because, at some level, they were fairly unremarkable, resolutely middle-class, benignly typical – their personal histories were unimportant for the work. It was their anonymity and consequently their emptiness as potential spaces for the inscription of meaning and the projection of fantasy that made them compelling. This anonymity initially impelled the spectator to consider these portraits at the level of surface, as occupying the flat dimensions of the screen. Without a sense of a particular person to whom one might begin to ascribe some meaning and identity, the faces that were presented to the spectator could only return his or her reading back onto themselves. Their blankness refused any narrative coding of the time of the pose. The emphasis on spectacularly large, formal, and simple screens also encouraged the spectator to see the screens as modernist objects, drawing attention to the elusive materiality of the surface of the screen itself, reinforcing the fact that, though it offered a representational depth, the screen was also an object that was absolutely without depth, absolutely thin: one could walk behind it.

These screens, though, also operated as sites for exposing the self under a certain duress. The subjects sat or stood for a whole hour in front of the camera, as still as possible, their concentration occasionally interrupted by the blink of an eye, a slight wriggle of the body or shifting of their pose. Under the imposition of the rigid terms of engagement they entered into a trance-like state, alternating almost imperceptibly between a subtle self-consciousness in front of the camera and a withdrawn meditative state, flickering in between the place of being and the requirement to become a sign. At times it seemed that these people were on the brink of becoming so self-absorbed that they might slip out of visibility itself, withdraw into some other imaginary space and leave one with only the surface of the screen to gaze at. The relationship between the surface materiality of the image and the performance was absolutely fragile and thin. But in that context the subject seems fragile too, holding him- or herself together for the sake of the recording. In this sense, despite the calmer tone of these works, which contrasts with those earlier video pieces I have discussed, Struth's works could, perhaps surprisingly, be seen to reinforce the sense of the screen as a site for the inscription of our psychic fragility.

One way of interpreting these portraits is as being about the way in which we are constituted as subjects in a technological culture; they dramatise the tension between technologies of surveillance and the self-determination of performance that is at the heart of my discussion here. But the works also raise important questions about the gaze and the significance it takes on in the gallery context. Struth's screens were suspended from the ceiling and hung, angled away from each other so that they could only be looked at one at a time. Holding their pose as still as possible for such a long period of time and staring straight into the camera lens was certainly an exercise in endurance for the subjects, one which had its own power dynamic in relation to the mobile, shifting audience that passed through the museum halls where it was installed. The spectator felt compelled to return the gaze, to watch back, but inevitably could not meet the challenge – was out-faced, and turned to move on to the next encounter uncomfortably aware of his or her irrelevance to the subject they had left behind. Part of the discomfiture was of course related to the fact that the gaze that seemed to be directed at the spectator was not directed at him or her at all, but at the camera. The very directness of the apparent form of address was in fact an illusion, masking the presence of the filmic apparatus. The camera in this work represented a blind spot in the visual field. It situated the spectator's gaze, but it was now absent and became a kind of vanishing point for a returning gaze that could never be met.

When faced with works like this, we also feel as though there is a sense in which, in front of the image, it is we who are positioned in the place of the visible. We are reminded of Lacan's discomfiture in his anecdote about the sardine can bobbing in the sea, glinting in the sun, not seeing him as he sits in the boat with the laughing fishermen, but nevertheless placing him in the field of the visible.[11] Now we become aware that the very fact that the subjects of these works don't see us exposes the space of the visible as far from being a continuous plane. It is in fact uneven, fissured, and folded, and we are reminded that this space of visibility is peculiarly complicated by the intervention of the apparatus. It is this fault-line in the visible, at the point of the illusory convergence of these two gazes – the subject's and the spectator's – that defines the difference and the distance between us.

Struth's work can be seen as typical of a genre of contemporary video portraiture centred on the large projected face. I have suggested that there is an ambivalence within this work about how it addresses the spectator, not only as the disengaged spectator of a modernist tradition, but also as an object of the gaze produced by the image, and finally and perhaps most fundamentally as a spectator who is 'diagnostic' and who can see and interpret the vulnerability of the subject portrayed. This is a hypothesised spectator who can clearly be traced back to the traditions of photographic representation that were discussed earlier in this essay. However, in many contemporary video installations we are no longer positioned as objective observers by our spectatorial position; we are positioned instead as embodied spectators in the space; the theatre includes us; it is fundamentally dialogic. In such works there is a convergence between a diagnostic gaze and a space of performance of the self within a dialogical framework. This establishes the space of projection as one that is bounded by the psychical parameters of the therapeutic relationship.

In 2006 Phil Collins installed a major piece of work, *gerçeğin geri dönüşü* (*the return of the real*) (2005), in the Tate Gallery Turner Prize show (figure 4.4). In a long darkened room, empty apart from benches for the spectators down each side, two projections faced each other. On one wall, at a large scale, there was a series of faces of Turkish individuals who had been participants in reality TV shows, each recounting in a series of lengthy interviews the impact that this experience had had upon their life. On the opposite wall a separate projection displayed their interviewer. He was himself a director of reality shows, but in this situation took the role of a kindly counsellor or therapist, eliciting their story, encouraging them to tell more, nodding his assent to their attempts to construct the narrative of their lives, sympathetically engaging with their confusion and despair, and, by his very neutral and non-judgemental presence, encouraging them to go further and tell more.

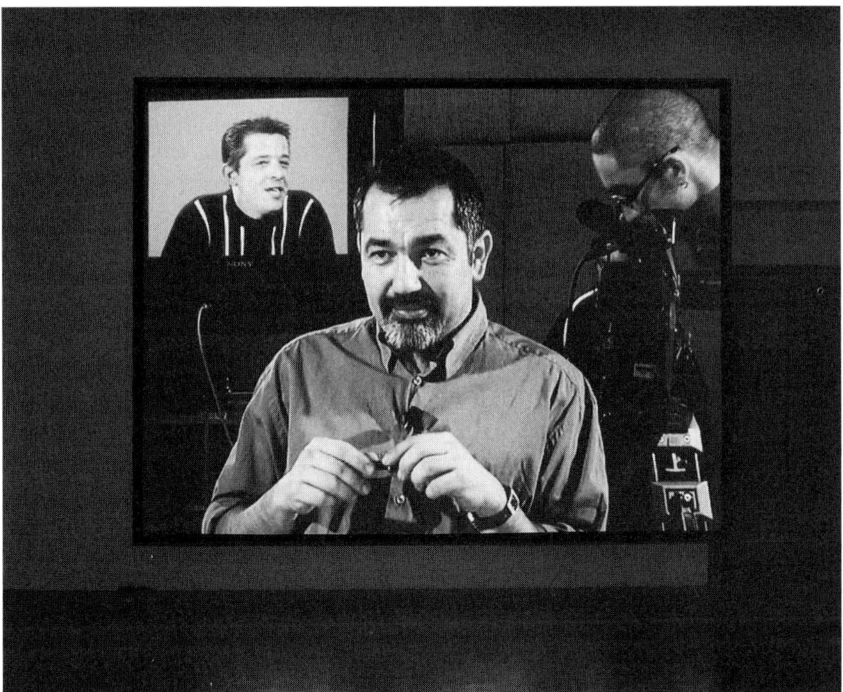

Phil Collins, *gerçeğin geri dönüşü* (*the return of the real*), 2005. Multi-channel video installation, colour, sound, 60 minutes. Installation view, Ausstellungshalle zeitgenössische Kunst Münster, 2007. Photo: Thomas Wrede. Courtesy Shady Lane Productions. 4.4

Whilst the former participants were represented against a blank backdrop – representing the neutrality of the 'studio' as a site of representation – the director was clearly seen in the studio that is the site of production, with all his equipment behind him, the interviewees' faces being simultaneously screened, as they spoke, on a monitor behind him. This screen, the one displaying the director, therefore represented not only the scene of production but also that of projection, and in this sense it also implicitly complied with the construction of the kind of narcissistic structuring of video space that was endemic to the forms of early video art referred to above. In such works artists performed to the camera whilst simultaneously being seen performing on the monitor, a form of practice which Rosalind Krauss has famously declared to be characteristic of the medium itself: 'The body ... [is] centred between two machines that are the opening and closing of a parenthesis. The first of these is the camera; the second is the monitor, which re-projects the performer's image with the immediacy of a mirror.'[12]

The interviews, then, in the way in which they were displayed, theatricalised a particular division of labour and power implicit in representation.

A space that seemed initially to be divided equally – two people in dialogue with each other – was actually the scene of a more complex allegorical representation of the very unequal power relations involved in any form of revelatory or confessional discourse, and of the role of technology in constructing the parameters of that discourse. Moreover, seated in the dark space between these two screens, it was clear that the audience were very clearly part of the space defined by that technological apparatus. The interviews, which were monologic in form, were extremely long – between forty minutes and an hour. In an important sense they were banal, undramatic, and apparently unedited. Non-Turkish speakers had to read the subtitles. Video art is no stranger to the epic representation of monotony, repetition, and the everyday; a generation of spectators have been armoured to endure hours of real time recording on the basis that this is an appropriate form for art to take in a consumerist society wedded to melodrama and spectacle. Nevertheless there was something interesting in the fact that so many visitors to the gallery were happy to relapse into a semi-somnolent state listening to the long, detailed biographies of a series of strangers – whilst reading the translations in subtitles.

The role of the spectator in such a space is fairly undemanding; indeed, it has passivity thrust upon it. There is no requirement here that he or she does anything but watch and listen. There is some comparison to be made with the immersive passivity of the cinema experience, but in this context the consequences of the conventions of unedited straight recording limit any sense of imaginative engagement; there is no dramatic structure to engage with, no tension to be felt, and even the requirement to seek some documentary truth has been stripped away. Yet there is still a sense that the spectator's passive presence is part of the apparatus, positioned physically at this empty interface between two projections. The spectator is a witness, one who scrutinises the face on the screen, looking for signs of self-possession or disintegration, seeking a glimpse of the truth, trying to match the fleeting expressions to the tone of the voice or the translated subtitles that flicker across the screen. He or she begins to take up a diagnostic gaze, a disinterested form of observation, matching words to gestures, fleeting expressions, seeing the screen as a surface made up of symptomatic signs rather than as producing a representation of a person.

Rosalind Krauss, in her discussion of the narcissism of video practice, saw the reflexive real-time loops that it created as being a mechanism that severed or disconnected the subject from 'text'.[13] In the collapsed present that is created by the mirror reflection of video, the subject, she argued, is severed from text, from language, from the public, and from their own psychic history. She saw this as a potentially regressive form of practice. Collins's installation, I would argue, suggests a different inflection of video's narcissism. His installation reconstructs the space of video projection as a therapeutic theatre or consulting room. The gallery space in this context has all the qualities of the communicational space of analysis. The temporal conflation that Krauss described is spatialised in this installation and, far from being about the evacuation of text, in this dramatised encounter we can see the subject becoming text, enacting the story through which they have become who they are. Their words are made visible through so many forms of recording and translation, their huge faces presented not as signs of identity but primarily as symptoms of some hidden unstable state. The projected image on screen in the gallery has become positioned as a peculiarly privileged site for the representation of the individual and for the definition of a modern form of unstable subjectivity. Stripped of all external contextual references, and subjected to the rigidity of the photographer's or filmmaker's stipulations, clinically interrogated by the lens, the individual's frailty is exposed at that very moment at which the video camera starts recording. Like the silent therapist in the chair at the end of the couch, the spectator's presence enables the symptomatic structure of the subject to be articulated, spoken, and made visible. The darkened gallery takes on the characteristics of a kind of consulting room, the screen becomes a site for the production of symptoms and the subject on the screen becomes that familiar 'clinical' subject that we have encountered before. In this installation the entire viewing space has been physically commandeered by a therapeutic discourse in which we appear to be literally placed inside the dialogical relationship created by the confessional structure of the piece.

Stephen Melville's observations about the instability of the relationship between viewer and viewed, and the problematic that he opens up when he asks how it is that we can be enabled to separate those positions, are important. They suggest a way of looking at the technologies that we use in the creation of artworks as mechanisms for the production of a problematised definition of the visible; it is an approach that implies indeed that visibility is hard-won and that spectatorship is something that has to be continually constructed and defined. In this essay I have tried to suggest that video projection as a technology for the production of art about the self has developed in the particular way it has partly as a result of a historically constituted set of discourses around mental illness and photography that stretch back into the nineteenth century. As a result of this the positions offered to the spectator by these works are always situated in a web of historically constituted discourses, discourses which suggest a clinical or diagnostic relationship between the spectator and the subject and which frame the modern self that is represented there as a set of symptoms. The argument is, perhaps, that the history of video installation is above all a cultural one, carrying the traces of discourses that have complex and entangled histories, the influence of which continue to permeate the spaces of projection.

Notes

1 Stephen Melville, 'Division of the gaze or remarks on the color and tenor of contemporary theory', in Melville, *Seams: Art as a Philosophical Context*, ed. Jeremy Gilbert-Rolfe (Amsterdam: G + B Arts, 1996), p. 121. Melville discusses the relationship between a Lacanian model of vision and Merleau-Ponty's concept of the embodied viewer in a way which has been helpful for my discussion here.

2 Georges Didi-Huberman's *Invention of Hysteria*, trans. Alisa Hartz (Cambridge, Mass.: MIT, 2003) is one of the key works to have drawn attention to this relationship.

3 Sander L. Gilman, *Difference and Pathology: Stereotypes of Sexuality, Race and Madness* (New York: Cornell University, 1985); Didi-Huberman, *Invention of Hysteria*; David Green, 'Veins of resemblance: Francis Galton, photography and eugenics', *Oxford Art Journal*, 7:2 (1984), pp. 3–16; Jessica Evans, 'The iron cage of visibility', *Ten.8 International Photography Journal*, 29 (1988), pp. 38–51; Suren Lalvani, *Photography, Vision and the Production of Modern Bodies* (Albany, N.Y.: State University of New York Press, 1996); Allan Sekula, 'The body in the archive', *October*, 39 (Winter 1986), pp. 3–64.

4 Sander Gilman, *Seeing the Insane* (New York: John Wiley and Sons/Brunner/Mazel Publishers, 1982). Gilman's discussion of this body of images can also be found in his 'The image of the hysteric', in Sander L. Gilman, Helen King, Roy Porter, G. S. Rousseau, and Elaine Showalter (eds), *Hysteria Beyond Freud* (Berkeley, Calif.: University of California Press, 1993), pp. 345–452.

5 Connolly, quoted in Gilman, *Seeing the Insane*, p. 168.

6 Charles Darwin, *The Expression of the Emotions in Man and Animals* (1871; London: John Murray, 1904). See Gilman's discussion of Darwin's use of photographs in his *Seeing the Insane*, pp. 179–90.

7 See Gilman, *Seeing the Insane*, p. 185.

8 There have been many studies of Charcot's treatment of hysteria, notably Didi-Huberman's *Invention of Hysteria*; A. R. G. Owen, *Hysteria, Hypnosis and Healing: The Work of J.-M. Charcot* (London: Dobson, 1971); Felicia McCarren, 'The "symptomatic act" circa 1900: hysteria, hypnosis, electricity, dance', *Critical Inquiry*, 21:4 (Summer 1995), pp. 748–73.

9 Ulrich Baer has made this aspect of Charcot's work the subject of a fascinating study in his *Spectral Evidence: The Photography of Trauma* (Cambridge, Mass.: MIT Press, 2002).

10 An extended discussion of the ethical implications of this work can be found in David Hopkins, '"Out of it": drunkenness and ethics in Martha Rosler and Gillian Wearing', *Art History*, 26:3 (June 2003), pp. 340–63.

11 Jacques Lacan, 'The line and light', in 'The gaze as *Objet petit a*', in *The Four Fundamental Concepts of Psychoanalysis*, trans. Alan Sheridan (London: Hogarth Press/Institute of Psychoanalysis, 1977), pp. 91–104.

12 Rosalind Krauss, 'Video: the aesthetics of narcissism', *October*, 1 (Spring 1976), pp. 50–64.

13 Krauss, 'Video: the aesthetics of narcissism', p. 53.

'You've got me under your spell': the entranced spectator 5

Maria Walsh

Strains of familiar music emanate from the space. I enter the gallery cube. A video is being projected. I know it is 3'48" in duration, so I watch distractedly, waiting for the loop to begin again. By that time, I have identified the music as one of Ennio Morricone's haunting scores for Sergio Leone's spaghetti westerns.[1] The film is *Lasso* (2000) by Finnish artist Salla Tykkä (figures 5.1–5.3). The loop begins.

A young girl in a blue tracksuit comes running down a street towards the camera. She stops at a house and, getting no answer to the house-bell, she walks around to the side and looks in the window. She sees a bare-chested young man in the sitting room frenetically lassoing the empty space around him. The incongruity of this scene is overridden by the choreography of his movements, which seem in sync with the hypnotic rhythm of the music. She stares transfixed. I gaze at

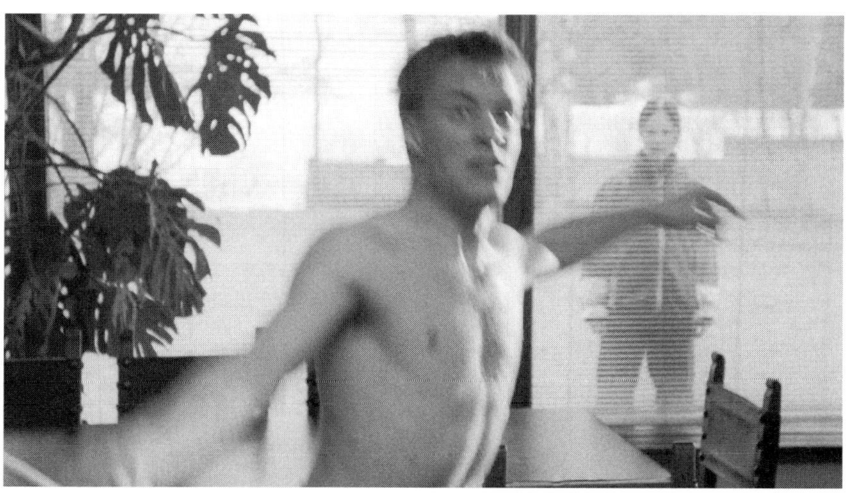

Salla Tykkä, *Lasso*, 2000 (video still). Video, colour, sound, 3 minutes 48 seconds. **5.1**

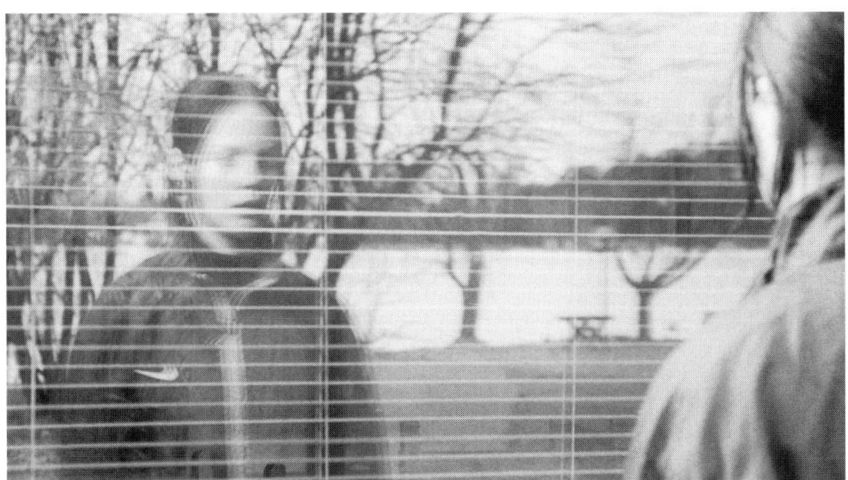

5.2 Salla Tykkä, *Lasso*, 2000 (video still). Video, colour, sound, 3 minutes 48 seconds. © Salla Tykkä. Courtesy of the artist and Yvon Lambert Paris, New York.

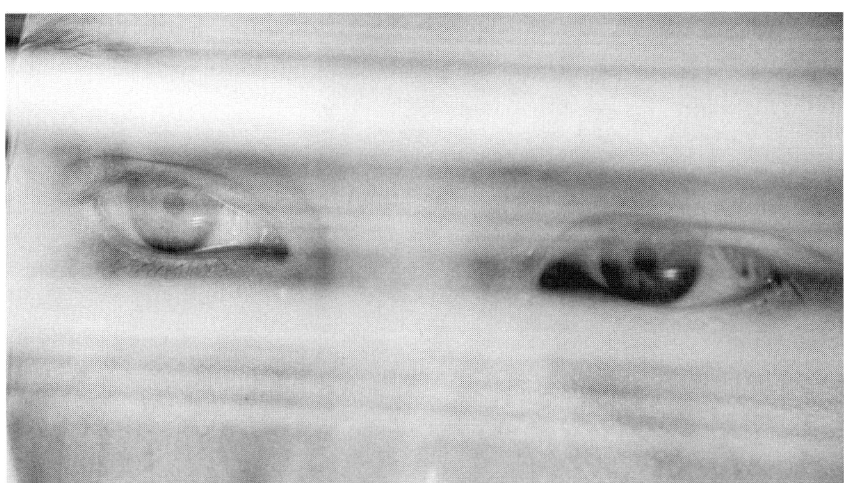

5.3 Salla Tykkä, *Lasso*, 2000 (video still). Video, colour, sound, 3 minutes 48 seconds. © Salla Tykkä. Courtesy of the artist and Yvon Lambert Paris, New York.

the space between them, as the camera moves from shots of one to shots of the other. It then cuts to a shot of the girl's face doubled. She looks, as if at herself, her image reflected in the window. This is followed by close-ups of the girl's face shot from behind and from in front of the window. Her blanched skin corresponds with her blank expression, its pallor slashed horizontally by the white strips of the window blind. I forget about the young man, captivated as I am by the surface of her skin and the various gradations of whiteness. Meanwhile, the young man brings the taut lasso to a standstill oblivious to the girl who continues to watch, impassive and fascinated, excluded from his world, as he is from hers. On one level, nothing further happens. There is no communication between them. A close-up of the girl's face reveals a tear. The psychological import of this is vanquished by the camera's movement, which dispassionately glides away from the girl and pans along the ground outside, stopping to focus on a fresh patch of snow, which bleeds into white video static, while Morricone's ode to spaghetti westerns continues. Now I stare transfixed by the screen's white glow. I am as if blinded in a snowstorm. My eyes are clouded by a shimmering haze that slips between my gaze and the image. I find myself suspended in the static pulsations of the white screen. Is there something emerging from the technological flakes? I cannot see in the white darkness.

In reflecting on my experience of this film, historical conceptions of spectatorship seemed unhelpful. It was obvious to me that I was seduced by the melodramatic intimations of a relationship between the protagonists and that I identified somewhat with the young girl's voyeuristic fascination and exclusion. However, the most captivating aspect of the film, the moment that really moved me and motivates this essay, is when the camera moves away from the girl's face and wanders over the snow encrusted ground, the image eventually bleeding into white technological static. Clearly, this was a moment of narrative dissolution, but I could not account for its significance in terms of distantiation. While my partial identifications disintegrated, this was not an occasion for taking up a critical position towards the seductive illusions of the image. On the contrary, I felt an even more intense proximity to an image quality that, for now, I shall call entrancement.

My deliberately personal trajectory here can be aligned with currents in contemporary film and video practice as well as with shifts in theoretical approaches to the moving image. Many contemporary film and video artists deploy forms of narrative inherited from Hollywood cinema to make moving-image works using similar means of producing pleasure and encouraging identification, but with the difference being that their modes of address are redirected. Tykkä's film installation, *Lasso*, one of a trilogy of short films, is a case in point.[2] In *Lasso*, Tykkä plays with genres such as the western and melodrama and with Hollywood codes of editing, but combines this with an awareness of fine art video history in which the materiality of the medium was often foregrounded at the expense of narrative. Her skewing of these different histories generates a kind of spectatorial engagement that is neither self-reflexive (the mode conventionally attributed to viewing avant-garde film), nor bound by narrative identifications (as when viewing mainstream cinema), but is instead immersive and affective, with the capacity of being emotionally moved by the more abstract filmic gestures of colour, sound, movement, and rhythm. The question therefore becomes one of how to theorise this mode of spectatorship.

In theories of the moving image, there has been a turn to affect in theorising spectatorial response.[3] This turn takes place in the wake of, and in conjunction with, Gilles Deleuze's emphasis on the affection-image, which he contrasts to the action-image in his books on cinema. In *Cinema 1: The Movement Image*, Deleuze distinguishes the triadic sequence of goal-oriented movement in the action-image, whereby perceptions of and affections about an object or situation culminate in action, from the time-image in which action is suspended.[4] In the latter type of image, which he situates historically as occurring in post-Second World War cinema, the preliminary experiential poles of perception and affection are magnified. Characters become seers who succumb to hypnotic encounters which exceed their capacity to respond or react. The image becomes hallucinatory and de-linked from narrative continuity, its autonomous intensity momentarily suspending the volitional structures that lead to action. Such an encounter is described by Deleuze in De Sica's *Umberto D* (1952), where the maid's series of domestic gestures, her weary busyness, is brought to a halt by the sight of her pregnant belly. A pause occurs and is filled by intense emotion, in this case 'all the misery in the world'.[5] While for Deleuze the concept of the spectator remains limited by linguistic conventions of film appreciation not conducive to the affective intensity of the time-image, his conception of the latter resonates with the scene of entrancement I encountered above in relation to *Lasso*. In both instances, the hypnotic arrest of the image induces an emotional capacity that absorbs and dissolves the autonomous perspective of the subject into a temporality outside of their control. However, in what follows, I shall maintain the category of the spectator as a site in which the transformation of narrative linkage to the felt dimensionality of qualitative affect is located.

The spectator determined by unconscious processes has gone out of fashion in recent film theory where the emphasis is placed on 'socially situated viewers' and the 'ethnography of film audiences'.[6] Such work relies on audiences' own accounts of their relationship to film rather than positing a spectator who, by contrast, cannot necessarily speak of the mechanisms of desire by which his or her relation to a film is constituted. Laura Mulvey, historically one of the most important advocates of the latter position, currently maintains a tenuous allegiance to this construct, putting forward the notion of the 'possessive spectator', whose unconscious desire seeks control over the film image's movement.[7] While I would question the status of the unconscious in Mulvey's conception of the possessive spectator, I want to hold fast to the concept of the spectator as a positionality determined by unconscious processes. Given that the particular kind of affective state I am exploring in relation to the positionality of the spectator is entrancement –

especially in relation to a pulsating, yet blank, image – what kind of psychoanalytic and/or other models of analysis might throw light on the embodied nature of this type of filmic engagement? And are there any moving-image precedents for it?

Does affect have a history in film theory?

While there is a current vogue for the concept of affect in contemporary film theory, this term only occasionally appeared in radical film theory in the 1970s and 1980s, where it was largely viewed in negative terms as resistant to discourse. As Freudian psychoanalyst André Green states, affect is caught between its chaining up in discourse and the breaking of the chain. For Green there are two types of affect: 'affect with a semantic function as an element in the chain of signifiers …, and affect overflowing the concatenation and spreading as it breaks the links in the chain'.[8] (The latter type is reminiscent of Deleuze's affection-image and its capacity to dissolve narrative.) Radical film theory in the 1970s and 1980s was dominated by Lacanian psychoanalytic theory, in which 'what matters is not the affect as it is "experienced" in the obscurity of immanence' but 'the affect as it is "transmitted by language"… that is, as it makes itself recognized in the transcendent exteriority of representation'.[9] Using this framework, a film such as Chantal Akerman's *News from Home* (1976) is considered by Lacanian-influenced film theorist Stephen Heath to both generate and block discourse. *News from Home* consists of a ninety-minute image track of mainly static camera shots of New York city and a soundtrack composed of Akerman reading the letters her mother sent her when she lived in the city. As the film progresses, the city sounds completely obliterate the clarity of the voiceover. In the final ten-minute sequence, the camera pulls out from the city, propped on the Staten Island ferry. The mother's words are silenced; the soundtrack consists instead of seagull cry and water lapping the sides of the ferry. In Heath's analysis, the film generates discourse, in the sense that one image is replaced by another in a continuous sequence of moving-image stills, but also blocks it, in the sense that the openness of the final sequence fails to resolve the problems of desire presented by the film's montage, both image and sound.[10] He considers this to be the film's strength – that is, that it poses the problem of female desire as an impossible limit of representation, as not having a signifier in patriarchal discourse. Heath's polarisation of representation and its gaps or ruptures is in line with classical psychoanalytic theory. As opposed to this, in a Deleuzian-inspired reading, the gaps or ruptures of affective intensity may be considered as generative of their own sensible economy. In relation to the final sequence of Akerman's film, an image of the New York skyline receding in the distance shot, this might be an economy of affective movement where the spectator is led through states of being over time, which resonate at a level not normally accessible to conscious reflection. Heath celebrates gaps in signification, but only as they point either to the mechanics of the apparatus or to the blind spot of dominant discourses – patriarchy in Akerman's case. However, for me, the final sequence of *News from Home* has positive signifying potential in itself, its dynamic openness shifting the viewer from the position of looking at an image to feeling its rhythm.

Tykkä's *Lasso*, while very different in terms of production, is not dissimilar to *News from Home* in failing to provide a definitive representation of female desire, instead portraying the motion of desire, its kinetics, via analogous images signified by the camera's panning over the snowy ground and the bleed into a suspended yet pulsating image of whiteness. The camera's coming to rest on the girl's face and on the snow might suggest contiguity between the girl and nature. This would be a commonplace association, as would a reading of the film in terms of an empowering female gaze, a simplistic reversal of Mulvey's analysis of the codes of conventional Hollywood cinema, in which active looking is considered male. More interesting for my purposes here is the pervasive hypnotic mood that accumulates from the protagonist's blank expressivity to the image of the white screen at the end of the film, which unhinges the distinction of figure and ground, subject and object. If not for this passage to the white screen and the dissipation of suspense preceding it, the film might be said to give us the usual story of femininity as caught between 'the deep blue sea of passive femininity and the devil of regressive masculinity'.[11] However, in Tykkä's *Lasso*, the affective dimension of the dissolve to the white screen exceeds an ostensible conforming to stereotypes. Seemingly impassive, this type of image has its own economy of affective movement. To cite Vivian Sobchack:

> The seeming passivity and immobility of the 'fixed' cinematic gaze is belied by the kinetic tension which informs the visibly quiescent 'moving image' such a 'fixed' gaze is always actively producing. Indeed, this most quiet and invisible mode of visual movement is an *arresting gaze* and never an *arrested* gaze – even in its manifestation of the 'freeze frame'.[12]

As I stare at this image, 'I' am faced with and fascinated by a luminous whiteness without on-screen borders. The barely perceptible motion of the image motivates a shift to an inner space where 'I' feel the qualities of motion and where 'I' engage in a dispersed relatedness with something other than myself. How might the re-negotiation of boundaries between viewer and screen that occurs in its space of entrancement be thought about? While Tykkä herself does not speak of her film in these terms, it might be useful to examine how other filmmakers in the past have done so. One such protagonist is Maya Deren.

One genealogy of trance in film: Maya Deren

The term 'trance film' was used by P. Adams Sitney to describe Maya Deren's films, specifically *Meshes of the Afternoon* (1943) and the Haitian footage she shot of spirit possession which was later made into the film *Divine Horsemen* (1977) by Teiji and Cheryl Ito.[13] Her films, he said, were peopled by 'somnambulists', 'initiates of rituals', and 'the possessed'.[14] Sitney characterised trance films as being interested in dream spaces and the erotic quest for the self, whereas I am considering trance as a space between viewer and screen, which was also something that interested Deren. Her description of viewing Gregory Bateson's Balinese footage encapsulates the affective sensibility of my experience of viewing both *Lasso* and *News from Home*. At first, a particularly uneventful long take bores her, then it induces '"a kind of suspenseful state of mind"'. In such shots, she claims '"just because nothing is happening in the developmental sense, and just because the shot keeps lasting, the scene crosses some strange boundary from 'activity' into 'state'"'.[15] This state expands the range of subjectivity beyond the narrow confines of the ego. Deren maintained that the motoricity of the camera could affect the human sensorium.[16] In seeking to create a physiologically contaminative film space that would induce states of entrancement via technical means, Deren was also inspired by shamanism and the collective staging of trance and spirit possession in Haiti:

> [J]ust as various mechanical devices such as crystals and light are employed in hypnotism, so I believe, drum rhythms are extremely important in inducing possession. As we know, rhythm consists in the regularity of the interval between sounds. Once this interval has been established, our sense-perceptions are geared to an expectation of its recurrence … Even more important, sustained rhythmic regularity and the fact that the source of it is outside the individual rather than within, means that consciousness is unnecessary, as it were, in the maintenance of this concentration.[17]

Deren extended these ideas about drumming in Haitian ritual to film, arguing in effect that film was a ritual means enabling the filmmaker to generate hypnotic rhythms that could in a sense possess the spectator. The filmic means used to produce trance extended not only to sound, but to the fact that '[t]he rhythm of twenty-four frames per second, the rhythm of light and darkness in the pictures, the rhythm of varying and repeating speeds in the films affect perception much more than the symbolic value of the pictures'.[18] While this is somewhat arguable in relation to *At Land* (1944) and *Meshes in the Afternoon*, it is the case that Deren's films became more and more about rhythm and movement, a trajectory figured in the final sequence of escape and dissolution in her *Ritual in Transfigured Time* (1946) (figure 5.4). I watched this sequence over and over again.

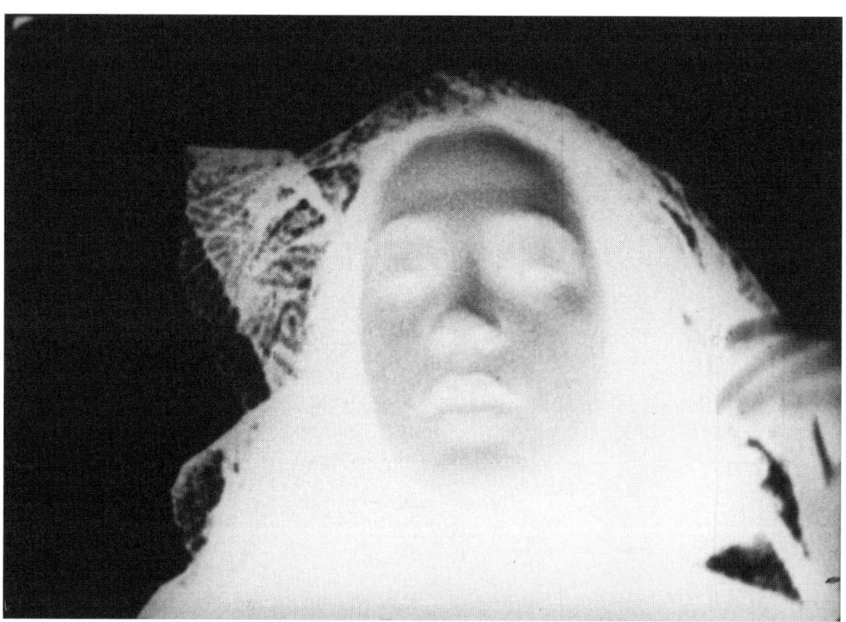

5.4 Maya Deren, *Ritual in Transfigured Time*, 1946 (film still). 16mm film, black and white, silent, 15 minutes. Courtesy of Anthology Film Archives, all rights reserved.

A man, dancing in leaps and bounds through a garden arcade, chases a woman. Earlier she danced with him, but his body turned to stone. She had run away, off screen, to reappear in the garden arcade enmeshed in this game of pursuit. The game stops as the film cuts to an image of water, black-and-white rivulets lapping the edges of the screen, while another woman in the distance is seen running, then wading into the water, waving her arms, her scarf flowing around her. The camera focuses on this second woman, as she writhes in the water, turning her head, her eyes shut tight, arms held out grabbing the air. Cut to arms plumbing the blank greyness of the sky, and then the first woman falls into and out of the screen. Another body plunges down through the screen, a white body against a black ground, an X-ray body with garments undulating like fronds around it. As soon as it reaches the bottom of the screen, its descent is repeated and it falls again from the top of the screen – is this the first or the second woman or a strange amalgamation of both? A female body plummets down another time, and then lifts a veil from her face. I fall between the two protagonists into depths I cannot fathom. Unseeing eyes stare out at me, solarised and still in an empty stare, their whiteness lit up neither from within nor without. I am pulled into the folds of this liquid space. I am losing myself in relation to a series of black-and-white variations forming between the bodies of drowning women, their flowing garments and wavy hair.

Ritual in Transfigured Time is structured around a series of dance movements by four dancers – one male, three females – who perform various poses in a mansion and its gardens, where a cocktail party is taking place. The poses are filmed in slow motion, repetition and freeze frame, which, as Alison Butler cogently argues, turns on an inherent contradiction in the film: '[I]n her efforts to reinvigorate dance in film, by drawing on the specific means of expression of the medium and the collective state of the culture, Deren inadvertently draws on some of the negative fantasies of the machine age, which revolve around alienation and the life-threatening propensities of technology.'[19] Butler suggests that the final sequence of *Ritual in Transfigured Time*, where two of the female dancers, Deren and Rita Christiani, plunge into the ocean, is a flight from this. In that sequence, the technique of solarised printing, where the image changes from positive to negative, merges their separable forms, so that they become as if one solarised figure emerging and drowning in the blackness of the image. For Maria Pramaggiore, the oscillating shots of the two women 'suggest a continuing process of relational identity rather than a transformation from one identity to another'.[20] More importantly for my purposes, this dispersed relatedness generates a similar psycho-physiological diffusion in the viewer. The entranced spectator might find herself becoming unhinged from gravity and carried away on waves of black-and-white gradations of form strangely akin to Deren's description of her own experience of Voudoun spirit possession in her book *Divine Horsemen: The Living Gods of Haiti*.

In the final chapter of her book, 'The white darkness', Deren presents an account of her own experience with spirit possession. While Deren's 'participatory observation' in the rituals of Haitian Voudoun is rightly considered by Joan Dayan to be problematic in terms of the exoticism it portrays, it has a value if taken as expressive of a desire to replicate such an experience in film.[21] Dayan writes: 'Hers is a glorious surrender, a loss that she can only remember in images of the rolling sea, fog, light, "a white darkness, its whiteness a glory and its darkness a terror"'.[22] Whatever fantasy or reconstructed dream space is being recounted here, the terms of this evocative description resonate with the final sequence of *Ritual in Transfigured Time*, where the women's bodies are transformed into a strange, glowing, whiteness fused with gradients of black by the negative printing process. In this re-articulation of the human form, 'woman' is emptied of to-be-looked-at-ness, becoming a purely gestural figuration that captivates the spectator by means of hypnotic movement alone. It was something of this quality that I felt in relation to the camera movements in Tykka's *Lasso*. The camera freed the girl from being cast as subject or object in relation to the look. Its movements also had this effect on me, freeing me from seeing her or my identification with her, as positioned in relation to a set of predetermined categories. Instead of Mulvey's 'possessive' spectator, who controls the image, in trance, the spectator is possessed by the image, willingly controlled and transported by its rhythm. What might be happening to the spectator in this film scene of entrancement? What kind of subjectivity might be emerging?

Affect at the borders of psychoanalysis

In psychoanalysis, entrancement occurs in the well-known phenomenon of transference, which is where the patient is so enamoured by the analyst that he or she transfers his or her affections to him or her in a replay of a past that cannot be remembered but only acted out. The various branches of psychoanalytic thinking have slightly different attitudes towards this phenomenon, but generally agree that it needs to be undergone and then eradicated by the therapeutic treatment.[23] In a radical rethinking of this phenomenon, the psychoanalytic historian Mikkel Borch-Jacobsen claims that Western society has an allergy towards trance.[24] Borch-Jacobsen critiques the Freudian/Lacanian emphasis on representation and discourse, which, it is worth repeating, is the school of psychoanalytic theory that influenced 1970s and 1980s film theory that proffered the critical spectator as a necessary foil to the deceptions of the film apparatus. According to Borch-Jacobsen, Freud, well aware of the proximity of his burgeoning science to older therapies, emphasised representation and discourse in the talking cure in an attempt to eradicate suggestion and hypnosis from psychoanalysis. What this does in effect is to amputate the affective and mimetic element from the cure and downplay the subject's origin in assimilative identifications. Borch-Jacobsen concentrates on and exposes the repudiated primitive affectivity of the subject, repressed in its bid to establish its identity as an individual. 'Desire (the desiring subject) does not come first, to be followed by an identification that would allow the desire to be fulfilled. What comes first is a tendency toward identification, a primordial tendency that then gives rise to a desire.'[25] In the trance state, one encounters once again this primordial tendency where identifications are in the process of being constituted but are as yet fluid and suggestible. Key to the trance state is a sense of depersonalisation, whereby the subject is possessed by a strangeness that neither comes from within nor from without, but from an intermediate zone of experience normally unattended to. This state overturns the 'ordinarily accepted borders' between self and other, constituting an 'incommunicable *lived experience*' as 'one cannot simultaneously *be* (an) other while distinguishing oneself from that alterity'.[26] The trance state is one where the possessed 'can in no way distance himself from the role that he plays'.[27] Following Surrealist writer Georges Bataille, Borch-Jacobsen insists that 'the experience of being-other, when pushed to the trance state, can only be "interior" and lived "from within" – any discourse on the trance ... can do nothing but miss its object, precisely because it makes an object of it'.[28]

In claiming that certain film moments can generate such entrancement, and then going on to find ways of theorising the experience, I am guilty of making an object of something that operates on the margins of sense, but there is perhaps a value in teasing out the subjectivity of this scenario. As I watched *Lasso*, my overt identifications were suspended and 'I' felt possessed by a pulsating whiteness that momentarily released me from the need to recognise and name things. 'I' felt my gaze was moving in a dispersed space where identificatory traits circulated without belonging to filmic characters, entities, or an individuated viewer. Through the intermediary of the camera's mechanical eye, the space between screen and viewer was contaminated by affects and percepts, partly generated by the film image itself, its rhythm, lighting, colour, and texture, and partly generated by the viewer's desire to incorporate these foreign bodies as her own. While Tykkä's pulsating image only lasts mere seconds as opposed to Akerman's ten-minute sequence, the endings of both films induce a state reminiscent of the experiential proximity of becoming other characteristic of trance, where 'I' cannot separate myself from the parasitic invasion of flows and intensities of unbound affects. 'I' become a host body, a site for a re-negotiation of boundaries between objects and subjects that expand and yet remain distinct. The trajectory from quantifiable narrative to qualitative duration in the shift from the female protagonist's gaze to the white screen (in *Lasso*) or from the daughter's mimicry to the relative silence of the vanishing horizon (in *News from Home*) intimates that the scene of entrancement incorporates a sense of futurity. While action is suspended, the continuity of affective movement is suggestive of a future re-incorporation of boundaries. This scene is a productive opening out of the self, trapped by its own mastery to a self open to the fluidity of its boundaries. Released from possessive desire, the trance state, in operating 'a passage between terms that from a symbolic point of view are diametrically opposed', provides the opportunity for other positionalities to emerge whereby the subject's patterns of identification might be reconfigured in less possessive directions.[29]

However, while trance can be used to proffer a mode of spectatorship conducive to the immersive environments and subject matter of contemporary film installations, the moments or tropes that will entrance particular viewers cannot be predicted, the scenario being dependent on an individual's particular affective ties, which are largely unconscious. As Tim Groves states, 'The logic of Borch-Jacobsen's argument is that affectivity does not depend on any "particular technique or power" in a film, but rather on the "rhetoricity of the affect *as such*, a rhetoric anterior to any verbal [or filmic] persuasion". While stylistic (or narrative) elements can contribute to the persuasion of spectators, the efficacy of any such technique depends on the suggestibility of viewers, which is always variable.'[30] For my part, I find myself captivated by those moments where the camera moves from a distal state to a more proximal one, altering the rhythm and focus in the film. In *Lasso*, this is the shift from the girl's white face slashed by white bands of window-blind to the pan of the snowy ground and on to the expansiveness of technological white static. In *Ritual in Transfigured Time*, it is the shift from a solidified architectural space to the liquidity of a monochromatic space where gravity is unhinged and identity dispersed. In Akerman's *News from Home* it is the shift from the noise of the city and the mother's letters to the zoom-out of a vanishing horizon line and the sound of water lapping. In all these cases it is the movement from one hypnotic space to its suspended intensification that displaces my ability to form symbolic identifications. As Akerman describes it in relation to her film *Hotel Monterey* (1972):

> When you look at a picture, if you look just one second, you get the information, 'that's a corridor.' But after a while you forget it's a corridor; you just see that it's yellow, red; that it's lines; and then again it comes back as a corridor. If you don't stay long enough, if you don't stare, you will never forget that this is information about a corridor.[31]

The entranced moments I have encountered in order to account for my experience of Tykkä's *Lasso* occur as a result and effect of kinetic and narrative accumulation and suspension. They are not all-pervasive, as in the coloured light effects in Stan Brakhage's hand-painted films from the 1960s, which Sitney also includes in his category of 'trance' or, more relevant to my argument, the slow motion of Douglas Gordon's installation *24 Hour Psycho* (1993), which in the contemporary landscape of film installation is the example that comes most readily to mind vis-à-vis the distinction I am arguing for here.[32] *24 Hour Psycho* stretches Hitchcock's classic suspense film into twenty-four hours, extending the twenty-four frames per second of film time into the human time scale of a day. Gordon's screen, propped on the floor so that it can be viewed front and back, induces a hypnotic spaced-out kind of viewing where the only action is the viewer's waiting for an event to unfold from the familiar Hollywood narrative. This attention is so imperceptibly slow that one becomes immersed in the drift of one's own perceptual processes. However, the distinction between this spectacular display of drift and the films that I have encountered in this essay is not only that the latter are engaged in attempting to rethink identity, particularly female identity, via the mechanisations of the filmic apparatus, but that the state of entrancement ultimately operates at an affective level delinked from narrative where there is a shift to a blank space of kinetic arrest. The address of *24 Hour Psycho* is lodged within the frame of narrative. The installation at its most critical enables a perspective from which the processes of drift can be objectified due to the fact that they are ultimately grounded by the ready-made nature of Hitchcock's narrative. In a sense, Gordon's installation could be said to put entrancement in parenthesis as a comment both on the alleged passivity of contemporary mediatised reception and on the film apparatus as a seductive, illusion-inducing machine.

Another example from contemporary film installation which compounds the deconstructive aspect of work such as Gordon's, and is relevant to the distinctions I am making, is Runa Islam's *Stare Out (Blink)* (1998). Islam's short film, a single-screen projection, is formally reminiscent of Deren's evocation of a trance space in the final sequence of *Ritual in Transfigured Time* via the technique of solarised printing. *Stare Out (Blink)* is a projection of the direct imprint, that is, the negative of a woman's face on a 1:1 scale staring straight into the lens and/or the eyes of the viewer. Every eight seconds there is a one-second flash of white where the negative is in fact blank and the light of the projector passes through it. This forces the viewer to blink, creating a positive after-image in the process. *Stare Out (Blink)* induces a hypnotic effect: the final image is found neither on the celluloid strip nor as an illusion on the screen, but rather as a physical imprint on the viewer's retina. However, this effect is purely physiological rather than, as in the films I have been discussing, psycho-physiological, whereby 'I' am transported to a space of blind seeing imbued with unbound potential. *Lasso* and *Ritual in Transfigured Time* generate trance-like elements that shift protagonists from being objects or subjects of gazes or desires, a shift that in turn produces an expansiveness in the spectator's psycho-physiology where she might feel the potential of becoming other than what she already knows herself to be. In making this claim, I am arguing for a view of mediatised reception whereby a supposed passivity - that is, entrancement – might have its own economy of transformative engagement. In the unhinged gravitational and temporal space-time of filmic entrancement, we can gain access to an experiential continuum not bound by the traps of the spectacular image. This is the spell that entranced spectatorship casts wherever or whenever we find it.

Notes

1 In the case of *Lasso*, the music comes from Leone's *Once Upon a Time in the West* (1969).
2 The other two films in Tykkä's trilogy are *Cave* (2003) and *Thriller* (2001).
3 See for example Vivian Sobchack, *The Address of the Eye: A Phenomenology of Film Experience* (New Jersey: Princeton University Press, 1992) and Laura U. Marks, *The Skin of the Film: Intercultural Cinema, Embodiment, and the Senses* (Durham/ London: Duke University Press, 2000). For a materialist account of affect, see Teresa Brennan, *The Transmission of Affect* (Ithaca, N.Y.: Cornell University Press, 2004).
4 See Gilles Deleuze, *Cinema 1: The Movement Image*, trans. Hugh Tomlinson and Barbara Habberjam (London: The Athlone Press, 1992).
5 Gilles Deleuze, *Cinema 2: The Time-Image*, trans. Hugh Tomlinson and Robert Galeta (London: The Athlone Press, 1989), pp. 1–2.

6 Mark Jancovich and Lucy Faire with Sarah Stubbings, *The Place of the Audience: Cultural Geographies of Film Consumption* (London: BFI, 2003), p. 6. See also Jackie Stacey, *Star Gazing: Hollywood Cinema and Female Spectatorship* (London: Routledge, 2004).
7 Laura Mulvey, *Death 24x a Second: Stillness and the Moving Image* (London: Reaktion Books, 2006), pp. 161–80. She also posits Raymond Bellour's concept of the 'pensive spectator', who oscillates between reflection and suspension in relation to the stilled film image, as another positionality determined by unconscious processes. For further discussion of Mulvey's position and a critique of her notion of the 'possessive spectator', see my 'Against fetishism: the moving quiescence of life twenty-four frames a second', *film-philosophy Journal: Continental Film Philosophy Today*, 10:2 (September 2006), pp. 1–10, at www.film-philosophy.com/2006v10n3/walsh.pdf.
8 André Green, *The Fabric of Affect in the Psychoanalytic Discourse*, trans. Alan Sheridan (London/New York: Routledge, 1999), p. 208.
9 Mikkel Borch-Jacobsen, *The Emotional Tie: Psychoanalysis, Mimesis, and Affect*, trans. Douglas Brick and others (Stanford: Stanford University Press, 1992), p. 80. The quote within this quote is from Jacques Lacan's *Ecrits: A Selection*, trans. Alan Sheridan (London: Tavistock Publications Ltd, 1977).
10 See Stephen Heath, *Questions of Cinema* (London/Basingstoke: Macmillan Press, 1981), pp. 98–99.
11 Laura Mulvey, 'Afterthoughts on visual pleasure and narrative cinema' (1981), reprinted in her *Visual and Other Pleasures* (London: Macmillan Press, 1989), p. 13.
12 Vivian Sobchack, 'Active eye', *Quarterly Review of Film and Video*, 12:3 (1993), pp. 20–36; p. 24.
13 Compounding the connection between Deren's psychodramatic trance narratives and the documentary footage, excerpts of 'spirit possession' from the Haitian footage were juxtaposed with the staircase sequence of *Meshes in the Afternoon* in the television documentary *Ancient Mysteries: A History of Voodoo* (A&E Networks, 1996).
14 P. A. Sitney, *Visionary Film: The American Avant-Garde, 1943–1978* (New York: Oxford University Press, 1974), p. 21. Sitney's category also included the early films of Kenneth Anger and Stan Brakhage.
15 Deren, quoted in Alison Butler, '"Motor-driven metaphysics": movement, time and action in the films of Maya Deren', *Screen*, 48:1 (Spring 2007), p. 15.
16 This idea was partly influenced by her father's research in psychiatry. In the years prior to the Russian revolution, Deren's father, Salomon Derenkowsky, had studied at the Psychoneurological Insititute of Vladimir Bekhterev. Bekhterev developed forms of physical therapy, using hypnosis and trance. One of the devices he used to prove the objectivity of mental activity was the camera.
17 Deren quoted in Ute Holl, 'Moving the dancers' souls', in Bill Nichols (ed.), *Maya Deren and the American Avant-Garde* (Berkeley/Los Angeles/London: University of California Press, 2001), pp. 151–78; p. 160.
18 Holl, 'Moving the dancers' souls', p. 160.
19 Butler, '"Motor-driven metaphysics"', p. 13.

20 Maria Pramaggiore, 'Seeing double(s)', in Nichols (ed.), *Maya Deren and the American Avant-Garde*, pp. 237– 61; pp. 255–56.

21 As Catherine Russell states, vis-à-vis the interest in trance in the work of Deren and Jean Rouch, '[p]ossession offers the dissolution of distance between spectator and text'. See Russell, *Experimental Ethnography: The Work of Film in the Age of Video* (Durham: Duke University Press, 1999), p. 235.

22 Joan Dayan cited in Moira Sullivan, 'Maya Deren's ethnographic representation of ritual and myth in Haiti', in Nichols (ed.), *Maya Deren and the American Avant-Garde*, pp. 207–36; p. 226.

23 For a concise, yet detailed account of transference, see Jean Laplanche and Jean-Bertrand Pontalis, *The Language of Psycho-Analysis,* trans. Donald Nicholson-Smith, with an introduction by Daniel Lagache (London: Karnac/Institute of Psychoanalysis, 1988), pp. 455–64.

24 Borch-Jacobsen, *The Emotional Tie*, p. 111.

25 Borch-Jacobsen, *The Emotional Tie*, p. 47.

26 Borch-Jacobsen, *The Emotional Tie*, pp. 100–1.

27 Borch-Jacobsen, *The Emotional Tie*, p. 96.

28 Borch-Jacobsen, *The Emotional Tie*, p. 101.

29 Borch-Jacobsen, *The Emotional Tie*, p. 102.

30 Tim Groves, 'Entranced: affective mimesis and cinematic identification', *Screening the Past*, 20 (2006), at www.latrobe.edu.au/screeningthepast/20/entranced.html. accessed 14 December 2006.

31 Akerman quoted in Gary Indiana, 'Getting ready for the golden eighties: a conversation with Chantal Akerman by Gary Indiana', *Artforum*, 21:10 (Summer 1983), pp. 56–61; p. 58.

32 Some of the work of Runa Islam, Pipilotti Rist, Doug Aitken, Gary Hill, and Bill Viola might also be said to induce hypnotic states of viewing. However, discussion of the differences amongst these artists exceeds the limits of this essay.

6 Screen eroticisms: exploring female desire in the work of Carolee Schneemann and Pipilotti Rist

Amelia Jones

This essay addresses a profound technological and ideological shift in the visualisation and conceptualisation of eroticism in screen-based culture from the 1960s to the 1990s through a comparative analysis of two major feminist screen-based projects: Carolee Schneemann's *Fuses* (1964–67) (figure 6.1) and Pipilotti Rist's *Pickelporno* (or, in English, *Pimple Porno*; 1992) (figure 6.2). By focusing on these two pieces, each produced by a key feminist artist at different periods in the history of contemporary art and in different locations the essay seeks to cast light on three major and interrelated shifts in the following areas: 1) feminist and broader social conceptions of eroticism and sexual agency; 2) the articulation of a vital female erotic power through specific screen-based media (16mm film and video, respectively), each having its own potential to render the human subject differently; and 3) artistic strategies for exploring the relationships among the body, the camera, the resultant screen image and space. Ultimately, by showing how each artist pushes the technological capacities of each medium (film and video) to render different modes of female sexual agency, the essay will point to broad transformations in beliefs about sexual identity and embodiment in the contemporary period.

The screen (cinematic versus televisual) is the operative pivot both in a literal and metaphorical sense for the visual culture works at hand, and understanding how screens function to articulate sexual subjects is essential in understanding how Schneemann and Rist produce contrasting possibilities of erotic subjectivity in *Fuses* and *Pimple Porno*. Dominant versions of subjectivity or ways of being in Euro-American culture, enacted partly through the screens of the mass media, position us most often, still, through binary codes relying on oppositional conceptions of identification – gender (male/female), sexuality (hetero/homosexual), race (white/not white), ethnicity (European/otherwise), class, nationality, and so on. These screens also position us literally as spectators in front of perspectivally constructed spaces: Albertian windows onto worlds, themselves presented as 'truth'. As such, we are encouraged to believe that when we watch screens we are in some way witnessing the 'truth'.

At the very least, we tend to absorb screen images as driven by bodies we engage with through reiterated codes of identification that in turn structure our ways of being in the world.

In contrast, although they both nominally narrate erotic encounters between two people who appear to be male and female (and thus to convey what, on the surface, appear to be hetero-erotic relations), both *Fuses* and *Pimple Porno* explore and produce embodied erotic possibilities for viewers which counter these conventional binary structures via screen-projected imagery. In the case of *Fuses*, this imagery is produced through the pellucid, glowing transparencies of 16mm film (although the film is often, today, viewed in a compromised VHS version marketed by Mystic Fire Video). In its original version *Fuses* is a dense, twenty-three-minute collage of abstracted images of a woman and a man (Schneemann herself and her lover of then ten years, James Tenney) making love, as viewed by her cat.[1] In the case of *Pimple Porno*, a twelve-minute-long PAL-format video, the erotic bodies are conveyed via the even, bright tones of digital video projection (originally produced as an analogue videotape to be viewed on a monitor, the work is most often today transferred to digital video and projected for public display).[2]

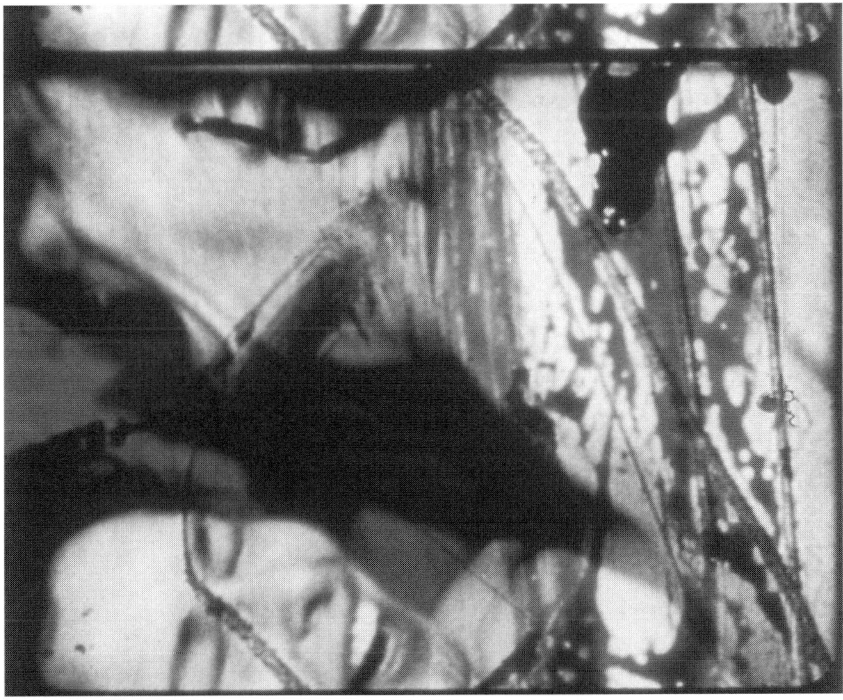

Carolee Schneemann, *Fuses*, 1964–67 (film stills). 16mm film, colour, silent, 23 minutes. Courtesy of the artist. 6.1

Working through the specificity of how the erotic screen bodies in each piece are conveyed and can be engaged by artists working in different parts of the world (Schneemann in New York and Rist in Zurich) and from different generations of feminist practice (Schneemann was born in 1939; Rist in 1962), this essay will conclude with thoughts about what these two projects tell us, in the most embodied of ways, about different modes of envisioning and enfleshing the erotic (gendered, sexed) screen subject in 1967 versus 1992. These thoughts will, of course, be provisional – the screen bodies I interpret will be evoked here through words as possibilities, not as fact. Part of my point, as the essay will make clear, is that screens make available visual fields (in this case, of eroticised bodies) which open out to the 'other' who views them; the appearance of the bodies and their particular relationship to the screens suggest identificatory responses, but do not legislate how these bodies come to mean in a final way. Screens are hinges between self and other, both literally and figuratively, not final sites where a body solidifies into a subjectivity. Screens are passageways, allowing us entry into eroticisms that might unhinge our usual static relation to the other(s) before us.

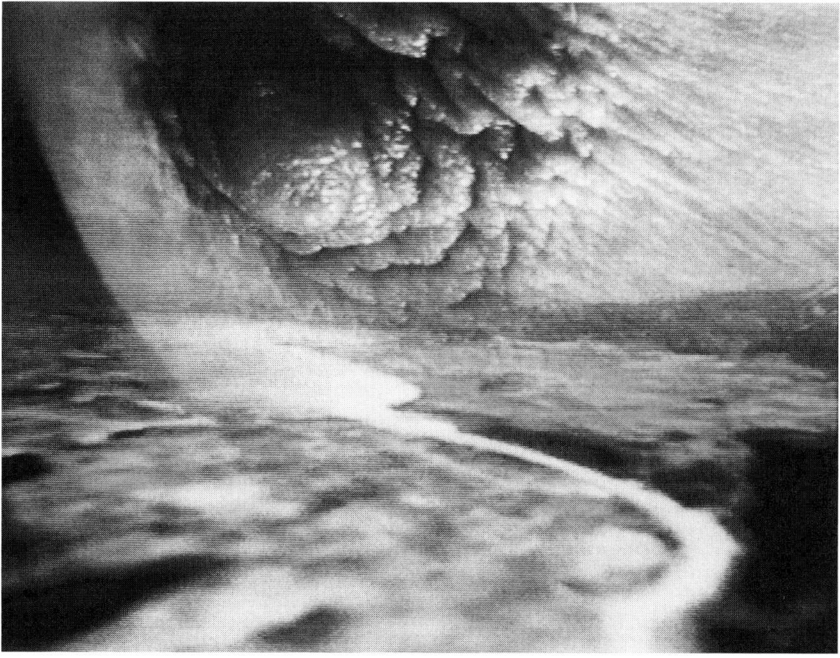

6.2 Pipilotti Rist, *Pickelporno* (*Pimple Porno*), 1992 (video stills). Video, colour, sound, 12 minutes 2 seconds. Courtesy of the artist and Hauser & Wirth.

Experiencing screen eroticisms: watching *Fuses*

I have watched *Fuses* about twenty times, once (oh joy!) as a 16mm film projection; many times on the twenty-three-minute VHS version of the original film I have shown to classes of young and eager students, who generally find its erotic textures quite radical even in the twenty-first century; and most recently in a newly re-edited and remastered twenty-nine-minute version on DVD, with original footage added by Schneemann.[3]

But now, autumn 2007 (before the remastered version is available), I am sitting with my lover, curled together on the sofa, watching it in preparation for writing this essay. The monitor of our small screen (attached to the bulky 'body' of the last generation of analogue television sets that will ever be manufactured) unfurls the film's skeins of deeply coloured montages. I remember watching the film version: a glowing rectangle of flame on the wall over there, I found myself sutured into it; with larger-than-life acts of heterosexual penetration hovering in my view, and hands rubbing gleaming taut muscles and wet folds of skin, I was enfolded in its erotic logic as my lover enfolds me in his embrace. Still, while not fully rendering the limpid jewel-like colours of the film version, the video version pulls me towards it with its flesh encounters.

Schneemann notes about *Fuses*, 'I wanted the bodies to be turning into tactile sensations of flickers … [The film is] is a painterly, tactile translation edited as a music of frames … That's why it is collaged, and cut and baked.'[4] This tactile manipulation of the film stock, which turned it into skin, makes the film itself *embodied*. I view the bodies making love there – the rhythmic thrusting of one into the other beautifully rendered, if in fragmented form with the scratched and scumbled surface of the film mitigating my full access to the bodies: I thus experience the screen itself as enfleshed, as having its own logic and depth; the screen like a kind of *skin*, the rippling contours of which signal a body (bodies?) writhing underneath.

Schneemann unfurls herself like a wave, both powerful and receiving. Her cunt is wet and red (the whole film is coloured in saturated rubies, tangerines, and at some points cool blues) stroked deliciously by her lover. His penis – glory be! we see the male organ without its explosive eruption and detumescence being the sole point of the narrative (as in hard-core porn) – appears again and again, lovingly rendered both as an object of desire, certainly female and potentially otherwise, and as a fleshy but vulnerable rod, slick with bodily juices, that works as a visual counterpart to her invaginated receiving body. Wet, is the operative feeling: wet and pulsating, alive, electric, sexed (the bodies, but also the body, the flesh, of the screen itself).

But *Fuses* is hardly simply a personal exploration in eroticism unattached to the vicissitudes of political history. By the early to mid-1960s Schneemann was an artist and simultaneously an activist working against the US government's actions in Vietnam. Training male friends how to avoid the draft, and others how to deal with police brutality, which was common at anti-war protests in the USA during this period, she was also creatively driven by a sense of outrage to produce two projects directly linked to the war: the 1967 kinetic theatre event *Snows*, an environment in which her 1965 film *Viet-Flakes* was projected. Both *Snows* and *Viet-Flakes* were created (as she has stated) 'out of my anger, outrage, fury, and sorrow for the Vietnamese'; the goal of producing *Snows* was 'to concretise and elucidate the genocidal compulsions of a vicious, disjunctive technocracy gone berserk … The grotesque fulfilment of the Western split between matter and spirit, mind and body, individualised "man" against cosmic natural unities.' Along with projected atrocity images from the Vietnam war as collaged in *Viet-Flakes*, she used film in the *Snows* event, projected through dual projectors (making live and filmed bodies collide in space) 'as integral to [live] performance … handled as tactile, palpable material'.[5]

The soundtrack to the *Snows* project, by James Tenney, included the noise of trains punctuated with 'sounds of orgasm'; this accompanied the live performances in which 'performers [were] … aggressor and victim, torturer and tortured, lover and beloved'.[6] So, too, in *Fuses* the body of the film, enacted through the erotic bodies of lovers, scratched and made into 'flesh', symbolises the manipulated flesh of bodies elsewhere. While *Fuses* is in no way directly a commentary on Vietnam, its visceral approach to embodiment clearly parallels Schneemann's strategic attempt in her other projects to unveil the political and military violence perpetrated by US troops abroad. I *feel Fuses* (in my gut, my womb) as an attempt to redeem the flesh through an eroticism that seeks to transcend the violence of nations through the personal euphoria of the orgasm.

This approach of activating live and film bodies as flesh across Schneemann's work during this period is very '1960s'. While harrowing and visceral, particularly in the case of *Snows* and *Viet-Flakes*, it is also very uplifting if one takes this attempt at transcendence – undoubtedly utopian and wilfully 'essentialising' (what other way, after all, did there seem to be to call Americans back to their bodies in an era of imperialist invasion on the part of the USA?) – in its brutal historical context: a context in which activating the body erotically meant to reclaim its capacity for positive union over its tendency to wreak bloody havoc.

Experiencing screen eroticisms: watching *Pimple Porno*

The footsteps of a high-heeled woman (apparently white, thin) walking over an urban grating, approaching a man who looks to be from an East Asian background, dressed in a blue suit: her eye in close-up *sees him* (it's the female gaze!). Their hands clasp, are solarised into a glowing meshing of skin and bone; he hands her a rather excessive pink flower; her body falls onto an artificially bright blue surface. As in *Fuses*, human eroticism is paralleled by the carnality of animals and the burgeoning of 'nature', in this case freewheeling animal locomotion. We see birds flying across the virtual sky of the televisual screen, landscapes (techno-colour, with the hyped hues of a vacation brochure), and flowers layered over, under, or within the contours of the two bodies, which in turn mesh, caress each other, and twirl in the strange gravityless space of the televisual box. Rist turns her camera around, refusing its authority as a stationary 'eye' and opening its purview into an intergalactic space in which landscapes turn upside down and bodies float, rotate, and spin in the dimensionless space of the monitor.

Bodies floating in space, a space textured through glorious skeins of techno-colour, ripples of skin, landscape, water. The infinitesimal line where one body begins and another ends is completely effaced: there are no borders, there is no binary separating 'man' from 'woman', 'black' from 'white'. His apparently Asian body and her apparently white body look equally luminous and sensual, in some cases distorted through a fish-eye lens, in others eaten into by the billowing layers of colour. A hand strokes a thigh (whose hand? whose thigh?), globes of fruit (tangerine-vibrant) against the downy-haired pitted skin of legs (whose legs?) mark human skin as infinitely soft compared to the rude, rubbery, and pock-marked skin of the citrus fruit. The screen itself dissolves (at one point shimmering away into an orange/yellow interference pattern, a televisual grain that's like technologised skin).[7]

Rist's project is profoundly televisual. While I have also seen it projected as it was intended to be, in the version I am studying now it is playing on my television, it is made like television, it is about television (not so much network television as its attenuated, more creative televisual forms such as MTV, the music television station founded in 1981, or to some extent artist's videos). The melting of the bodies together is the melting of experience into the screen, the flesh into the televisual, that people born after 1960, like myself (b. 1961) and Rist (b. 1962) have learned (in our bodies) to accept as the way things 'are' – call this the 'real' or call it 'simulation'. Either way, it is how we know the world around us.

As much as we allow ourselves to be lured into the world of the televisual, we know (we feel in our bodies) that the televisual is artifice about artifice: the smell of fire rarely accompanies the image of a fire visible on the screen. In *Pimple Porno* the orgasm between the man and woman is signalled by an increasingly frenetically paced visual and aural extravaganza, a feast of images of lava, fire, meshing bodies, a hard cock floating through a flower-filled field, a cunt opening itself into/as the screen. Synaesthetically, *fire*, simulacrally rendered via televisual representation, both symbolises and is signalled (through the saturated reds and the images of flames and exploding volcanoes) as *hot*, with *hot* linked to the 'heat' of consummated desire. One experiences the *images* of fire – the explosive, hot effects of which are exacerbated by the 'heated', rapid cadences of the music and the overlaid sounds of people moaning in pleasure – as having a (metaphoric) temperature. We can 'feel' the texture and friction of the sex between the man and the woman.

Perceived racial, gendered, and sexual identifications condition how we experience (synaesthetically view and apprehend) bodies in the world, in 'real' time/space or in representations. *Pimple Porno*, with its seemingly white female and Asian male bodies mixes up our (Euro-American) expectations about how such bodies would interact sexually: the woman is at least as aggressive in her desire-driven touch; the man is both sculpted in his physique (masculine) and ephemerally sensual, desiring; the white person is an object of desire as well as 'colonising' subject; and the Asian person, his penis shown hard in its active pursuit of his object of desire, full with agency.

At the same time, the seeming visible differences of the two bodies beg the very question of the binaries through which we give bodies (and other kinds of interactions) meaning. Thinking we know a body is that of an 'Asian man' or a 'white woman' is already a fraught enterprise of categorisation based on presumed identifications connected with visible codes. Rist participates creatively in the growing interrogation of beliefs about identity and of the role of identity politics in conceptions about what visual images *mean*. *Pimple Porno* is a visual examination and refutation of the dominant Euro-American idea that we can 'know' what or who we see based on our interpretation of visual cues. As Peggy Phelan notes in the introduction to her important 1993 book *Unmarked*:

> Identity cannot, then, reside in the name you can say or the body you can see ... Identity emerges in the failure of the body to express being fully and the failure of the signifier to convey meaning exactly. Identity is perceptible only through a relation to an other – which is to say, it is a form of both resisting and claiming the other, declaring the boundary where the self diverges from and merges with the other. In that declaration of identity and identification, there is always loss, the loss of not-being the other and yet remaining dependent on that other for self-seeing, self-being.[8]

What Rist, like the other most interesting artists and visual theorists of our time, makes clear is that visibility is never enough. Thinking that we see what we know belies the constructedness of the visual field, not to mention the contingency of our interpretation of what we see (a seeing that is always dependent on multisensory input). While life is now, arguably, fully 'representational' and simulacral, our experience is still embodied, synaesthetic, not only visual and aural. But saying it is fully embodied is not saying it is knowable or in any way essentialised in relation to the body. So much *Pimple Porno* explores through its confusion of boundaries between bodies and identifications, and its solicitation of an array of sensory responses.

Thus, in *Pimple Porno*, as in all of Rist's work, the interconnection of image and sound is crucial, as is the way in which she narratively depicts touch across these multiply identified bodies (much of *Pimple Porno* is devoted to images of bodies touching, rubbing, caressing). The touch of skin and the touch of sound mesh bodies, blurring their boundaries. Rist's eerie soundtrack conditions our experience of the bodies on the screen: it includes Rist singing in German with Les Reines Prochaines (the feminist punk group for which she was lead singer from 1988–94), her voice filled with longing, the sounds of moaning and chanting, noises from a hyped-up version of nature (birds twittering, water rushing), and various techno-sounding versions of acoustic instruments.[9]

As I hope my descriptions enact, *Pimple Porno* exemplifies the way in which Rist's work evokes what Laura U. Marks calls a 'haptic visuality', a 'feminine' (rather than penetratory and perspectival, as is typical in Western visual culture) visual relation, wherein the viewer is encouraged to engage with the surface of the image as having substance – as if it could be touched, 'haptically'. Haptic visuality encourages an 'intersubjective eroticism', not only (in the case of *Pimple Porno*) between figures or characters *within* the work, but between these bodies and ours. Marks notes, '[w]hat is erotic about haptic visuality, then, may be described as a respect of difference, and concomitant loss of self, in the presence of the other … [It is a] giving-over to the other'.[10]

Elsewhere, Marks has noted, 'We cannot help but change in the process of interacting'.[11] Giving over to the other (Rist's lovers; Rist; perhaps even the 'other' in ourselves, or our imagined/actual lover) through synaesthetic visual encounters can open up a process of change. This is the radical potential opened up by *Pimple Porno*'s erotic televisual scene. And it is a radical potential signalled in an early, nascent state by *Fuses*.

The screen 1967/the screen 1992: two feminist eroticisms

Schneemann's and Rist's two projects, I argue, are profoundly complementary in effect and in apparent motivation, but mark two different feminist eroticisms – themselves linked to two different relationships to visuality, and to two different technologies of imaging the self, from the two different periods and locations in which they were produced. To some extent they can be viewed as informed by two different generational approaches to the erotic body. As noted, Schneemann was born in 1939 and Rist in 1962. Their approaches are profoundly informed by the very technologies that end up conveying them (film versus analogue video and then digital video projection). They are also informed by feminist views about how various representational media function to reinforce particular gender and sexual identifications and about allowing for women's agency in relation to the visual field – attitudes that are critical but also celebratory of ways of articulating women's sexual pleasure.

Both artists respond critically to the Western history of positing or assuming a mythical centred subject of vision in relation to the visual field – one who is implicitly white, male, and heterosexual. The increasingly common location of vision in the subjectivity of the viewer in Euro-American visual culture after 1960 led ultimately to a new regime of knowledge in which meaning and value would no longer be viewed as existing 'out there', inherently in objects, but as constituted in *reciprocal* relation between the perceiving subject and the object. This shift away from the idea of the meaning of the text as generated from an originating author to the visual agency of the viewer (linked to the insights of poststructuralism) marks the difference between most visual works made before the 1960s and many works made afterwards.[12]

Schneemann's *Fuses* straddles the two belief systems (as my analysis makes clear, she is central to our apprehension of the work – both as we see her within the text and as we imagine her authorial agency producing the text). Rist's *Pimple Porno*, in contrast, relinquishes authorial coherence to a greater degree, locating the meaning of the eroticism in our embrace of the bodies on the screen, bodies that we may associate with her but that don't seem to 'be' her (or even to stand in for her). To different degrees and in different ways, Schneemann's and Rist's works are thus exemplary of the kinds of visual works produced out of this new understanding – they mine the capacity of film and video to open out the reciprocity between seer and seen. The remainder of this essay will tease out technologically and ideologically driven differences between Schneemann's and Rist's projects.

Fuses and the 'skin of the film'

While *Fuses* straddles older and newer modes of screen culture, it still clearly occupies the tail-end of a modernist trajectory in the history of art and film, one originally taking shape in the historical avant-gardes of the 1910s and 1920s in Europe and resurfacing in the post-Second World War period, particularly in the context of North American cinema with the work of filmmakers such as Maya Deren and Stan Brakhage, with whom Schneemann worked for a period before making *Fuses*. This kind of avant-garde work seeks to disrupt the visual field via strategies of montage and disjunction in order to distance the viewer, ultimately aiming to shift and contest dominant beliefs – in the case of Schneemann's film, the key belief system addressed is that relating to the positioning of women as objects of heterosexual male desire, but not as agents of their own sexual experience and identification.

At the same time, one of the most important things about Schneemann's work, and *Fuses* in particular, is that it crosses over this kind of avant-garde strategy with a feminist strategy of deploying what Laura U. Marks calls the 'skin of the film' (the film's capacity to engage viewers in a circuit of identification that is embodied and potentially highly politicised).[13] This strategy, in its feminist variant, produces bodies in such a way as to preclude the simple fetishisation of the woman's (and in this case man's) body. In Schneemann's *Fuses*, both the male and female body offer potential sites of identification, motivating the viewer to position herself differently in relation to heterosexual difference and thus perhaps to challenge the structures of fetishisation that are foundational to conventional Hollywood cinema.

Schneemann was one of the artists who developed this strategy in the most dramatic and successful way. In this way, *Fuses* moves us towards what comes to be defined as a postmodern kind of cultural production, one that is not avant-gardist in any simple fashion (not oppositional or distancing) but that still attempts to intervene in (or create friction in relation to) the structures of capital and subject formation in a critical way.[14] By manipulating the flesh of the celluloid itself, 'burning, baking, cutting, and painting it, dipping my footage in acid, and building dense layers of collage … held together with paper clips', Schneemann broke apart the conventional film text, enacting her own agency as a making (and active sexual) subject.[15]

Schneemann in this way *enfleshes* the film itself, literalising Marks's concept of the skin of the film on a material as well as narrative level (its potential to spark embodied engagements); as 'flesh', *Fuses* precludes the distancing effect necessary for fetishism to take place. The skin of *Fuses* enacts the skin of Schneemann and Tenney as they make love. The enfleshed movie de-objectifies the lovers' bodies, turning them into limpid surfaces that are also depths (and yet there is a tension between this effect and our identification of Schneemann as the author of the film).

It is crucial to stress, as well, that Schneemann's relationship to the binary of gender identification was never clear-cut. Unlike many feminists working in the 1960s and 1970s, she did not seek simply to reverse the poles of subject (male) and object (female) to empower women as subjects; rather, in this early work she confused the binary, while at the same time keeping 'male' and 'female' as intact entities, involved as they are in a clearly heterosexual romance. Schneemann's activation of herself as a subject (rather than only object) of the visual field in *Fuses* is thus not at the cost of the 'other' with whom she makes love. Of *Fuses*, she emphasises that she worked in complete collaboration with Tenney, situating his participation 'as both object and subject'. Her goal was pointed: 'I really wanted to see what "the fuck" is [from a woman's point of view] and locate it in terms of a lived sense of equity … we have to remind ourselves that throughout the sixties, only men maintained creative authority: women were muses, partners.'[16]

Schneemann's project thus complicates dominant models of interrogating structures of sexual difference in feminist film theory from the 1970s and 1980s. Film, as many feminist theorists from Laura Mulvey onwards have pointed out, is predicated as a medium on the binary logic of hetero-normative sexual relations and identifications. But in *Fuses*, as film theorist David James argues, 'a new copulation between the filmic and the erotic is traced, in which female sexuality is enacted in a practice of mutuality'.[17] *Fuses* blurs the boundaries of the binary and thus interrogates the cinematic itself, as well as heterosexual gender conventions. It does this partly through its character as a deeply painterly (rather than seemingly strictly 'photographic' and indexical) film: as noted, like Brakhage, Schneemann manipulates the very film stock itself, treating it like flesh; the scratched and rubbed celluloid, through which light is projected onto the screen, moves and gyrates and pulsates like erotically charged patches of flesh (paralleling, for example, the pulsating skin of Tenney's scrotum, visible at one point in the film, or the moist labia and opening of Schneemann's cunt, stroked by Tenney at another point).

While it is materially and sensually resolutely cinematic, through this meshing of flesh and screen image *Fuses* refuses simply to render the bodies 'indexically' as somehow representatives of clearly demarcated bodies in the 'real'. In this way, while *Fuses* is cinema, it radically moves towards, while not fully embracing, what I will call a *televisual sensibility*, one newly available to American artists coming of age in the 1950s and 1960s just as televisions became ubiquitous in American households. *Fuses* includes some cinematic landscape views (notably of Schneemann running across a beach), but it is primarily structured through close-ups that interweave and layer the bodies of Schneemann and Tenney into and as their environment, pressing them into the screen (and thus into *our* space). The film thus merges certain cinematic structures and qualities with what at the time was a relatively new televisual approach to representing the body (often in close-up, with camera angles that render the body as if pressed into the screen).

Fuses thus marks one of the earliest and most successful instances of the enactment of what Marks calls haptic visuality. The screen in *Fuses* becomes a site of exchange (both within the film's internal narrative and between the images on the screen and the viewers).

Pimple Porno and the shift to televisuality

As noted, Marks argues there is an erotics in haptic visuality, which indicates a 'respect of difference, and concomitant loss of self, in the presence of the other

… [It is a] giving-over to the other'.[18] Expanding on the potential opened up by *Fuses*, Rist's *Pimple Porno* is a further exploration of the potential of *televisual* screen space to enact multiply identified bodies that mesh and intertwine, that merge both with the surface of the televisual monitor and with the paradoxical space 'behind' it (which seems both infinite and contained by the box).

But *Pimple Porno* pushes the dissolution of the binary logic of fetishism even further than does *Fuses*. In *Pimple Porno* the embodied (three-dimensional) space of the monitor parallels the embodied, yet simulacrally rendered (dissolved, solarised, twirling in space) bodies of the lovers. Rist's piece draws on the erotic content and visual and editing strategies of *Fuses*, but pushes this content and these strategies further in the direction of a radically disorienting televisual screen texture in which we are encouraged to give over to the other, to recognise (via a haptic visuality) the impossibility of remaining 'outside' the image, as one is to some extent forced to do in viewing a projected cinematic text.

This giving-over takes place technologically, via the specific spectatorial mechanisms made possible through video art, as well as ideologically and psychically, in terms of identification. While we 'give over' to otherness in *Fuses*, the otherness is still marked in terms of conventional and heterosexual, white middle-class versions of sexual difference as articulated through the fundamentally modernist medium of cinema (albeit radically opened out into the skin of the film). In *Pimple Porno* the otherness is metaphorically marked in terms of a sexual difference that is understood *as determined in relation to in the highly marked terms of racial difference*. The meshing of flesh is marked in terms of a web of interrelated identifications in Rist's piece, where the woman, while apparently white, is also marked as racially/ethnically identified rather than 'neutral' or (as Peggy Phelan would put it in her 1993 book by this title) 'unmarked'. Rist articulates bodies that are *identified* but not knowable, as if in answer to Phelan's argument about identity cited above (published, as noted, in 1993, just a year after Rist's project was produced): 'Identity cannot, then, reside in the name you can say or the body you can see … Identity emerges in the failure of the body to express being fully and the failure of the signifier to convey meaning exactly.'[19]

It has been rightly noted by writers such as bell hooks that feminism was dominated by whiteness from the 1960s through the 1980s, and this whiteness was largely invisible to most (white) feminist artists, critics, and art historians.[20] Feminist film theorist Mary Ann Doane puts this critical point otherwise, in a way that resonates with Schneemann's work and that of many white feminists from the 1960s into the 1990s, including my own early publications on feminism: 'what can a white woman know about racial difference or oppression when her social regime is constituted as the denial or evacuation of racial identity … ?'[21] While the majority of feminists working in North

America and Europe in the 1960s through the 1980s were white middle-class women who thus didn't (or couldn't) see beyond their whiteness to explore the structures hooks and Doane identify as co-articulating sexual and racial difference, by the 1990s Rist is able to articulate a feminist screen eroticism that foregrounds (without overemphasising) racial/ethnic identifications as constitutive of gendered and sexual identifications – with these identifications (as Phelan suggests) never fully knowable through visual cues.

The dissolving of binaries into complex multiple networks of interrelated identifications is related to the specific representational mode through which *Pimple Porno* was made and is displayed. Technologically, *Pimple Porno* offers a related but ultimately different experience from that offered by *Fuses*. Rist grew up with the ubiquity of television, hand-held video cameras, and, by the mid-1970s and into the 1990s, VHS players and MTV. As noted, she was herself the member of a female punk band from 1988 until 1994, and her work is deeply informed by the aesthetic of the MTV generation, as well as by the history of artists' video. Although elsewhere in her video work – pieces such as *I'm Not the Girl Who Misses Much* (1986) and *Absolutions (Pipilotti's Mistakes)* (1988) – Rist scrambles the video signal in order to play with the texture of the interference, so rupturing the integrity of the bodies on the screen, in this case it appears that Rist does not mess with the representational medium at the level of its technological formation (the signal itself). She does manipulate the image, however, using various strategies of solarisation, fades, and other distorting techniques that render the bodies both more visible as central tropes and less stable as material entities (at many moments we are even made unsure which body we are seeing).

While it is now often projected digitally on a large screen, *Pimple Porno* was made for a monitor and remains resolutely 'of the box': the bodies take on dimensionality as they twirl in a televisual (monitor) space, not as they mesh into a projected film image (as occurs with the bodies in *Fuses*). Video viewed on a monitor encourages a particular viewing relation. There is at least a perceived intimacy with televisual screens that prompts those who make television shows or those who made art videos in the days when these were confined to monitors to produce different narratives, which tend towards fragmented stories that adapt to commercial breaks and the vicissitudes of everyday life as it interrupts television viewing in the home, but also to structure the narratives through much more intimate kinds of images, which are often close-up – a composition more amenable to the visual format of the televisual screen.[22] In a monitor-based piece such as *Pimple Porno*, too, the bodies are perceptually contained in what is experienced as a piece of furniture (at least until the advent of flat screen televisions).

Placed in the 'box' of the monitor, the video screen is a container. As Rist notes, the video monitor swallows up the viewer: 'At first you look at the box, at the screen or projection, but when you concentrate on the sequences you feel as if you're inside the box, behind the glass, within the wall. You forget everything around you and concentrate completely on the box: you're swallowed … *Reconquering the space inside the TV set: that's one of my aims* …'[23]

If classical Hollywood film labours to position the viewer so as to purvey a traditional binary structure of subject and object, with the filmic body *over there*, then television as produced in the centres of the entertainment industry seeks to suture the viewer, but in a different way – via positioning itself as 'furniture', but also as conveying stories that 'swallow' the viewer up, bringing her into the televisual world as a space of everyday 'truth'. If Schneemann's project purveys the body of the film as flesh in order to extend but also disrupt avant-gardist strategies of rupture, opening the door to a meshing of bodies and screen space, Rist's project pushes this further. 'Reconquering the space inside the TV set', using tools from rock video and from earlier avant-garde film projects such as Brakhage's and Schneemann's, Rist produces liquid bodies the texture of whose flesh is reciprocally defined in relation to the grained texture and box structure of the traditional televisual screen.[24]

Conclusion

Fuses is a radical work that enacts bodies as what Marks calls the skin of the film, drawing us in to a cross-gendered (if still apparently heterosexual and white-identified) relation with a man and a woman making love. Manipulating the film itself, Schneemann turns the movie into a body (known to be *her* body) with which we engage to find ourselves in a different space vis-à-vis female agency. In contrast, *Pimple Porno* enacts male and female bodies that are apparently raced as Asian and white in the pixellated depths of the video monitor; in so doing, Rist's video gives up the clear and politicised activation of female artistic agency (dissolving authorship to some degree and relinquishing the meaning of the work to the viewer) in order to produce an erotic haptic visuality that (to repeat Marks's formulation) offers the potential of inspiring 'respect of difference, and concomitant loss of self, in the presence of the other … [It is a] giving-over to the other.' In other words, Schneemann (as had to be the case in the 1960s) strategically retains the master/slave binary, and articulates her own agency clearly within the film, while Rist, partly due to being empowered through earlier works such as *Fuses*, is freed to interrogate the very oppositional terms of this binary.

Schneemann's *Fuses* works through the self–other dialectic of dominant (white, middle class) heterosexual relations, enacting on a personal (turned political) level the way in which such lovers can trouble the easy binary structuring both sexual difference and photographic and cinematic imaging technologies. Rist's *Pimple Porno* gives over to the other – the viewer, and metaphorically the potentially non-white, non-heterosexual other left out of dominant Euro-American models of sexual difference (even, until recently, feminist ones). If, as Marks notes elsewhere, '[w]e cannot help but change in the process of interacting', then both projects offer ideal openings for such change in the cutting-edge versions of the technologically and ideologically inflected languages of their times.[25]

Notes

1 Schneemann has noted of the film, '*Fuses* was made as an homage to a relationship of ten years – to a man with whom I lived and worked as an equal. We are perceived through the eyes of our cat. By visualising the cat's point of view I was able to present our coupled images in the contexts of the rectangles and the seasons surrounding us.' Schneemann, 'Notes on *Fuses* (1971)', in Schneemann, *Imaging Her Erotics: Essays, Interviews, Projects* (Cambridge, Mass.: MIT Press, 2001), p. 45. By 'animalising' the gaze, as it were, Schneemann repositions the body outside the human gaze (although the film can also be viewed, as it most often is, as conveying the sexual act through a woman's point of view).

2 For full credits on *Pimple Porno*, see www.videoart.ch/en/videodetail.php?v_id=5. I first viewed Rist's piece at the 'Screen/Space' conference in Edinburgh in March 2007 – the presentations of which provided the basis for this volume – via a DVD projected onto a large screen via a digital projector.

3 The new version, available through Anthology Film Archives, has additional footage of the couple's lovemaking. I am deeply grateful to Schneemann for making a study copy of the film available to me while I was finishing this essay.

4 Schneemann in 'Interview with Katie Haug', originally published in *Wide Angle*, 20:1 (1977), pp. 20–49, reprinted in Schneemann, *Imaging Her Erotics*, p. 43.

5 Schneemann, 'Snows', in Schneemann, *More Than Meat Joy: Performance Works and Selected Writings*, ed. Bruce McPherson (1979; Kingston/New York: Documentext, 1997), p. 129.

6 Schneemann, 'Snows', pp. 131–32.

7 I expand on these issues in chapters four and six ('Cinematic self imaging and the new televisual body' and 'The televisual architecture of the dream body') of my book *Self/Image: Technology, Representation and the Contemporary Subject* (London/New York: Routledge, 2006).

8 Peggy Phelan, *Unmarked: The Politics of Performance* (London/New York: Routledge, 1993), p. 13.

9 Les Reines Prochaines is a shifting group of women who straddle the music and visual arts and performance worlds; Rist was active in the group as a founding member from 1988 into the 1990s. See www.cityofwomen.org/archive/root_found/reinesprochaines.html. I am grateful to Sus, current member of Les Reines Prochaines, for providing dates on Rist's activities with the group in an email of 31 October 2007.

10 Laura U. Marks, *The Skin of the Film: Intercultural Cinema, Embodiment, and the Senses* (Durham, N.C.: Duke University Press, 2000), pp. 7, 183, 192–93.

11 Laura U. Marks, *Touch: Sensuous Theory and Multisensory Media* (Minneapolis: University of Minnesota Press, 2002), p. xvi.
12 See Roland Barthes's distinction in his later work between readerly and writerly texts, noting the shift to the reader as 'writer' (or maker of meaning) in contemporary literature.
13 See Marks, 'Introduction', *Skin of the Film*, pp. 1–20.
14 As Sean Cubitt has noted, early twentieth-century-style avant-gardism has no purchase under global late capitalism: '[r]esistance … is not a practicable political strategy in the age of infinitely flexible corporate control'; cited by Marks in *Touch*, p. xiv.
15 Schneemann, 'Notes on *Fuses*', p. 45. She also notes here that she shot the film over a three-year period, belying the sense one gets of a single intense erotic encounter. As Schneemann has observed, she was motivated to make *Fuses* by her long experience of being positioned as an object in men's work, including in Brakhage's films and in the now famous 1964 performance work *Site*, attributed to Robert Morris, but initially collaboratively designed by Schneemann and Morris (from conversations by the author with Schneemann, 1996).
16 Schneemann in 'Interview with Katie Haug', pp. 26, 23.
17 David James, *Allegories of Cinema: American Film in the Sixties* (Princeton: Princeton University Press, 1989), pp. 317–18.
18 Marks, *The Skin of the Film*, pp. 192–93.
19 Phelan, *Unmarked*, p. 13.
20 See bell hooks, 'Black women shaping feminist theory' (1984), in *Feminist Theory: From Margin to Center* (London: Pluto Press, 2000), pp. 1–17.
21 Mary Ann Doane, 'Dark continents: epistemologies of racial and sexual difference in psychoanalysis and the cinema', in her *Femmes Fatales: Feminism, Film Theory, Psychoanalysis* (New York/London: Routledge, 1991), p. 247.
22 See Tania Modleski on soap operas, and this kind of fragmented, repetitive narrative time as specifically female, in her classic book *Loving with a Vengeance: Mass-Produced Fantasies for Women* (Hamden, Conn.: Archon Press, 1982).
23 Rist in Hans Ulrich Obrist, 'Interview [with Pipilotti Rist]', in Peggy Phelan, Hans Ulrich Obrist, and Elisabeth Bronfen, *Pipilotti Rist* (London: Phaidon, 2001), p. 15; my emphasis.
24 Of course, with the advent of flat-screen televisions in the last few years this structure has shifted somewhat. Now televisions are often hung like pictures on the wall – a configuration that makes them into 'artworks' rather than 'furniture' and affects our relationship to the screen images.
25 Marks, *Touch*, p. xvi.

Part III
Space

Windows in the white cube 7

Andrew V. Uroskie

In the mid-1960s, the Sony PortaPak changed the history of the moving image, cementing what many film critics of the 1970s and 1980s proclaimed as a 'death of cinema' through the increasing proliferation of a video and television culture. Around thirty years later, in 1995, the Sony digital camcorder helped to inaugurate another cultural transformation: together with the non-linear editing software and digital projectors introduced in the early 1990s, its digitisation of video would, ironically, herald a widespread transition away from the single channel video works of the 1970s and 1980s, towards what has been called an aesthetics of 'the cinematic' within contemporary video installation.[1]

Yet 1995 was also the year Stan Douglas produced one of the most iconic works of contemporary projected-image art, and his project – *Der Sandmann* – was both shot and projected using the supposedly anachronistic medium of 16mm film. Through this unusual choice of support, one quite intentionally out of sync with its historical moment, Douglas foregrounded his interest in the cultural history of the moving image across different technological forms, and the diverse sites of its production, exhibition, and reception. Already in his first work, *Breath* (1982), the artist had begun to interrogate the site of the cinematic without even employing the technology of cinema. Within a Vancouver movie theatre, Douglas played an audio recording of '*O ma belle rebelle!*' a love poem by sixteenth-century French poet and lyricist Jean-Antoine de Baïf, together with a series of slide projections. Yet the 'images' Douglas chose to accompany this song were all a simple, uniform grey, with a translation of the song's verse at the bottom like a running subtitle. Thus, within a cinematic theatre, Douglas effectively negated the expected 'narrative space' of the feature film and its particular mode of phenomenological transport. Just as the song's protagonist projects his desire upon an absent figure, Douglas's audience saw only the projection of their own desire upon the screen. Nevertheless, for all its austere self-reflexivity, the work is not simply a negation of cinema's concern with affect and movement, but is instead an attempt to re-imagine these dynamics for a new model of artistic practice – one which seeks to engage a hybrid phenomenological situation between the proximity and material presence of the material object within the art gallery's brightly lit white cube, and the kind of distance and mobility promoted by the dematerialised image within the cinematic theatre's black box.

Within the general field of projected images, the particular technologies Douglas has employed vary greatly. He used slide projection in *Breath* (1982), *Mime* (1983), and *Onomatopoeia* (1985); 16mm film in *Overture* (1986), *Pursuit, Fear, Catastrophe: Ruskin, BC* (1993), and *Inconsolable Memories* (2005); analogue video projection in *Hors-Champs* (1992) and *Evening* (1993); and digital video within *Nu*tka* (1996) and *Vidéo* (2008). His *Television Spots* (1988) and *Monodramas* (1992) took place over the networks of broadcast television, while his recent 'recombinant narrative' works such as *Win, Place or Show* (1998), *Journey into Fear* (2001), and *Klatsassin* (2006) have utilised computational algorithms to sequence short clips into changing structures of near-infinite duration. Thus even the most superficial survey reveals that Douglas's production does not follow any straightforward trajectory from film to video under the sign of novelty, nor does it display a single-minded commitment to 'outmoded' technologies in some kind of nostalgic refusal of contemporary audiovisual culture. Rather, Douglas's oeuvre presents us with a serious, sustained engagement with the heterogeneous and often ambivalent location of the moving image as it enters and transforms the space of contemporary art.

Jean-Christophe Royoux has suggested that contemporary installation is a post-cinematic medium – that in the present moment, visual art takes place within a cinematically structured world.[2] Rather than simply propose an investigation of the material conditions of projection within literal space (the anti-illusionist paradigm), or a totalising attention to the narrative space of the cinematic image considered as a world in itself, a post-cinematic analytic explores the conjunction and imbrication of these two models through the hybrid form of moving-image installation. To understand today's most ambitious work in moving images – work such as Douglas's – it is necessary to examine a genealogy that leads not to structural film, single-channel video, or the so-called sculptural film, but to a less studied body of artist-filmmaking which takes up the cinematic image as a support for affective engagement and subjective dislocation. These practices engage with the cinematic as a transport away from the confines of a local material environment, even as they persist in maintaining a connection with the sedimented cultural and institutional histories of the 'white cube' that marks the site of their enunciation.

Writing in 1916, Hugo Münsterberg theorised film as an external materialisation of our internal psychic life, citing its uncanny ability to project an image of our basic capacity for attention, affect, memory, and imagination.[3] In her consideration of the contemporary intersection of film and museographic space, Giuliana Bruno has recently reconsidered Münsterberg's theories in light of a heterogeneous pre-cinematic culture of installation as 'site-seeing'. Within devices such as the cabinet of curiosities, she suggests, we find a physical analogy of cinematic spectatorship – 'a mobilised architectonics of scenic space in an aesthetics of fractured, sequential and shifting views.'[4] We might here recall Walter Benjamin's account of the collector and the way in which his objects *screen* a spatial and temporal displacement: 'as he holds them in his hands, he seems to be *seeing through them* into their distant past as though inspired'.[5] Diverse practices of nineteenth-century visual culture, from the institution of the Paris Salon to the commonplace curiosity show, promoted a spectatorial labour of imagination and perambulation or 'site-seeing' as a kind of cognitive and affective displacement.

Developing from these architectures of 'site-seeing', cinema would become, in Bruno's words, 'an agent of intersubjective and cultural memory' by means of its particular ability to collapse distance – 'to bring things "closer" spatially and humanly', as Benjamin famously put it in his essay on the condition of art 'in the age of mechanical reproduction'.[6] Whilst the rise of commercial narrative cinema traded the physical engagement of spectatorial perambulation for a greater affective and cognitive immersion within the single 'narrative space' of the projected image, Bruno finds it 'only appropriate that the cinema and museum should renew their convergence' at a cultural moment in which the efficacy and legitimacy of both has been called into question.[7] For, while cinema has not died, it has become old. Like modernism itself, it is a history accumulated and archived to the point where its last hundred years of development are now both curiously familiar and increasingly distant to us in the present.

From canvas to window

The 'Expanded cinema', as identified by Sheldon Renan in 1967, can be understood as a reaction to this historical situation, as artists of the postwar period increasingly felt constrained by the pseudo-autonomy promised by abstraction and medium-specificity, and sought to wrestle with the profound transformations wrought on distance, time, and subjectivity by film and televisual media.[8] Whilst the rich and complex history of these practices lies outside the scope of the present essay, a single metonymic example might suffice to indicate the way in which this work sought to navigate a path between materialism and immersivity, between Minimalism's phenomenological concern with the local environment, and the internal landscape of the psyche transformed through the identificatory displacements produced by the moving image.

Coincident with the rise of sculptural Minimalism, Robert Whitman's *Cinema Pieces* (1964–65) complicate any straightforward phenomenology of the sculptural object or site through their incorporation of the dislocating technologies of the moving image. These technologies allowed Whitman to investigate an entirely non-material property that, if not specific to the cinematic medium, was at least centrally evident within it – namely, the importance of affective identification in the workings of aesthetic spectatorship. Lynne Cooke has written that, 'while ostensibly sculpture, these works introduce mediated representation … they allow a new level of intimacy between the viewer and the work, a relationship that is familiar from cinematic experience (via the close-up and the zoom), and proper to sculpture (by means of a direct encounter in real space and time) but virtually unknown in the theatre'.[9] This new level of intimacy is indeed 'familiar from cinematic experience', but it far exceeds the spatial information afforded by the magnification of the close-up. Rather, it is an intimacy bound up with the processes of cinematic identification, and with the gendered form this identification often takes.

As if ripped from a dream, *Window* (1964) presents us with the concretisation of a metaphor. In it, a rather quaint-looking domestic window is physically set into the wall of the exhibition space. Looking through this window, into the space beyond, we see a pastoral landscape through which a woman will pass and disrobe. The scene of the nude in the garden may be as old as the picture-window of painting itself, but this window on the world provokes a spectatorial experience fundamentally different from that of the traditional painterly tableau. For one thing, the material construction of the work is a decidedly heterogeneous mélange. The window is a real, physical object – ordinary window glass and an ordinary wooden frame are physically set into the wall. Beyond this frame lies a darkened space – its physical dimensions uncertain – in which some real tree branches have been arranged like a crude diorama. Beyond that, space seems to continue back, deep into a forest glen, branches faintly shifting in a gentle breeze. But, of course, this final movement is not really beyond anything in the spatial sense – for it is upon the illuminated surface of a rear-screen projection that the 'space' of a forest, and a woman within that forest, is photomechanically depicted. Our phenomenal experience of space, in this construction, is thus split between that which we can navigate with our corporeal body and that which we navigate through our affective imaginations. The distinction is at first obvious, inconsequential, and even trite. But over time, as we fix upon the moving image depicted in the world beyond, the experience of space itself becomes strange and uncanny.

The glass and wood window calls attention to the putatively neutral gallery space as a specific, material site through the act of destruction that we realise the creation of the window would have necessitated. Cutting directly into the support of the gallery space, Whitman's act recalls Italian painter Lucio Fontana's infamous slashed canvases of a few years before. Fontana's cuts, conjoining surface and depth, repudiated the picture plane itself through a physical act of incision. Yet Whitman's hole was less a cut than a peephole or viewfinder through which the viewer could exit the physical space of the museum, in order to enter the different space of the cinematic image. And, like a peephole, Whitman's window exchanges Fontana's purely formal articulation of presence and absence for a much more affectively oriented perceptual experience. Lacking the putative grace and stillness of the classical nude, the actress is presented in the process of disrobing, a temporal interaction which immediately suggests not so much the 'high art' of the classical nude as the 'low' genre of the striptease. But it is ultimately aligned with neither. The woman is a fleeting presence – like an apparition, she appears only for an instant before she is gone again. The majority of the time, we are watching an empty forest glen, waiting. Yet we yearn not for flesh but immersion, to be drawn more fully, more totally, across the threshold of the spectacle.

In the moments after the woman has walked out of the frame, or has simply vanished, but before she unexpectedly reappears a moment later, our gaze moves into the deep space of the forest glen. But alongside these branches, swaying gently in the wind, intrude those others, the real branches located in that curiously intermediary space beyond the window but before the rear-projection screen. These branches make an awkward incision into the cinematic tableau, drawing our uneasy attention out of the cinematic world and back into the physical, material space of the gallery – at least for a moment, before the screen's flickering movement, the subtle action within the cinematic tableau, grabs our attention again, beckoning us back inside, across the portal and into the space of the film. With this constant back-and-forth movement, we are asked, in effect, to look *at* the screen at the same time that we are being conjured away by a spectacle transpiring *on* the screen. Within *Window*, this specific materialisation of the screen and the quality of mediation or transport it effects is troped by the materiality of the wooden window-frame and the real foliage diorama. We are accustomed to understanding the cinematic image as a world unto itself, cordoned off by the impermeable frame of the darkened theatre. Yet here we are made to reconfigure our basic understanding of space around a phenomenological hybrid – gazing through a real window and real branches into the illusory space of a forest that begins to seem ever more real.

Reflexivity seems too blunt a concept to describe this delicate interplay of spectator, affect, screen, and material. For it is not simply a matter of the cinematic apparatus calling attention to the fact of its own materiality or to its own mechanical operation. Rather, the fetishistic transport or mediation of the cinematic screen – and the affective registers upon which this transport depends – is simultaneously invoked while being laid open to view. Whitman's field of operation is the subject's own desire for illusion, for transport – the fetishistic disavowal, 'I know very well, but all the same …' which subtends the entire history of the moving image, from the first Hale's Tours of the nineteenth century to the CGI special-effects wizardry of the twenty-first. This incorporation of media technology brings with it a whole other scene of cinema – the workings of desire and identification, as well as the desire for identification – that takes us away from the white cube, transporting us into an imaginary, fantasmatic space. The scenes Whitman constructs within these works stand opposed to the phenomenological specificity of the Minimalist object in its relation to the space of the gallery as a material container. Rather, Whitman's *Cinema Pieces* take place within a newly hybrid, fantasmatic locale. They construct an other scene somewhere between the logic of the gallery's white cube and the cinematic theatre's black box, between the concrete perception of physical space and temporal duration, on the one hand, and the dream-like logic of the primary process, the identificatory conflation of subject and object, and the very different temporalities inherent in the space of the cinematic image.

In keeping with its hybrid location, the space within Whitman's cinematic Garden of Eden is a disjunctive one. Within this haunted, flickering space, the leaves and branches of the foliage alone remain constant, whereas the woman walks into and out of the frame, appears, then is suddenly gone, like the logic of a dream. This liminal visibility keeps us focused on the woman as spectacle, undercutting the reality of the narrative space as a stable and coherent site. Yet, even as we are pulled into the world of the projection, we are denied the fiction that it *is* a coherent world we might occupy. In constructing such a liminal space, Whitman focuses our attention not on the alternative world to which the theatrical cinema has become so adept at transporting us, so much as on the affective qualities of the mechanism of transport itself – our desire to pass over the threshold, to cross the screen.

It seems important that *Window* is not a sculpture, in the traditional sense, in that it does not rest wholly and visibly within the gallery space. The work is built directly into the gallery wall, literally trespassing upon the architectural boundary of the space, necessitating a separate and concealed location within which its scene can unfold. Thus, in quite material terms, it is not exactly 'within' the four walls of the gallery space. Yet the fracture, the breach it opens in the very space of the gallery, is indeed symptomatic, for it also operates outside the conventions of traditional aesthetic production and spectatorship that characterise that space as a *sociocultural* site. Thus, both literally and figuratively, we pass outside the white cube as we attend to these works, and are caught up in their operation.

Under the influence of Minimalist sculpture, as Brian O'Doherty has shown, the gallery space was in the 1960s becoming understood as a kind of illuminated laboratory, a container allowing everything within it a perfect and total visibility.[10] By contrast, the black box of the cinema theatre is not only dark, but the various devices making up the cinematic illusion are quite deliberately concealed. The sound system is covered over by the cinematic screen. The projector is not only above and behind the audience; it is also sealed from the audience in a noiseproof room. To ensure the seamlessness of the cinematic spectacle, the brute materiality of the apparatus must be concealed from both visual and audible perception. *Window* integrates media technology to introduce a distant spatio-temporal incident into the present time and space of the gallery. The fleeting image of a woman passing before us, disrobing, or moving out of the frame, captured by a camera some time before, and far from this particular site, is re-presented before us, *inside* a physical installation with its own experience of obdurate presentness. *Window* quite obviously rejects the idea of the self-contained object. Deliberately staging the work of technological mediation, it similarly foregrounds the historical association of erotic voyeurism with the development of moving-image technology. Like a striptease, Whitman's work both reveals and conceals its illusionistic operation. Rather than aiming to annihilate illusion in the name of a fully transparent and self-conscious reality, it speaks to the importance of the affective and the imaginary, drawing concrete, material space together with affective, fantasmatic space in order to explore their structural interdependence in an increasingly mediated age.

The expanded field of this sculptural practice includes not only the material technology of cinema, but also the identificatory or fantasmatic relations that have dominated the cultural history of that technology. Thus, within *Window*, real objects are presented interacting with realistic images, and vice versa, the illusory existing alongside the actual in a state of imbrication. Whitman writes, 'Fantasy exists as an object, as a central physical entity, and as part of the story that you tell about other objects', and clearly his sculptural practice is one in which the notion of 'object' must be expanded to include a whole range of phenomena outside the purely material.[11] Chrissie Iles has noted that Whitman's *Cinema Pieces* were 'one of the earliest examples of the projected image's shift away from the cinema screen into the medium of sculpture'.[12] But, perhaps more importantly, *they were also the reverse*: for Whitman, the tactile, material space of the sculptural installation – and, by its Minimalist extension, the whole physical space of the 'white cube' – becomes imbricated with the dematerialised dreamspace of the cinematic.

In creating this hybrid, ambivalent situation, with its complex intersection of real with imagined space, psychological affect, and concrete materiality, Whitman's *Cinema Pieces* model an engagement with place that eschews the literal emphasis on materiality or presence in favour of an often spectral engagement with the affective and mnemonic. Functioning between the habits and traditions of the cinema theatre's black box and the art gallery's white cube, these works made an early and prescient move away from an 'anti-illusionist' rhetoric of political modernism, with its dream of an affectless sphere of deliberative rationality, towards an embrace of the cinematic as a source for a reconceptualisation of the political: examining the myriad ways in which our understanding of self and society are established through the sedimentation of media histories and networks of fantasmatic identification.

'Topical history: places remember events'[13]

By introducing this complex terrain of identificatory and fantasmatic relations, Whitman's *Window* sought to open up an expanded field of sculptural practice, one through which the richly sedimented cultural history of moving-image exhibition and spectatorship might be made a subject of investigation within contemporary artistic practice. Yet Whitman's *Cinema Pieces* invoked the history of these media histories only implicitly and in the most general sense. Stan Douglas, by contrast, has worked for over a quarter-century exploring the modes by which specific histories of media exhibition become intertwined with specific mnemonic sedimentations of place.

Guiliana Bruno writes, 'museums, like memory theatres, have genealogically offered to cinema the heterotopic dimension of compressed, connected sites', and throughout her works Bruno has laboured to establish an inherently *cartographic* dimension to the work of cinematic exhibition and spectatorship.[14] Similarly, Tom Conley recently cited Michel de Certeau's remark that the cinematic image, like a landscape, is a 'multiplication of texts and of their readings upon a single surface' in support of his conception of a 'cartographic cinema'.[15] Yet rather than remaining on the surface of the map, we might restore a depth to de Certeau's remark by invoking its properly archaeological or stratigraphic dimension. In his 1970 film *The Spiral Jetty*, Robert Smithson famously depicts a map, torn into pieces, falling past the striated layers of a broken landscape. In so doing, he links the work of location not only to space, but also to time – the invisible sedimentation of history through which the site is slowly built up. Rather than pieces of a puzzle laid out upon a table, the multiple texts of de Certeau's account might be understood as stacked one upon the next, where the most recent and familiar serves to actively conceal those supporting it just underneath. Smithson's evocation of what I have elsewhere described as a 'stratigraphic temporality' functioned as both theme and form within his own multilayered construction of *The Spiral Jetty*, a framework strategically enabling the artist to reach beyond the material dynamics of space of his earlier 'site/non-site' works, towards a more temporal investigation of cultural and representational history.[16] In his own complex and multilayered practice of moving-image installation, Stan Douglas has long sought to mine the depths of the 'cinema cavern' which Smithson's tragically foreshortened investigations sought to open.

It is this stratigraphic conception of cultural archaeology that animates

Douglas's moving-image installations in general, and is perhaps most hyperbolically and metonymically figured within Douglas's *Der Sandmann*. Like Smithson's *Spiral Jetty*, *Der Sandmann* is not a singular, contained work, but rather a complex intertext built from distinct and heterogeneous forms of representation.[17] The dominant component of the piece is the black-and-white film which is projected inside the gallery space on a bare wall using two linked 16mm projectors. Set in one of the UFA (*Universum Film AG*) studios legendary in the heyday of German Expressionist cinema in the 1920s, the film's sombre aesthetic is deliberately juxtaposed with a series of large, colourful 'location photographs' that Douglas made during the course of the project. Set in present-day Germany, these feature modest gardens and brightly coloured foliage, and convey a pastoral, even bucolic sensibility that seems tellingly disjunctive. A text by the artist, entitled 'historical background', provides the connective tissue between these disparate elements.

In the text Douglas explains how the so-called *Schrebergärten*, which emerged at the beginning of the nineteenth century coincident with the beginnings of urbanisation and industrial modernity, were razed after German reunification for a new phase of capital development and real-estate speculation. Originally called *Armengärten* or 'poor gardens', these individual small plots were instituted, under strict state regulation, as a means by which workers could grow food as a supplement to their meagre wages. An early form of social welfare, they were also a bulwark against the economy of industrialisation, a residue of the life the newly urbanised peasant farmers had left behind. A garden, offering growth, harvest, and seeding, is a quintessentially cyclical, natural phenomenon. Yet these particular gardens were kept under strict state regulation as to what could be harvested, how, and when. Thus, already at their origin, we can find a tension between natural cycles and political intervention that would mark the history of the *Schrebergärten* over the last two hundred years, a tension that seems to mimic the very complexities and contradictions of modernity itself as they came to be variously shut down and reinstated at various times for various reasons across the political spectrum. The Socialists used them to foster 'class consciousness', and were accused of reinforcing class divisions. The National Socialists managed to bury the socialist origins of the gardens in order to ground their nationalistic projection of 'blood and soil'. And the bourgeois social reformers of the late nineteenth century imagined the gardens as an individual therapy against the ravages of industrialisation.[18] The man who gave his name to these gardens, Moritz Schreber, was one of the latter group. He had been particularly concerned with industrialisation's effect upon adolescents, and saw the gardens as a place for refuge, exercise, and relaxation. Yet Schreber's therapeutic ideas would bear strange fruit. One of his innovations involved the construction of a mechanical chair by which a child's slouching at the dinner table could be 'corrected' by a sharp tug to their head and neck. Schreber's sons Daniel Gustav and Daniel Paul were the trial subjects for this new mode of discipline. Schreber's first son committed suicide in his thirties, while the second became famously psychotic, recording his unbearable episodes in his *Memoirs*, and inspiring psychoanalytic philosophy from Sigmund Freud and Jacques Lacan to Gilles Deleuze, Elias Canetti, and Eric Santner.[19]

These cycles of nature and history, of nurturing and repression, are embodied in the cyclical format of *Der Sandmann*'s film. Using a motion-control device, Douglas shot a 360–degree arc of a fictional *Schrebergarten* on the outskirts of Potsdam, constructed in the aforementioned UFA studios. In its circuit the film depicts studio and garden both as a kind of split subject. But then the subject is split again, for Douglas shot an identical arc over a newly transformed set, made to appear as if twenty years later, with the gardens apparently being razed for development (the cabbage patch now dead, with cement blocks strewn about, and various parts of the house appearing aged and fallen into disrepair, etc.). Both loops were then projected onto a single screen, with half of each masked over, and the cycle one complete rotation out of phase (figure 7.1). The result was the creation of a 'temporal wipe', a split image that circles around the garden like the movement of the hands of a clock, within which, however, time jumps radically as it passes the central seam. The seam around which the passage is enacted is at first faint and barely visible. Our first encounter with it is likely to come as we pan across the narrator's face, as he stands reciting his lines from a page. We have been hearing a voice off screen, and as he becomes visible we expect to find him the source of the perceived narration. Something is wrong, however – the words he mouths do not correspond with the words we hear. Only when, over the course of time, we pass over that seam – or the seam passes over his face – do his lips suddenly come into sync, the sound and image now unbroken.

Nathaniel, the narrator of the story by E. T. A. Hoffmann, 'The Sandman', from which Douglas's work takes its name, is himself a kind of ghost, split between present and past. He is frightened by the sight of an ordinary gardener working outside in his small *Schrebergarten*, and is at a loss to explain why, but knows it has something to do with his childhood. 'It was as if I had seen it all before', he writes to his brother.[20] He is reminded that the gardener was not only their childhood neighbour, but the garden itself was the site of a profound trauma. As a child, he had been told the tale of the Sandman, who steals the eyes of children who refuse to go to bed. He had decided their neighbour was the Sandman, and had sneaked into the next-door garden late one night to find his sack of eyes. But the gardener had seen him and, shouting, terrified him. Returning home, his mother confronted him with horrible news: his father had died. Nathaniel thought the Sandman had done it to punish him, and that he was responsible for his father's death.

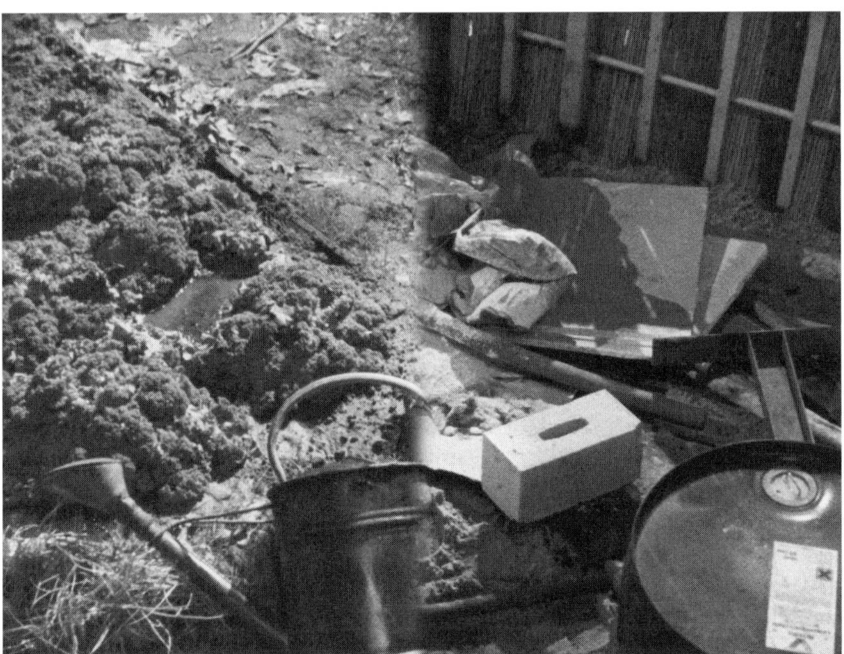

Stan Douglas, *Der Sandmann*, 1995. Installation composed of: two 16mm films, two manipulated optical sound 16mm projectors, two loop devices. 9 minutes 50 seconds (loop), black-and-white, sound. Dimensions vary. Courtesy of the artist and David Zwirner, New York. 7.1

Hoffmann's story contains another element which at first may seem absent from Douglas's rendition of the story: the figure of Olympia, the mysterious woman with whom Nathaniel falls in love, and who ultimately is revealed as a machine. Olympia is, however, not forgotten or repressed within Douglas's retelling, but is rather displaced onto the cinematic apparatus itself. Douglas's film not only takes place within the UFA studio, but also references it as the site of a particular cinematic and representational history. For it was here that Paul Wegener adapted Edgar Allan Poe's 1839 story of the *Doppelgänger* 'William Wilson' (a tale of Poe's own childhood, written seven years before Dostoevsky's 'The double'). Wegener's film *The Student of Prague* (1913) prompted two major psychoanalytic investigations of the subject – the first in Otto Rank's 'The double' (1914) and the second in Sigmund Freud's 'The uncanny' (1919).[21] The film was remade in 1926 by Henrik Galeen at the height of German Expressionist cinema, and exploited the new possibilities of the medium to present audiences with the first living *Doppelgänger* they had ever seen.[22] Galeen shot his actor with one half of the screen veiled; he then ran the same film through the projector to shoot the act again while veiling the opposite half. Douglas's technique in *Der Sandmann* cites but inverts this historic moment of the German 'New Vision'. Rather than 'covering over' a split recording in order to present a unified spectacle, *Der Sandmann* brings together two individual recordings within an uncanny split projection in order to 'uncover' or 'unearth' a complex cultural and cinematic history. Douglas's film itself thus constitutes the uncanny, machinic 'double' – the equivalent of the figure of Olympia – by virtue of its own doubling and redoubling of cinematic history.[23]

Turning the soil: re-enactment and return

Freud interpreted Hoffmann's story as providing a quintessential example of that special 'class of the frightening' which he calls the 'uncanny'.[24] Freud bases his theorisation of this idea on his postulation of a fundamental proximity between the familiar and the uncanny, in a manner which he compares to the way in which the word *Unheimlich* contains within it an etymologically buried *Heim*, or 'home'. Thus Freud argues that the frightening effect of what we perceive as disturbingly 'other' arises from the repression of what is really 'known of old and long familiar'.[25] Douglas's cinematic *Schrebergarten*, however, moves the source of trauma from the repressed history of the individual subject to the repressed histories of the nation state, its cyclical break or tear seeming to stand in for both the continuity and the rupture of historical time. Within Douglas's installation, Freud's geography of the unconscious becomes the repression of 'other' histories and 'other' subjects: namely, those many who may live on the same soil, but are excluded from the collective *Geschichte* (both 'history' and 'story') of the nation (*Heimat*, or 'homeland'.) Like Freud, Douglas seeks to uncover a network of associations buried just beneath the soil or, as the expression goes, 'buried right in our own backyard'.

One aspect of the history Douglas's remake seeks to 'uncover' is made visible the moment the narrator appears on screen. Addressing us in English, yet in a German accent, the role of Nathaniel is played by a young, dark-skinned man of uncertain ethnicity. That such a figure may seem neither particularly striking nor unusual as a contemporary German attests to the historical and cultural displacement between our present moment and the early twentieth century of Schreber and Freud and, even more so, the early nineteenth century in which Hoffmann's story is set. A Canadian of African descent, Douglas's works have long explored the complex ways in which race comes to stand for (and against) particular conceptions of nationhood – specifically in the repressed 'others' whose historical association to particular places has been culturally effaced. Through the displacement of the traditional European protagonists from his stories, he challenges us to consider how these repressed histories live on within the present by observing our own reaction to the transformation.

Here we might again recall the large, colour 'location photographs' Douglas incorporates as part of the project. The aesthetic transition they provoke, from black-and-white to colour, recalls Alain Resnais's evocation of a living past hidden just below the calm surface of the present in his *Night and Fog* of 1955. In that film, we are led seamlessly from the empty, abandoned buildings of a concentration camp shot in colour into the black-and-white documentary footage of the Nazi period, and back again. Robert Smithson cites this landmark of stratigraphic cinema in the conclusion of his essay 'Art through the camera's eye', written just as he was planning *The Spiral Jetty*, and attempting to formulate his own vision of a post-cinematic practice of contemporary exhibition.[26] As we have seen, Douglas's landscapes ineluctably body forth a psychosocial geography, one grounded in the complex historical formations of culture. His conception of site – like Smithson's before him – lies at the intersection of a number of social, cultural, and even intellectual histories. But these large photographs constitute a paradoxical form of representation in this regard, for they seem less about imparting any specific information to the viewer than about depicting their own failure or inability to represent. We come to understand, over the course of our attention to the project, the complex histories to which these images are related. But perceptually and aesthetically the images persist at a distance from these histories. Unlike the complex staging and dramatic formal construction of his split-screen film, these photographs – taken with a large format camera, elegantly composed, colourful, and rich in detail – are deceptively traditional in form. Their superficial beauty plays off the obdurate, allegorical fragments they contain.

One way of reading this photographic practice is as a deliberate, almost programmatic refusal to represent. Not an inability to represent *tout court* – this is not a postmodern critique of representation – but rather an attempt to address the different forms historical representation can take, and the particular dangers it involves. In his book *Sustaining Loss: Art and Mournful Life*, philosopher Gregg Horowitz contends that the commercial cinema's attempts to represent history – and particularly traumatic historical events – have paradoxically given rise to an 'obscene visibility' on account of the 'fullness' of their representational goals.[27] For Horowitz, it is not particular representations of history which are obscene, but rather the ways in which historical re-enactments reinforce a sense of the past as a distant, foreign land, a place safely consigned to the imagination alone. However noble its intentions, the coherent world within which fictional re-enactments are set functions to create an unbridgeable chasm between the present and the past. Keeping the past at arm's length, these simulacra ask nothing from their spectator. In so doing, they work to efface history's motive force as a living, perpetual intervention within the present.

Douglas's historical 're-enactment' within *Der Sandmann* is, by contrast, quite palpably incomplete. The visibility of the scaffolding, the artificiality of the space, and, above all, the temporal schism created by the 'seam' running through the centre of our field of view all reinforce the idea that this representation of history remains a 'work in progress'. This progress, this process, is one with which we, as viewers, are crucially involved. *Der Sandmann* thus contains both representational plenitude and lack. Unlike the theatrical feature, we are refused access to a coherent cinematic diegesis, unable to enter fully into the 'world' of a cinematic 'narrative space'. Yet, far from simply returning us to ourselves, spinning in space in a purely formalist, self-reflexive gesture, the film encourages a whole range of travels outside our present time and local space. This travel comes both as a result of the narrative voiceover, and the chain of associations and correspondences it effects, and as a result of the imagery itself, as key elements function allegorically to participate in this metonymic chain.

While Douglas's conception of historical re-enactment is one which certainly partakes of Bertolt Brecht's suspicion regarding representational plenitude, his work cannot be easily situated within a neo-Brechtian art-historical discourse of 'institutional critique'. Douglas's chosen sites are not laid bare, but revealed as densely layered palimpsests whose meaning and relation to the present solicit our careful attention. Grounded in what Jeffrey Skoller has described as the unseen, unspeakable, and ephemeral impact of history living on in the present, the work of historical connection is left to the individual viewer to perform.[28] Rather than presenting a coherent, encapsulated story, these works stage an open-ended encounter, addressing the viewer like an invitation. Neither expressive nor polemical, Douglas's mode of post-cinematic exhibition is a kind of allegorical assemblage – an invitation to explore a particular web of cultural histories and their living, motive force within the present. Formally and thematically, these works require – and reward – an active, inquisitive, and interrogatory mode of spectatorship. Yet this vision of active spectatorship is quite different from the rigorous austerity traditionally associated with the framework of political modernism. Rather than aggressive confrontation, Douglas's works seduce the viewer deeper and deeper into their web of allusion and reference.

Der Sandmann affords us a window into the dynamic reconceptualisation of place occurring within contemporary moving-image installations. While not beholden to a material or even strictly geographic conception of 'site-specificity', the particular 'placelessness' invoked by the cinematic form does not float ungrounded, but is rather tied quite specifically to a foundation of land and history. Yet this foundation is neither uniform nor stable; it exists as an interlocking matrix of allusion and reference, constantly remade within the space of media representation. For Douglas, the 'post-cinematic' installation is a stratigraphic engagement with history, made tangible and sensuous through a polyphony of dislocation. His works create a portal through which the spectator can travel, while underscoring the extent to which the most foreign lands are frequently those closest to home.

Notes

1 See Chrissie Iles, 'Issues in the new cinematic aesthetic in video', in Tanya Leighton and Pavel Büchler (eds), *Saving the Image* (Glasgow: Centre for Contemporary Arts, 2003), pp. 129–41.

2 Jean-Christophe Royoux, 'Towards a post cinematic space-time', in Sara Arrheius, Magdalena Malm, and Cristina Ricupero (eds), *Black Box Illuminated* (Stockholm: IASPIS, NIFCA and Propexus, 2003), pp. 107–20; and Royoux, 'The conflict of communications', in *Stan Douglas* (Paris: Centre Georges Pompidou, 1993), pp. 56–57.

3 Hugo Münsterberg, *The Film: A Psychological Study: The Silent Photoplay in 1916* (New York: Dover, 1970).

4 Giuliana Bruno, 'Collection and recollection: on film itineraries and museum walks', in Bruno, *Public Intimacy: Architecture and the Visual Arts* (Cambridge, Mass.: MIT Press, 2007), p. 17. See also her *Atlas of Emotion: Journeys in Art, Architecture, and Film* (New York: Verso, 2002).

5 Walter Benjamin, 'Unpacking my library' (1931), in Benjamin, *Illuminations*, ed. Hannah Arendt, trans. Harry Zorn (London: Fontana, 1973), p. 61; my emphasis.

6 Bruno, 'Collection and recollection', p. 4; Walter Benjamin, 'The work of art in the age of mechanical reproduction', in *Illuminations*, p. 222.

7 Bruno, 'Collection and recollection', p. 17.

8 Sheldon Renan, *An Introduction to the American Underground Film* (New York: E. P. Dutton & Co, 1967). A much fuller genealogy is elaborated in my forthcoming study, *Between the Black Box and the White Cube: Site, Specificity, and the Emergence of an Expanded Cinema in Postwar Art* (Chicago, Ill.: University of Chicago Press).

9 Lynne Cooke, Karen Kelly, and Bettina Funcke (eds), *Robert Whitman: Playback* (New York: Dia Art Foundation, 2003), p. 64.

10 Brian O'Doherty, *Inside the White Cube: The Ideology of the Gallery Space* (1976; Berkeley, Calif.: University of California Press, 1999).

11 Robert Whitman, as quoted in Michael Kirby, *Happenings: An Illustrated Anthology* (New York: E. P. Dutton, 1965), p. 136.

12 Chrissie Iles, *Into the Light: The Projected Image in American Art: 1964–1977* (New York: Whitney Museum of American Art, 2001), p. 86.

13 James Joyce, preparatory notebook for *Ulysses*, cited in Edward S. Casey, *Getting Back into Place: Toward a Renewed Understanding of the Place-World* (Bloomington, Ind.: Indiana University Press, 1993), p. 277. Casey writes, '[T]he initial spatio-temporal equipose of the phrase "topical history" is subverted by the claim that the active agent is place and not historical events, the former actively remembering the latter. Joyce calls into question the characteristically modern conception of viewing memory as exclusively time-bound, i.e. as recollection of the past. The

inherent localism of memory also obtains for narration, in which places, instead of merely settings or scenes, are active agents of commemoration.'

14 Bruno, 'Collection and recollection', p. 33.

15 Giuliana Bruno and Tom Conley have together written several book-length studies of the intersection of cinema and cartography. In addition to Bruno's *Atlas of Emotion*, see her *Streetwalking on a Ruined Map* (Princeton: Princeton University Press, 1992) and, more recently, Conley's *Cartographic Cinema* (Minneapolis: University of Minnesota Press, 2007). Conley cites de Certeau on p. 215, n. 4 of the latter work.

16 I elaborate this idea in my '*La Jetée en spirale*: Robert Smithson's stratigraphic cinema', *Grey Room*, 1:19 (Spring 2005), pp. 54–79.

17 I discuss the contemporary cinematic installation as intertext in my 'Siting cinema: Janet Cardiff and Pierre Huyghe', in Tanya Leighton (ed.), *Art and the Moving Image: A Critical Reader* (London: Tate Publishing, 2008), pp. 386–400.

18 See Douglas, '*Der Sandmann*, 1995: historical background and script', in Scott Watson, Diana Thater, Carol J. Clover, and Gilles Deleuze, *Stan Douglas* (London: Phaidon Press, 1998), pp. 124–30.

19 Sigmund Freud, 'The Schreber case (psychoanalytic remarks on an autobiographically described case of paranoia (dementia paranoides))', trans. Andrew Webber (New York: Penguin Classics, 2003); Jacques Lacan, *The Psychoses: The Seminar of Jacques Lacan, Book III, 1955–56*, trans. Russell Grigg (New York: Norton, 1997); Gilles Deleuze and Félix Guattari, *Anti-Oedipus: Capitalism and Schizophrenia* (Minneapolis: Minnesota University Press, 1983), pp. 1–50, 273–382; Elias Canetti, *Crowds and Power* (New York: Farrar, Straus & Giroux, 1984), pp. 434–64; Morton Schatzman, *Soul Murder: Persecution in the Family* (New York: Random House, 1973); Eric Santner, *My Own Private Germany: Daniel Paul Schreber's Secret History of Modernity* (Princeton: Princeton University Press, 1997).

20 Stan Douglas, '*Der Sandmann*, Script, 1994/97', from Watson et al., *Stan Douglas*, p. 128.

21 E. T. A. Hoffmann, 'The Sandman' (1816), in *The Tales of Hoffmann* (London: Penguin Classics, 1982), pp. 85–126, and 'Die Doppelgänger' (1821, untranslated); Edgar Allan Poe, 'William Wilson' (1939), from *The Complete Tales of Edgar Allan Poe* (Castle Books, 2003), pp. 555–68; Fyodor Dostoyevsky, *The Double: A Petersburg Poem*, trans. Constance Garnett (Dodo Press, 2008); Ernst Jentsch, 'On the psychology of the uncanny', in *Angelaki: The Journal of Theoretical Humanities*, 2:1 (1997), pp. 7–16; Otto Rank, *The Double: A Psychoanalytic Study* (Chapel Hill: University of North Carolina Press, 1971); Sigmund Freud, 'The uncanny' (1919), in *The Standard Edition of the Complete Psychological Works of Sigmund Freud*, trans. and ed. James Strachey, vol. 17, pp. 217–56. Andrew Webber teases out the relations between many of these texts in his *The Doppelgänger: Double Visions in German Literature* (New York: Oxford University Press, 1996).

22 Galeen's particular *Doppelgänger* was only the latest in a thirty-year history of illusionistic ghosts and doublings that began with Georges Méliès and his followers. Friedrich Kittler discusses the cultural dislocation of the double from the novel to the screen in his *Gramophone, Film, Typewriter*, trans. Geoffrey Winthrop-Young and Michael Wutz (Stanford: Stanford University Press, 1999), p. 153.

23 On the identification between the cinematic apparatus and the female body as a key fantasy of the cinematic form, see Annette Michelson's 'On the Eve of the future: the reasonable facsimile and the philosophical toy', *October*, 29 (Summer 1984), pp. 3–20.
24 Freud, 'The uncanny', p. 220.
25 Freud, 'The uncanny', p. 220.
26 Robert Smithson, 'Art through the camera's eye' (c. 1971), in *Robert Smithson: The Collected Writings*, ed. Jack Flam (Berkeley, Calif.: University of California Press, 1996). Interestingly, Danièle Huillet and Jean-Marie Straub's *Geschichtsunterricht* (*History Lessons*) was completed this same year, and employed a comparable stratigraphic or archaeological conception of historical inquiry.
27 Gregg Horowitz, *Sustaining Loss: Art and Mournful Life* (Stanford: Stanford University Press, 2001).
28 Jeffrey Skoller, *Shadows, Specters, Shards: Making History in Avant-Garde Film* (Minneapolis: University of Minnesota Press, 2005).

8 Inside the film-machine: architecture and apparatus in British women's film since the 1990s

Tamara Trodd

In recent artists' film – roughly, since the mid-1990s – a spatial model of great distinctiveness and interest has emerged. Time and again, in individual works made over the past ten years or so by artists working separately, our screens are filled with the camera's exploration of a found, architectural structure. Furthermore, the camera work in these films is such as to achieve a 'mapping' of found physical structure to the film's own material apparatus (lens, projector, screen, etc); whilst at the same time developing a spacious new 'interior' to the screen. The result, I propose, is a new imagining of what used to be called the filmic 'apparatus'; and what I propose we call here the 'film-machine'.[1]

The emergence of architecture as a support on which to map the filmic apparatus represents, I suggest, a displacement of the sculptural model which had been so important to artists' film of the 1960s and 1970s and which had helped define that era's sense and presentation of film's materiality.[2] In individual works by contemporary artists the architectural model is explored in different ways, but overall the effect is to produce a powerful sense of spatiality within the projection screen, into which the viewer's consciousness is projected. This new 'interiority' of the screen pulls against the simultaneous emphasis found in many of these works on the materiality of the film apparatus and the physical space of installation. At the same time, in certain core examples, this is an interior space producing rich resonances with earlier avant-garde movements.

In this essay I propose to articulate these effects in relation to the examples supplied by three major artists to have emerged in this period: the twins Jane and Louise Wilson, Tacita Dean, and an artist who has emerged more recently, Rosalind Nashashibi, together with her occasional collaborator, Lucy Skaer. Taken together, my contention is that their work offers the example of a powerful current in contemporary work, which operates to remap the history of artists' film. Furthermore, I shall suggest, this helps supply an alternative critical framework to existing critical paradigms for the projected image.

Spatial imaginaries

One of Jane and Louise Wilson's earliest major works, *Crawl Space*, of 1995, is built around the camera's exploration of an empty, derelict house. The camera, and with it the viewer's gaze, repeatedly passes through doorways, enters rooms, tracks down corridors, and probes around corners and into cupboards. One room in particular, with a red-painted floor and terracotta walls and an empty white chair, is returned to again and again. Red is the predominant colour of the film: the walls of one of the long corridors are painted red, and at another point red light from a stained-glass window spills out, staining a windowsill. Sometimes a red filter seems to have been used to achieve the overall reddish hue of a scene. The rooms are mostly empty and rubbish-strewn, lit only by the light coming from the windows.

The architecture of this film is supplied by the abandoned house; however, a second architecture, doubling this first, is supplied by the beginning and end sequences of the film. The film opens with a shot from below of a woman's face leaning down, submerged in water (figure 8.1). Slowly she opens her mouth and a bubble appears, on which is repeated the image of her own face, eyes shut, straining against the water. This bubble pops out of her mouth and becomes the travelling motif of the film, drifting into room after room of the empty house; always with the same female figure visible within it, stretching her arms against the confines of the bubble. Thus from within the woman's own body a form has emerged, which encases the image of her double (as though in an egg or uterine sac), and which at the same time redoubles our sense of her spatial confinement, first within water, and then within the house. We are presented with a set of bodily architectures, each housed within the other.

The sense of the house and the spatial interior of the film as together comprising a quasi-uterine space is made quite explicit in the end sequence of the film. After following a female figure as she walks across one of the house's empty rooms, up some stairs, and around a corner, suddenly the shot changes and we see the submerged woman's face again, this time from the side, her lips again stretched around the bubble on which again appears the image of her own face. As we watch she slowly and with difficulty swallows the bubble and withdraws her face from the water. Suddenly the shot changes again, and we see a woman's stomach, rising and falling with the sound of someone breathing (figure 8.2). At regular intervals a red light – like the infrared light used in a darkroom – flashes on screen. The light seems to 'develop', as though photographically, words which slowly begin to appear, written in a kind of clear gel on the woman's belly: 'Crawl Space', we gradually read. The clear jelly and its sensitivity to the red light suggest a photographic quality, as well as reminding the viewer of the gel smeared on pregnant women's bellies to obtain camera pictures of a foetus. This sequence establishes an explicitly bodily, feminine

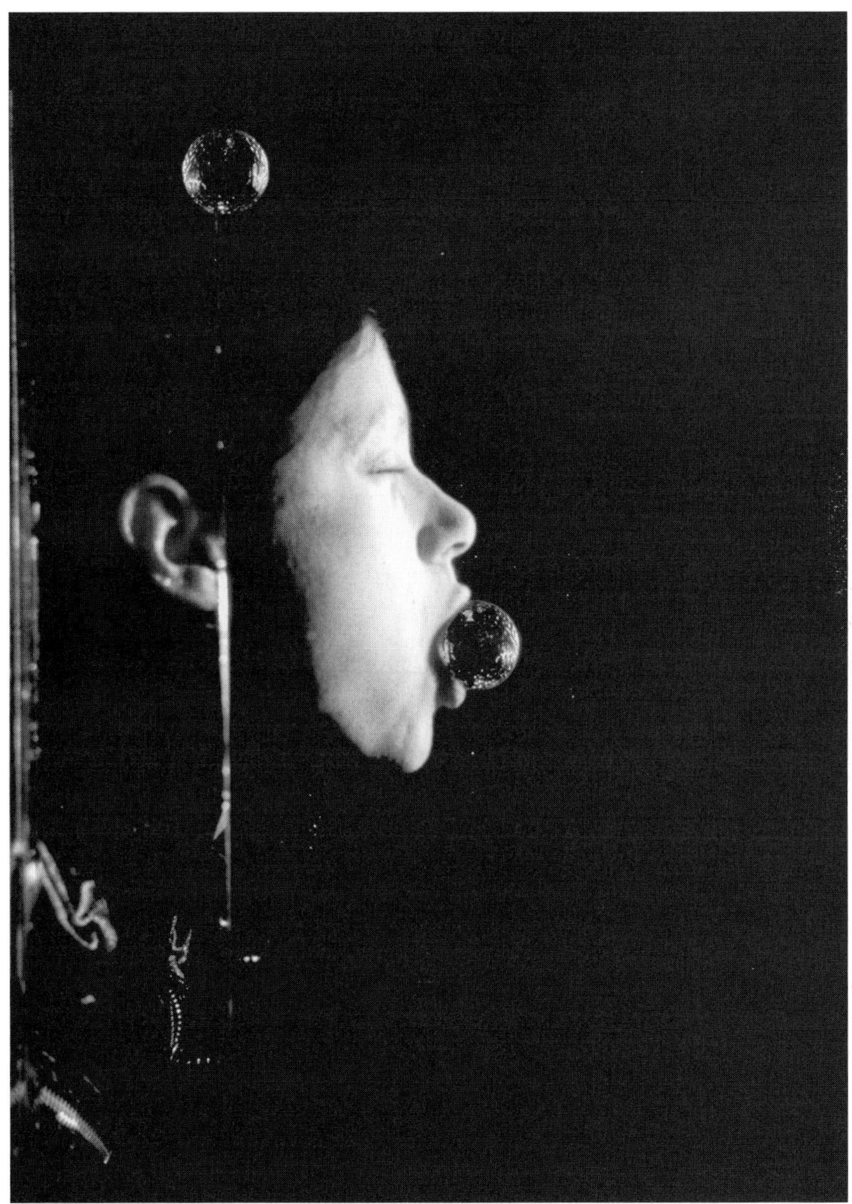

8.1 Jane and Louise Wilson, *Crawl Space*, 1995. C-type print. Courtesy of the artists and 303 Gallery, New York.

valency for the 'Crawl Space' of the title, which, it is suggested, means both the space of the mother's body and the space of the derelict house.

The sense of figures trapped within the fabric of the house is reiterated in

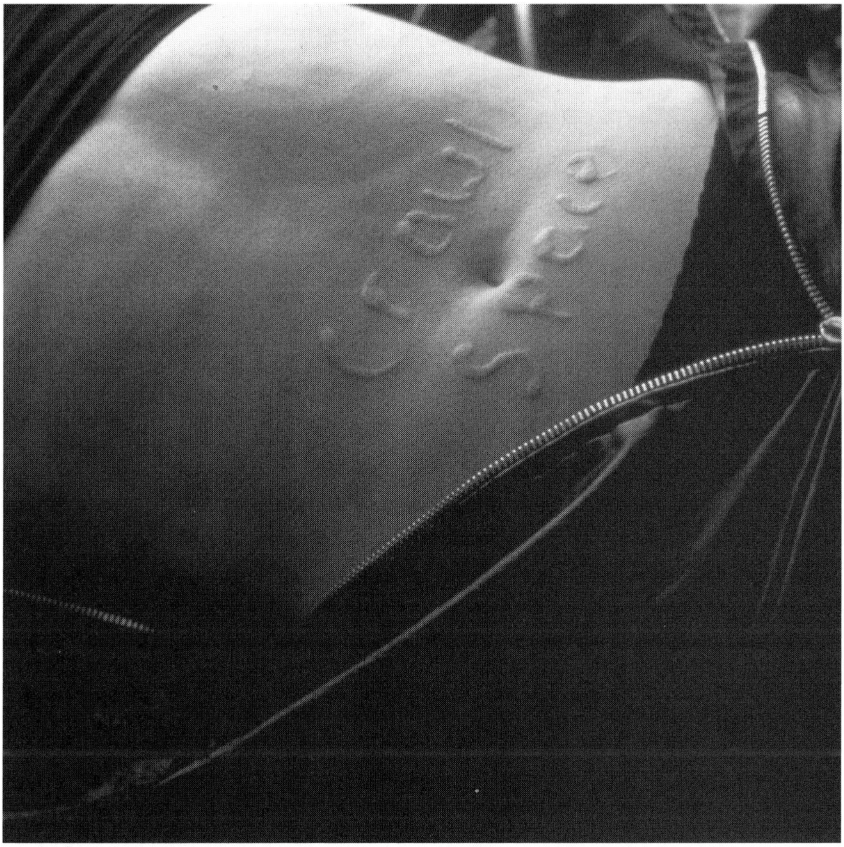

Jane and Louise Wilson, *Crawl Space*, 1995. C-type print mounted on aluminium. Courtesy of the artists and 303 Gallery, New York. 8.2

a shot repeated a number of times in the film, showing the flock wallpaper on one wall bulging outward in a regular pulse (like a heartbeat), as though a figure were trapped within it. As well as evoking the plot of Charlotte Perkins Gilman's cult novel *The Yellow Wallpaper* (1892) (in which a woman apparently in the grip of post-partum psychosis hallucinates a woman trapped behind the wallpaper in her room), the specific form of the bulge suggests a more art-historical reference, to Duchamp's plaster-cast-cum-drawing *With My Tongue in My Cheek* (1959), which bodily reference serves to further 'embody' the surface of the house, as well as suggesting the playful, slightly satiric spirit in which perhaps such references are meant.

In *Crawl Space* references are also established to mass-market cinema. (Indeed, the house itself was used by film companies, and when the Wilsons filmed there it was full of disused sets, 'partial film sets', as Jane Wilson described them.[3]) In particular a number of horror films focusing on terrifying women, made from novels by Stephen King, are referenced throughout: a scene of quick-cut doors slamming in response to a woman's glances recalls the prom-night bloodbath scene in Brian De Palma's *Carrie* (1976) (the splash of red paint on the wall confirms the sanguinary reference), whilst a shot of a woman dragging a wheelchair up a staircase recalls a similar scene in *Misery* (1990). The long, red-carpeted, sinister corridors of Stanley Kubrick's *The Shining* (1980) are clearly quoted by the Wilsons' long tracking shots through the red-painted hallways of the house, but even something as light, magical, and apparently harmless as *The Wizard of Oz* (1939) is referenced in the motif of the bubble encasing a figure, which floats through the scenes of the film. These glancing references come quick and fast, forming a forest or thicket of visual cues and reminders.[4] The 'Crawl Space' pictured on screen is a 'space of cinema' too; a squirming space of the cinematically constituted imaginary, corporealised or realised physically as the fantasmatic interior of a specifically female body.

The importance of the female body to the viewing structures and codes of cinema has been noted by numerous critics. Annette Michelson, in particular, has argued that '[t]he female body … comes into focus as the very site of cinema's invention and we may … see the philosophical toy we know as cinema marked in the very moment of its invention by the inscription of desire.'[5] This 'marking' or inscription of cinema is revealed by the Wilsons, who, in this work, appear to return to the female body and to the cinematic imaginary simultaneously, not so much mapping the two onto one another as revealing their mutual imbrication. It is my argument that the architectural shell, or cinematically 'haunted house', is used by the artists in *Crawl Space* as precisely the 'apparatus' which enables their excavation of cinema's multiple previous inscriptions on women's bodies – as it is used also by the other artists whose work I shall examine here.

In the film work of Tacita Dean – also dating from the mid-1990s on – we see a very different treatment of found architectural structures which nevertheless works to a similar purpose in hollowing out an interior to the screen. Dean's first major film was *Disappearance at Sea* (1996), in which her shots switch between the interior of a lighthouse lamp-chamber and exterior shots of the surrounding curve of land and sea. This was followed by later films such as *Bubble House* (1999) and *Teignmouth Electron* (2000), which again are built around interchanging shots, the camera moving slowly first over the exterior of these rotting and abandoned forms, then switching to their insides. Her treatment of these found physical structures is semi-sculptural, but cross-references the sculptural with an architectural model, referencing Robert Smithson's *Partially Buried Woodshed* (1970), as I have argued elsewhere.[6] As is the case in the Wilsons' *Crawl Space*, Dean's films explicitly map the filmic apparatus onto her depicted spaces. Where the Wilsons double the derelict architecture of an empty house – which we never seem to get 'outside' – with a woman's body, and, in repeated shots, parallel a pulsing form, bulging and receding behind the wallpaper, with the rising and falling of a woman's belly, Dean's camera work is more austere and slower-paced, and her imagery less bodily. The fraught, claustrophobic, and fantasmatic atmosphere of *Crawl Space* is replaced in Dean's works with a quiet opening of architectural shells to the sea and sky and sounds of the outside. Nevertheless, Dean's use of architecture enables a similarly physical and medium-specific construction of the filmic apparatus to that which is developed in the Wilsons' work. The apertures and windows of the abandoned house in *Bubble House* and the boat in *Teignmouth Electron* visually recall the shape of a cinema or TV screen, or the frames of a filmstrip. The turning lamp in the lighthouse, together with the glass of the lighthouse window, recall the lamp and lens which are constitutive of the filmic apparatus. The beam of the lighthouse lamp, cast out across the sweeping, dark sea, reminds us of the projection beam of film.

Thus, Dean's is a different model of the creation of an interior filmic space to that of the Wilsons in *Crawl Space*, but it still holds important things in common with it: principally, that the central business of the film work in both cases is to map the filmic apparatus onto a found, physical structure. In both cases, this represents a recovery of film's potential to construct and invite us to inhabit alternative spatial structures, and dimensions, which in these artists' hands come to constitute imaginative landscapes. This is an historically important recovery of film as a territory of imaginative escape and expulsion, and as the material to form a spatial structure into which the viewing consciousness, and viewing desire, can be projected.

After *Crawl Space* the Wilsons moved on to a series of films of abandoned government and military installations, including the ex-Stasi headquarters in Berlin (in *Stasi City*, 1997), the American military base on Greenham Common (*Gamma*, 1999), and the British Houses of Parliament (*Parliament*, 1999). At the same time they moved on to a more complex and explicit treatment of space in their installation strategy, adopting a multi-screen method of projection which they still use. Typically the works of the 1990s I have mentioned were designed to be shown on two pairs of corner-mounted screens, placed opposite each other to create an immersive, doubled and all-surrounding type of screen-space, and enabling a formal structure of mirror-like reflections to be established amongst their multiple projections. (Neville Wakefield, writing in 1998, referred aptly to the 'Rorschach-like symmetries' of the Wilsons' work.[7]) The placing of the doubled screens in the room's corners has the result that the images shown on each mirrored pair flow in opposite directions away from each other, the tracking shots of the camera producing a stream of as-if mirror reflections streaming away from the corner seam. Within their chosen architectural locations, a focus on gleaming surfaces contributes further to the 'hall of mirrors' effect.[8] Formal structures of tessellation, interlocking, and doubling make these works a fabric of surfaces and angles, animated by a visually complex language of machine-gleam and dazzle, as though in an update of 1930s New Vision aesthetics. Yet, at the same time that these works emphasise the buildings they explore as surfaces, redoubled and glimmering, the camera work on screen in each case produces a sense of spatial interiority, owing to the endless winding corridors which are explored and corners which are turned by the twins' ceaselessly moving camera, contributing to what Darian Leader has called an 'endoscopy of architectural space'.[9]

In most of these works the architectural structures are activated by the figure of a walking woman. We are never shown the woman's face, but the camera follows her as she enters buildings, walks through doorways and up or down staircases, before disappearing around a corner. The Wilsons' exploration of these spaces has often been interpreted as examining specific power structures, regimes of the Cold War and other military-political ideologies.[10] Certainly this is one effect of their camera's dispassionate examination of the surfaces and machinery of these buildings; however, this never amounts to an angry or even precisely oppositional critique, but instead remains a more formal, visual excavation of these architectural forms. In the Wilsons' handling, these architectural structures are constructed as machines for viewing, revealing buried fantasy potential as well as echoes to earlier artistic movements.

Sometimes their handling may be seen as revivifying specific legacies of European art – for example, Constructivism, as in *A Free and Anonymous Monument* (2003). Here the camera's exploration of a derelict modernist architectural structure is married to an examination of the political ambitions of earlier utopian modernist movements, in a way which might be compared to Dean.[11] Like Dean's *Teignmouth Electron*, *A Free and Anonymous Monument* seems to reference abandoned utopian hopes, configuring modernism as a found, ruined structure, even as their work also spins these structures into new excavations of shared psychic and fantasmatic space.

More recently in the Wilsons' work, Surrealism seems to be the legacy activated. In *Sealander* (2006), hulks of concrete buildings by the sea – abandoned Second World War military bunkers – are treated like found sculptural objects, the camera tracking endlessly over their scarred and pitted surfaces. Footage of the bunkers is paired, on facing screens, with film of an underwater sea creature (the rare 'vampire squid'), its clear, liquid eye rolling and bulging at the screen, its tentacles and sleek body undulating against the glass lens of the camera and the surface of the screen (figure 8.3). This film marks an important new departure from colour in the Wilsons' work: it is their first film entirely in black-and-white. The lush, velvety black and creamy white of the footage, however, makes an even more sensuous, and not austere, viewing environment. The darkened space of the viewing room, merging with the dark space of the sea surrounding the sea creature, is illuminated by the splashes and gleams of its light flesh.

This recent film demonstrates a new way of producing an interior filmic space – unlike in their previous work, the artists' camera does not travel inside the concrete bunkers, but instead a quasi-bodily space is created *between* the two sets of filmic objects. The squid effortlessly, repeatedly, flips itself into reverse, unrolling its body inside out like a glove. The effect of the camera bouncing off the scarred concrete surfaces of the bunkers – as though in a form of visualised echo-location – interchanging with shots of the squirming sea creature is a kind of *undoing* of the shoreline as a boundary between the two spaces, underwater and on land. This fortified border, bristling with obsolete defences, is undermined by the rhythmic camera work and the pulse of the squid's body. The bunkers at the edge of the sea appear remaindered, as though the shells or skeletons of creatures long ago expelled from underwater; an impression which is intensified by the exchange between these monstrous, long-dead hulks and the blind, bright creature inside the sea. The camera work

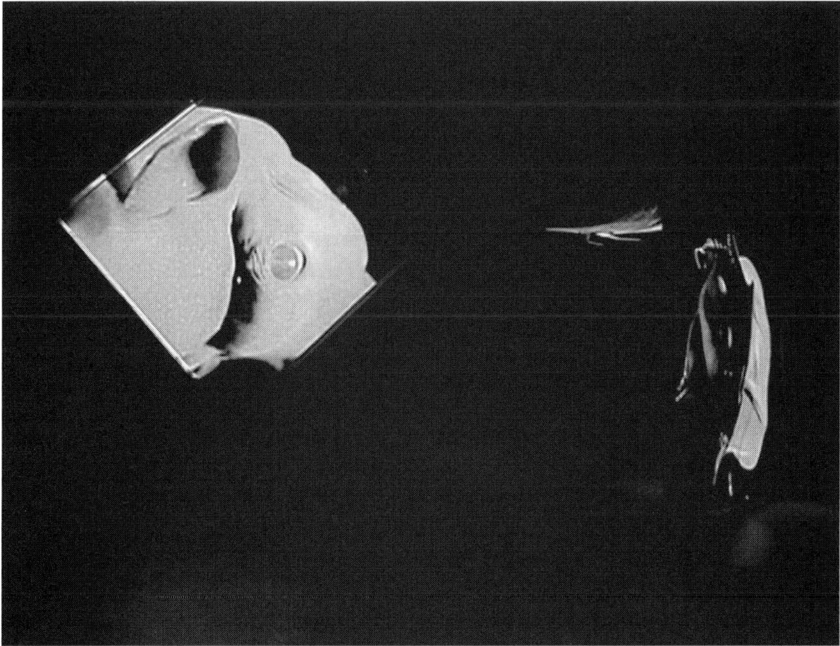

Jane and Louise Wilson, *Sealander*, 2006. Three-screen video installation (suspended screens with mirrors) with sound, 8 minutes 40 seconds. Photographed as installed at Haunch of Venison, Zurich, 2006. Courtesy of the artists and 303 Gallery, New York. 8.3

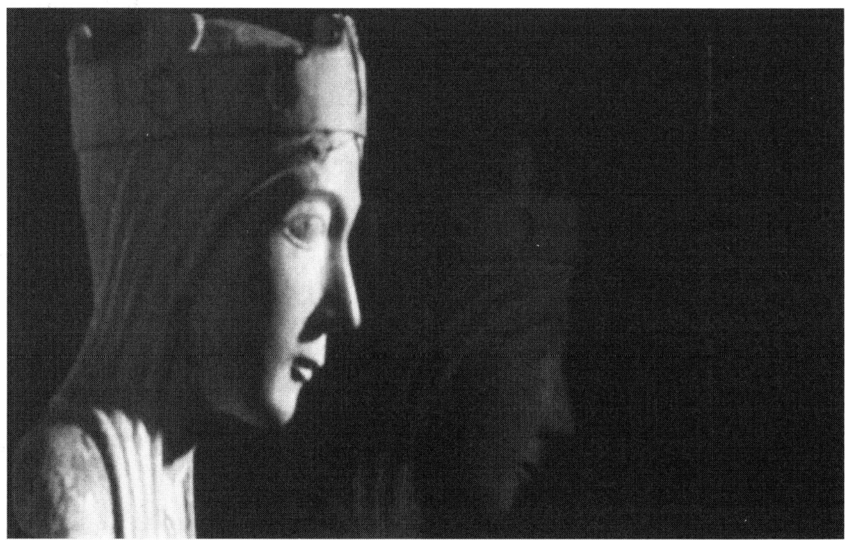

8.4 Rosalind Nashashibi and Lucy Skaer, *Flash in the Metropolitan*, 2006. 16mm film, colour, silent, 3 minutes 25 seconds. Edition of 3 + 2 AP. Commissioned by Spike Island. Supported by the Elephant Trust. Courtesy of the artists and doggerfisher, Edinburgh.

interlacing the space within the sea and the space outside, at its edge, rhythmically and repeatedly joins these two locations, inside and outside, and eventually succeeds in pulling space inside out, rendering outside as inside and vice versa, and producing an uncomfortably bodily and 'underwater' effect in the installation space itself. As Darian Leader has suggested, we might see an especially close relationship between this work and *Crawl Space*, since, as he argues, the motif of the bubble expelled from the woman's body in the earlier film may be seen as mimicked here by the expulsive/propulsive movements of the squid.[12]

Surrealist legacies are also explored in another recent film by two British women artists, *Flash in the Metropolitan* (2006) by Lucy Skaer and Rosalind Nashashibi. Again in this work we see a use of architectural space to 'house' something like the psyche of film. The roughly three-minute film was made at night, as the two women walked around New York's Metropolitan Museum of Art. As we watch, artefacts are illuminated in the beam of the women's hand-held flashlight, which passes quickly over them before the screen returns again to darkness (figure 8.4). The film is almost entirely dark, punctuated by these glimpses of sculptural forms, stone reliefs, and precious, unidentifiable objects, which only come into view for a moment. We see a brief 'flash' of the object, which in almost all cases is repeated. A doubled rhythm, like the quick–slow, dotted rhythm of a heartbeat, is established, only to be interrupted in one or two cases, where after the two showings we are unexpectedly shown the same object again, for a third time. In the context of the established rhythm of viewing, like a psychic pulse, this comes as a joke – it is unexpected, yet obvious, and somehow it makes us laugh. There is something of the Victorian parlour game about this exercise: Can you see what it is? Have another look – now, what about this? But the doubled, rhythmic pulse of light illuminating the buried object in the dark is also like a heartbeat, and so is carnal. The darkened space of the museum is recast as a bodily, perhaps womb-like interior. At the same time, because of the mystery and seeming ancientness of the objects which are uncovered, it becomes like the space of the unconscious. The Surrealist treasure trove of *objets trouvés* which are uncovered by their light and camera suggests a level of unconscious content brought to the surface of the mind, or glimpsed in a flash in the mind's eye, constructing filmic as psychic space and turning the cavernous museum into a fantasmatic interior.

Thus in each of these examples, by three sets of women filmmakers, architectural space is established as a model for filmic structure, meaning that in all these cases films are made around exploring and excavating architectural spaces. At the same time, within these architectural structures a kind of psychic interior to film is established. Within the interior spaces which the architectural model enables contemporary artists to establish, as I have shown, we witness the excavation of buried resonances to earlier avant-gardes. But even further back than these, older filmic narratives are reawoken, which suggest the possibility of retrieving a historical version of modernism against the grain, producing an alternative 'future history' for artists' film and, as I shall show, producing an importantly altered sense of the materiality of the filmic apparatus.

The film-machine

The Argentinean writer Adolfo Bioy Casares's 1940 novella *The Invention of Morel* tells a strange kind of fable about film.[13] The narrator, believing himself alone on an uninhabited island, explores the large, abandoned villa he calls a 'museum', which, together with a church, a mill, and a swimming pool, are the only built structures there. He finds a gigantic, engine-like projection-machine in the basement of the 'museum' which, he comes to realise, generates the images of people he encounters when what seems to be a holiday party appears on the island, dressed in 'clothes from another era' and listening incessantly to outmoded dance tunes on phonograph records ('Tea for Two' and 'Valencia' are the only records they seem to play). At first mistaking these illusions for real people, he is afraid and hides, learning about their movements and relationships by spying on them. Quickly, he falls in love with one woman in particular, whose name, he learns, is Faustine. The party are on the island at the invitation of a scientist, Morel, whose invention the projection-machine is, as our narrator discovers towards the end of the book, when he overhears Morel explaining to his guests that he has secretly recorded them. When he realises that Faustine is only a projection and cannot see or hear him, he is at first in despair, until he discovers that he can record himself, apparently interacting with her 'scenes', seemingly exchanging glances and occasional sentences, and so eventually can join her in the semblance of a relationship. The side effect of so recording himself is that his real, material body slowly dissolves and falls to pieces, bringing a painful, and lingering death; but this is a consequence he willingly accepts for the chance to join his beloved in an eternal life of images.

The book's imagining of the recording/projection-machine is one of its most distinctive and interesting features. Explicitly a compound apparatus, composed of several smaller machines with different functions (recording machines, projection machines, an electricity generator, etc.), the assemblage quality of this machinery seems mirrored in the architecture on the island, organised as it is into a sort of compound with three essential components – a church (which, like an unexplained part of the machinery, appears functionless in the novella, and is never referred to again), the villa, a swimming pool – and one satellite structure, the watermill down by the coast, whose function it is to harness tidal energy to power the machinery. This loose assemblage of locations provides a rudimentary scenery for the repeated encounters between the characters, as certain locations and conversations are returned to again and again over the course of the story. The characters' interactions loosely bind the scenery together, as though the projected people were only moving parts in the gigantic, architectural machinery of the island.

This overall model of assembled machine parts powered by a central motor, housed in a basement room – imagined as a kind of 'engine-room' – presents a large, mechanical, generative machinery lodged deep in the matrix of an architectural structure, which is productive of unfolding sets of scenarios. The eponymous 'invention' of Morel is, basically, a souped-up version of *film* – but this word is never mentioned. Instead the whole fable is written as if from an alternative world where phonograph records, radio, and photography have been invented, but film has not. (Morel's own description of his procedure refers to 'recording' and to 'photography' – 'My abuse', he says, in the 'explanation' scene, 'consists of having photographed you without your permission. Of course, it is not like an ordinary photograph; this is my latest invention. We shall live in this photograph forever.'[14]) Thus the project of the fable is to describe film as though for the first time. The descriptions proceed through a set of clumsy, imperfect analogies to other existing technologies. Indeed, film is explicitly imagined as the amalgamation of these other, slightly older devices

– phonograph records, radio, photography, plus new recording and transmitting devices for the olfactory, tactile, and visual senses – as though they had all been chained and harnessed together. In descriptions of the machinery there are repeated references to dials and switches, helping the reader to imagine the clumsy materiality of the generating machine.[15]

As we have seen, the film-machine (not exactly a camera, nor a projector, but a compound condensation of the filmic apparatus, necessitating this appropriately clumsy, doubled term) produces a series of alternative narrative scenarios, which are played out over the course of the novella.[16] One effect of this is to ally film explicitly to memory, as a machine invented to preserve and replay past times. However, the machinery has an even more specific stake and purpose. When Morel is explaining his invention to his assembled guests, he uses the example of a woman named 'Madeleine' whose illusory presence his machine will conjure. Not only is this surely an allusion to the *madeleine* which was the 'engine' of Marcel Proust's novelistic invention *In Search of Lost Time* (1913–27), thus making the link between Morel's machine and the work of memory explicit, but in addition Morel's choice of example, and his sensuous description of the absent woman, further intensifies the identification of the film work with a fantasmatic female body.[17]

Whilst Morel's machine is designed to enable the replaying of past *time*, what I want also to emphasise is the way in which his invention is enabled to act as an engine generating *space* by its harnessing of architecture. The engine housed in the basement of the 'museum' produces a set of dimensions, an atmosphere, or *medium* which the novel's characters populate. The characters' existence is only as projections, flickering in and out of dimensions whose whole matter is filmic. The medium of film superimposes itself over the geography and even meteorology of the island (the characters are oblivious to rain, and sun themselves in a perpetual, invisible summer). At one point the narrator finds himself trapped in a version of the tiled basement engine room, the entrance hole he had made in the wall apparently sealed over. Trying and failing to break a new hole in the walls, he realises that the stuff that surrounds him is absolutely impermeable and unbreachable, since it is entirely filmic; the impalpable and yet utterly solid stuff of projections. Gradually every spatial thing on the island is overlaid by its filmic double (and so on to infinity): a key, uncanny moment in the book occurs when two suns appear in the sky, and two moons; the one, 'perhaps a reflection of the other', which is 'much more intense'.[18]

Finally, the fact that the energy of the machine is supplied by a pipeline hook-up to a watermill further intensifies the slightly archaic sense that this filmic technology has. The overall temperament of this imagining of machinery, and the inclusion of a watermill in particular, suggest a parallel to the machinery pictured in Duchamp's *The Bride Stripped Bare by Her*

Bachelors, Even (1915–23), also called *The Large Glass*.[19] Indeed, the function of the two sets of machinery is similar. The projection-machinery in *Morel* has been invented in order to enable a bachelor's – first Morel's, but then the narrator's – access to, and eventual possession of, a woman he desires to be his 'Bride'. The whole machinery of the projection is designed to enable his leaving his own realm to enter hers – that is, to leave the material realm of the island and join Faustine in her realm of projected images. It seems an irresistible suggestion that, in Bioy Casares's fable, film is modelled as a gigantic 'bachelor machine', constructed to enable the passage 'from the Bachelor to the Bride'.[20]

Of the contemporary artists' films I have discussed, the work which bears the closest parallels to the material of Bioy Casares's novella is Tacita Dean's *Boots* (2003). Like the earlier work, Dean's film has as its central object a quasi-classical villa (a structure redolent of anachronism and bad historical conscience) – an extraordinary found architecture, seemingly deserted or else peopled by those who don't live there, and possessing, importantly, a quality of seeming out-of-time.[21] The villa in *The Invention of Morel* is described by the narrator as a 'museum', despite the fact that, as he acknowledges, 'It could be a fine hotel for about fifty people, or a sanatorium.'[22] The confusion seems significant. The building houses temporary visitors but cannot be called a hotel because the guests are not living people. A sanatorium seems perhaps closer to the mark, were it not the fact that the disease infecting the inhabitants had already proved fatal. The house is a 'museum', then, for people who are literally moving images. It is, we might say – though this word appears carefully avoided by Bioy Casares – a veritable cinema. This, it turns out, is exactly how Dean perceived the house she filmed in *Boots*, saying she saw the house, when she found it, as 'already a film set'.[23]

Dean's film follows an elderly man walking with a cane as he wanders through the villa's collection of rooms. The film comprises three one-hour parts or versions, which are projected simultaneously in different, adjoining rooms wherever the work is shown. Each replays the same repertoire of rooms with slight variations each time. In each, the old man's spoken reminiscences are slightly different; in each, he speaks in a different European language (English, French, and German), in none of which he seems quite 'at home'.[24] Altogether, *Boots* is Dean's most complex exploration of an architectural structure to date. Three interlocking films, which don't quite fit together but maybe tessellate, sit adjacently and spin off from each other in different dimensions like the reflections in the marble-walled, mirrored bathroom which is featured in all three films. In each film the man returns to this bathroom, which seems, somehow, the heart of the structure; the myriad reflections of the room seeming to further mirror the relationship of each film to the other, supplying a visual image for the layers of alternative spatial environments pictured in each version of the work.[25]

There is the whisper, or shadow, in *Boots* of an erotic dynamic similar to that which subtends Bioy Casares's story. In *Boots* the narrator tells the story of visiting his former lover here, Blanche. Unattainable, loved by many men, he remembers that he never quite possessed her, and in the present his differing memories perform a similar failure to capture her image now. It is her absence that has propelled his return here and which generates his rambling movements around the house, powering his drifting memories. Yet this male desire is framed and coolly exposed by a female artist, and in the end it is her camera's pursuit of him – a lame father figure – which overwrites in the present the older, remembered-at-a-distance tale of his romantic love.[26] In later films Dean's camera has continued to pursue old men, demonstrating a quietly insistent rewriting of a certain filmic machinery (which supplied the motive-force or engine for Bioy Casares's work), so that the old story takes on echoes and resonances with a new, female, filmic agency.

The rewriting of this drive is also made visible in the Wilsons' films, in which, as Giuliana Bruno observes, 'the technique of revealing the internal mechanism of a disused architecture recurs'.[27] Indeed, their works stage repeated scenes of the discovery of an inner engine room in some disused plant or building, as though returning again and again to some kind of 'primal scene' for film. Perhaps they are: as Bruno has noted, the particular atmosphere of terror and surveillance evoked by their formal strategies contributes to a sense that the particular machinery they are concerned to uncover is that of the visual and ideological formation of the subject. Describing the Wilsons' *Stasi City*, Bruno writes that '[d]evoid of human presences, with the closed doors that once imprisoned the investigated subject now pushed wide open, the construction of the very space of fear is revealed. We can now see the cheapness, even the fakeness of the psychic mechanism staged here – the mechanism that runs a theatre of terror.'[28]

At the same time, the desuetude of these architectures of the subject is an important dimension to their treatment at the hands of the Wilsons, as Bruno observes. Discussing the Wilsons' *A Free and Anonymous Monument*, Bruno writes that this work 'shares with many other works the pair has made the form of a meditation on matters of desuetude, post-industrial ruination and technological waste. In fact, these artists have long shown a predilection for visionary, machinic installations – mental architectures that are barren landscapes and deserts of the mind.'[29] This last description may recall for us the tenor of Duchamp's *Large Glass*, particularly as photographed by Man Ray under a thick layer of dust. This photograph was reproduced by the Surrealists in 1922 in their journal *Littérature*, where it received the following, evocative caption: 'This is the domain of Rrose Sélavy. How arid it is! How fertile! How joyous! How sad!' The stipulation that this dusty, barren surface is the 'breeding ground' (suggested in the title Man Ray and Duchamp gave the photograph,

Élevage de poussière, or *Dust Breeding*), for the 'rising up' (an alternative translation of '*élevage*') of a fantasmatic woman's body reinforces recognition of the ways in which this work, as an instrument of perspectival drawing or spatial 'projection', and as an architectural integer in whichever room it is displayed, is deeply linked to the problematic of cinema, as conceived by the early avant-garde and as I analyse it here.

Thus what seems to me of importance about the emergence of filmic architectures in the works I have described is that it enables excavation of an alternative model for the projected image – not the sculptural object, which was important to the utopian aspirations of an earlier generation, but instead a recovery of film's potential to be a desiring-machine, housing the viewer's imaginative projection. While it had been a desiring relationship on the part of a male narrator to a perfect and unattainable female image which provided the narrative motor or engine for fundamental early myths of cinema (as is made evident in Bioy Casares's book, and by Alain Resnais, who followed him), the women filmmakers I have studied here critically excavate this machinery and show it to have accrued a thick layer of dust.[30] The Wilsons, Dean, Nashashibi, and Skaer make their own journeys to the engine room of film and uncover its apparatus-like machinery, exposing its architecture and setting it going to house new desires. In their works the camera's gaze is re-engineered as enquiring – probing, in each case, a set of rooms and an unfamiliar architecture, glimpsed in the dark and illuminated in flashes. Peering through windows and structural gaps and holes, excavating, paring away, and holding filmic architecture to the light like a filmstrip, we might even say their work helps to constitute a new, feminine, desiring language for film.

Book of film: book: film: boat

One of Dean's most recent films, *Amadeus (swell consopio)* (2008), shows a fishing boat leaving the French harbour of Boulogne and travelling through the night to the small English port of Folkestone, arriving finally with the morning light (figure 8.5). Many of Dean's previous works were structured around the passage from day into night (we see this, for example, in *Disappearance at Sea* and in *Boots*), but in *Amadeus* that more familiar trajectory is reversed, and here we watch night turn into day. Starting in the darkness, behind the boat (Dean and her cameraman were apparently in a second boat, travelling close behind the first), we watch the boat's rushing wake churn the black water and its port and starboard lights move out into the wider darkness of the sea. Switching camera angle to look back, the glitter of the harbour lights dancing up and down recedes into a glimmer of strung-out dots and dashes along the shore, recalling a Moholy-Nagian type of light-play. The whole film is structured, using Dean's characteristically long takes, by these quiet, repeated switches of camera angle back and forth, between the view forwards, in the direction the boat is travelling, and the view back, towards the open sea. As the boat moves away from France it becomes harder to distinguish these two directions. The boat's continuous swaying motion making it sometimes hard to tell whether it is moving forwards, backwards, or staying still.

Gradually the cold light of early dawn begins to leach colour out of the scene. The vivid glimmer and dance of the gold lights in the dark grows pale. There is an extended moment between day and night when there is no colour, and the sea and sky together exist in a kind of monochrome. This undoing of darkness, and of colour, to reach a protracted, in-between point of no-colour is sensual: silver light spills loosely over everything, nonchalantly, richly, in complete suffusion, as though it had conquered colour. The poise of this moment seems essentially photographic: the way everything seems sealed in silver recalls the marmoreal polish of a silver gelatin print, and, like a photograph, we know that this is a brief, precarious moment caught in time. At any second the inevitable blue, pink, and yellow of dawn will begin to colour the sky, and the scene will vanish. This protracted moment, held for a few minutes, is, then, like a magically moving and yet still photograph, and because we know it can't last, we wait, almost holding our breath, until blue and pink and yellow make their inevitable appearance in the sky.

Characteristically, Dean's decision to structure her films around the passage from day to night or vice versa supplies a clear measure of passing time, and gives a narrative shape to her films. That her films describe the passing from one to another clearly distinct state lends a psychological trajectory to her films, as the viewer waits for and observes the changes coming. The fact that this film has a known end point, the end of the boat's voyage, in Folkestone, which is redoubled by the known end point of the night's arrival in morning, supplies an inevitability to the film's long duration which oddly intensifies anticipation rather than decreasing it.

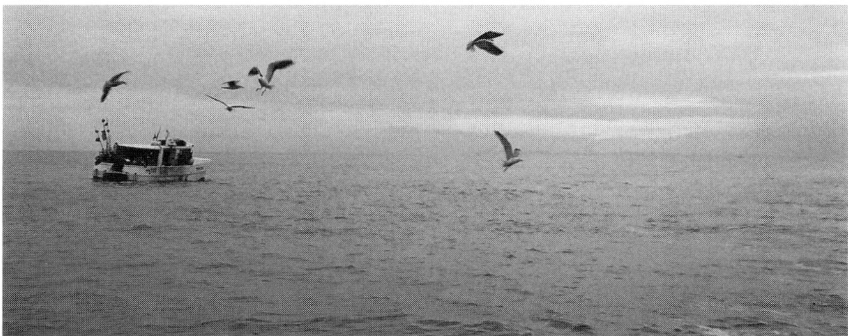

Tacita Dean, *Amadeus (swell consopio)*, 2008. 16mm colour anamorphic film, mute, 50 minutes. Courtesy of the artist and Frith Street Gallery, London. **8.5**

The inevitability of the film's steady trajectory, and its subject matter, immediately suggest a parallel to Michael Snow's iconic *Wavelength* (1966–67), long hailed as foundational to structural film. *Wavelength* comprises a forty-five-minute, fixed-viewpoint, single-angle camera zoom towards a postcard pinned up to the opposite wall of the artist's studio, which depicts a black-and-white view of the sea. During the course of the film a few narrative incidents occur – people appear in frame and fall out of it, seemingly, there is a death – but the camera never wavers from its slow, continuous zoom forwards. Snow's film was analysed in two influential essays by Annette Michelson as exposing the psychological anticipation which undergirds the diegetic drift of film and tying this expertly to the material apparatus of film, materialised in the camera's narrowing view.[31] She described the result as a 'hypostatisation', or intensified materialisation of the filmic apparatus, physically literalising the perspectival point-of-view construction which is at the root of the film-camera's structuring of vision.[32]

The materiality of *Amadeus* is, like that of *Wavelength*, strongly physical. However, in contrast to the intense, narrowing focus and fixed-angle glare of Snow's film, Dean's has a rather different quality. Whereas the waves remain frozen still in the postcard in Snow's film, and the camera's zoom is pointedly unanimated by any movement, throughout the whole fifty-minute length of Dean's film the camera moves with the ship, tilting and swaying on the water. Dean's camera work, which can look so cool when it dispassionately excavates architectural spaces in her earlier works, is here given if not exactly a more passionate, certainly a more sensual, inflection. Here the movement of the camera on the water recalls the action of *Delft Hydraulics* (1996), which she insists always on projecting at hip height, since it is, she says, a 'very sexy film'.[33]

Like structural film, Dean's delineates the materiality of the filmic apparatus. The simple three elements of this film – boat, sea, shoreline – form an assembled apparatus. The boat travels along the sea as if threaded on it; its *Endpunkt* is the shoreline towards which it moves steadily. Given the medium-specificity which so many of Dean's earlier films are notable for having performed (the lighthouse in *Disappearance at Sea* mirroring the lamp and lens and rotating motor of the film projector; the house in *Boots* and the cinema), it is perhaps not too far-fetched to see in the simple assemblage of *Amadeus* a loose modelling of the filmic apparatus. Here the unspooling ribbon of grey sea would be the filmstrip running through the projector, modelled by the tiny, hollow boat, which beams its small lights outwards towards the 'screen' or shoreline against which, like the projected film, it will eventually come to rest. The analogy is not exact; too firm or tight a modelling would not be the point. Rather at stake is a loose, but intense imagining of the materiality of film – housed now in the travelling form of the boat, in a development of the architectural model I have previously described. The gain of the new imagining is a looser, more flowing, more fluid, and more sensual rendering of the feel of film's materials and the kind of spaces they can describe. Where Snow's *Wavelength* materialised the apparatus by 'hypostatising' perspectival vision, Dean's materialisation of the apparatus allows for a looser assemblage of parts and more expanded space, producing filmic vision as hypnotic, expanded, carnal, and spacious.

Dean is not the only one of the group of contemporary artists I have discussed here to have turned her attention recently to the form of the boat.[34] In 2007 Nashashibi made a solo work filmed aboard a large cargo ship, travelling on the Mediterranean. Beginning at the exterior of the ship, Nashashibi's camera soon moves to the interior, filming the ship's all-male crew as they work and eat. Called *Bachelor Machines No. 1*, the title references the lower half of Duchamp's *Large Glass*. At first it may seem unclear what the 'bachelor machine' of the title is. But then one realises – like the joke in which a baby sardine, seeing a submarine, says to his mother, 'Look, mum, a can of people!' – of course, the 'bachelor machine' is the ship. Traditionally referred to in English as 'she', the ship's cool exterior houses an all-male crew. This is, then, a machine full of bachelors, experiencing an enforced separation from women for the duration of their voyage on the sea. Filmed by a woman, the segregation of the sexes (the men at sea, the women on dry land) is repeated in the dividing line between the two sides of the camera: the filmed men and the filming woman. Thus the line dividing the realm of the Bachelors from that of the Bride in Duchamp's *Glass* is here represented both by the line, somewhere in the distance, where the shoreline meets the sea, and by the glass lens of the camera, behind which is Nashashibi: the unseen 'bride' filmicly courting her bachelors.

But another reference we might find in this work by Nashashibi is to the Conceptualist Marcel Broodthaers's short film *A Voyage on the North Sea* (1973–74). In this work Broodthaers films a painting of a boat, his camera minutely traversing the painting's surface. Shots of the painted sea and ship filling the screen are regularly interchanged with black intertitles giving page numbers: 'page 1', etc. Nashashibi similarly uses black-screen intertitles, which in her case give theatrical divisions (for example, 'scene 1'), which, as they do in Broodthaers's film, here suggest that the form of the film has been spliced with the form of a page-based support.

In 1999, Rosalind Krauss argued this film of Broodthaers's shows film finding a support – a new 'medium' – for itself in the form of a novel; the hybridity of this exercise itself, she argued, inspired by the compound form of the filmic apparatus (comprising camera, projector, screen, etc.).[35] The work is spliced, and intermedia, she acknowledged, but finds a form of renewed, modernist medium-specificity in modelling itself after film's compound apparatus. Where Broodthaers remains at the surface of the boat, however, Nashashibi's film fills out the space of her support, her film travelling into the interior of the ship.

Where Broodthaers's film tracks across the surface of the painting, as if wishing for an interior to travel into, but stopped by the material surface of the paint, Nashashibi's camera-work freely cuts inside and outside the ship; engaging the workings of both narrative and psychological projection and finding an alternative materiality in the ship itself as a large film-machine, producing and generating space. The ship – moved by the sea, hollow, with its cast of bachelors stuffed inside it – becomes the model for a filmic apparatus with a new interior sense of space.

In place of Krauss's idea of the reinvented medium, then, I want to suggest that the more fruitful model taken by the artists I have discussed here is that of the machine – or, more specifically, the 'bachelor machine'. This term is appropriate because it captures the reference to Duchamp's clumsily carnal imagining of machinery which so many of these film works seem to make in their reimaginings of the apparatus of film, and which above all they materialise by mapping film onto found architectural structures, carving out a spatial structure for film's housing of desire. The clumsy, archaic machinery of the 'bachelor machine' which, in Duchamp's model, runs on 'love-juice' and produces a 'cinematic blossoming', thematises the work of filmic production and photographic projection as erotic, as well as fundamentally generating a doubled, split, alternative-dimensions model of space (which in *The Large Glass* is pictured by the divide between the two 'realms' of the glass). Film articulated as a 'bachelor machine' by these artists is a projection-machine for desire.

Thus, above all, in its insistence on a poetics and thematics of interior space – founding itself on a new, architectural model for film – the women artists I have studied here create a new aesthetic for gallery film: one which returns to and excavates certain dream forms from modernism's past, even as it remakes these in an explicitly feminine mode. In so doing, these artists remake avant-garde poetics, too. In place of a materialist emphasis on the space of projection in the gallery, these women's works hymn a certain slipping out of true, a distortion of the space of projection in which the viewer's subjectivity slips into an expanded spatial metaphorics of displacement. Slip-sliding through found architectural windows, out through the screen, and further out on voyages of discovery, this work constitutes an emphatically different poetics from that of structural or Minimalist filmmaking of the most recent 'heroic' generation. Activating Surrealist legacies in rich and productive ways for the present, in ways which are distinct from the glossy, hyper-real or spectacular, hysterical, or thwarted enthrallment with and/or opposition to cinema which fixates male filmmakers of their generation (such as Douglas Gordon or Pierre Huyghe), the works I have discussed here suggest alternative futures for artists' film.

Notes

1 Defining essays on the idea of the filmic apparatus include Jean-Louis Baudry, 'Ideological effects of the basic cinematographic apparatus' (1974), and Baudry, 'The apparatus' (1976), both reprinted in Theresa Hak Kyung Cha (ed.), *Apparatus: Cinematographic Apparatus: Selected Writings* (New York: Tanam Press, 1980), pp. 25–40, 41–67. See also the essays collected in Philip Rosen (ed.), *Narrative, Apparatus, Ideology: A Film Theory Reader* (New York: Columbia University Press, 1986), and in Stephen Heath and Teresa de Lauretis (eds), *The Cinematic Apparatus* (London: St Martin's Press, 1980).

2 I have discussed the sculptural model for film in 'Lack of fit: Tacita Dean, modernism and the sculptural film', *Art History*, 31:3 (June 2008), pp. 75–95.

3 Jean Wainwright, 'Interview with Jane and Louise Wilson', *Hotshoe International* (July/August 1999), pp. 18–23; p. 23.

4 References to films noted by other commentators include *The Exorcist*, *Whatever Happened to Baby Jane?*, *Repulsion*, and *The Tenant*. See Cherry Smyth, 'Psychic trails', in *Jane and Louise Wilson: Normapaths* (London: Chisenhale Gallery, 1995), no pagination.

5 Annette Michelson, 'On the Eve of the future: the reasonable facsimile and the philosophical toy', *October*, 29 (Summer 1984), pp. 1–22. See also Giuliana Bruno, 'The architecture of science in art: an anatomy lesson' (1992), reprinted in Bruno, *Public Intimacy: Architecture and the Visual Arts* (Cambridge, Mass.: MIT Press, 2007), pp. 87–116, and Andreas Huyssen, 'The vamp and the machine' (1981), reprinted in Huyssen, *After the Great Divide: Modernism, Mass Culture, Postmodernism* (Bloomington, Ind.: Indiana University Press, 1986), pp. 65–81. It will be clear in what follows that each of these articles has been important for my work here, which in certain respects may be viewed as a continuation and development of the arguments set out by Michelson in particular.

6 See my 'Lack of fit'.

7 Neville Wakefield, 'Openings: Jane and Louise Wilson', *Artforum* (October 1998), pp. 112–13; p. 113.

8 In the case of *Gamma*, the artists did in fact add large mirrors to one wall of the building, to intensify the mirror-reflections on screen. See Wainwright, 'Interview', p. 20.

9 Darian Leader, 'The architecture of life', in *Jane and Louise Wilson* (Zurich/London: Haunch of Venison Gallery, 2007), n.p.

10 See, for example, Claire Doherty, 'Awaiting oblivion', in Claire Doherty and Jeremy Millar, *Jane and Louise Wilson* (London: Ellipsis Books, 2000), pp. 74–78.

11 Giuliana Bruno discusses this work in these terms in 'Modernist ruins, filmic archaeologies: Jane and Louise Wilson's *Anonymous Monument*' (2004), reprinted in Bruno, *Public Intimacy*, pp. 43–82.

12 Leader, 'Architecture of life'.

13 Adolfo Bioy Casares, *The Invention of Morel*, trans. Ruth L. C. Simms (New York: New York Review of Books, 2003). I am grateful to Isla Leaver-Yap for bringing this book to my attention.

14 *Invention of Morel*, p. 66. This fluidity of conceptualisation between photography and film, the still and the moving image, is by no means unusual and is indeed

characteristic of theorisations of film and photography in the 1920s and 1930s (it may be seen also, for example, in Walter Benjamin's writings and in André Bazin's).

15 Because it is a machine for projecting visual plus olfactory and tactile illusions, the invention of Morel may remind us of what André Bazin described in 1946 as 'the myth of total cinema': 'There are numberless writings, all of them more or less wildly enthusiastic, in which inventors conjure up nothing less than a total cinema that is to provide that complete illusion of life which is still a long way away.' This, Bazin argues, is '[t]he guiding myth ... inspiring the invention of cinema.' Bazin, 'The myth of total cinema' (1946), reprinted in his *What is Cinema?*, vol. 1, ed. and trans. Hugh Gray (Berkeley: University of California Press, 1967), pp. 17–22. Michel Carrouges, discussed below, also uses the term 'total cinema' for Morel's invention, although he does not mention Bazin's essay.

16 Hollis Frampton uses the term 'film-machine' and discusses the idea in ways which resonate with my discussion here in his article, 'For a meta-history of film: commonplace notes and hypotheses', *Artforum*, 10:1 (September 1971), pp. 32–35.

17 'With my machine a person or an animal or a thing is like the station that broadcasts the concert you hear on the radio. If you turn the dial for the olfactory waves you will smell the jasmine perfume on Madeleine's throat without seeing her. By turning the dial of the tactile waves you will be able to stroke her soft, invisible hair and learn, like the blind, to know things by your hands. But if you turn all the dials at once, Madeleine will be reproduced completely.' Bioy Casares, *Invention of Morel*, p. 70.

18 Bioy Casares, *Invention of Morel*, p. 50.

19 Another parallel, I suggest, might be to the machinery for space travel described by J. G. Ballard in his short story 'Myths of the near future' (1982), reprinted in *J.G. Ballard: The Complete Short Stories* (London: Flamingo, 2002), pp. 1061–84. Climbing into a drained swimming pool, the main character explains to his female companion, 'It's an engine, Anne, of a unique type ... It's no coincidence that the Space Centre is surrounded by empty swimming-pools' (p. 1077).

20 Indeed, this is the suggestion made by Michel Carrouges in the revised and expanded edition of his *Les Machines célibataires* (Paris: Chêne, 1976). (The first edition was published by Editions Arcanes in 1954 and did not include discussion of Bioy Casares's book.) Taking its name from his analysis of the lower portion of Duchamp's *Large Glass*, Carrouges's highly original book (which is still not translated into English) set out the argument that the kind of machinery pictured by Duchamp provides an interpretive key to a range of literary works, Bioy Casares's novella amongst them. This is not the place to go further into the intellectual history of the idea; suffice to say that Carrouges's model of the 'bachelor machine' is in important ways different to the popularisation the term has received via Gilles Deleuze and Félix Guattari in their book *Anti-Oedipus: Capitalism and Schizophrenia*, trans. Robert Hurley, Mark Seem, and Helen R. Lane (1972; London/New York: Routledge, 2004), which cites Carrouges's idea, basing their account on the first edition of his book.

21 'It has a shabby decadence and charm, but also a quantifiable sadness', Dean has written. 'Somehow, the villa feels like it never quite fulfilled its potential; never became the house it should have done.' Tacita Dean, 'Proposal for a film project', unpublished manuscript, n.p.

22 Bioy Casares, *Invention of Morel*, p. 14.
23 Dean, 'Proposal'.
24 Dean has said she sees this quality of the man as mirroring a quality of the house: 'In a way, Boots is the perfect equivalent of many of the places I have been attracted to ... There is something very dilapidated about him, and he is also a true anachronism. His charm and personality feel the same age as the villa.' Dean, 'Proposal'.
25 In the returns to this room, we may see perhaps the most explicit parallel in *Boots* to *The Invention of Morel*, in which the room housing the projection machinery is described similarly: 'I entered a many-sided room ... The walls were covered with strips of a material that resembled cork and with slabs of marble, arranged symmetrically. I took a step: through stone arches I saw the same room duplicated eight times in eight directions as if it were reflected in mirrors. Then I heard the sound of many footsteps – they were all around me.' Bioy Casares, *Invention of Morel*, p. 18. The echoing, uneven sound of the old man's footsteps and the tap of his cane are also the predominant aural features of *Boots*.
26 Dean has spoken of a resemblance to her father in her text accompanying her film *Mario Merz* (2002), which, like *Boots*, is built around her camera's fascination with the figure of an elderly man. See her 'Mario Merz', in her *Selected Writings* (Paris: Paris-Musées/Göttingen: Steidl, 2003), n.p. She has discussed her interest in the theme of Oedipus in her 'Zen and the art of film-making', *Guardian*, G2 supplement (15 October 1997), pp. 12–13.
27 Bruno, 'Modernist ruins', p. 73.
28 Bruno, 'Modernist ruins', p. 73.
29 Bruno, 'Modernist ruins', pp. 75–76.
30 A further layer of complexity intervenes in the French reception of Casares's novella, which I don't have space to treat here. Alain Resnais's ninety-minute, black-and-white film *Last Year at Marienbad* (1960) seems loosely based on *The Invention of Morel*. Indeed, Resnais's title appears to have been suggested by a remark made by the narrator of Casares's book, who at one point describes the visitors to the island as 'people who dance, stroll up and down and swim in the pool, as if this were a summer resort like Los Tequos or Marienbad' (Bioy Casares, *Invention of Morel*, p. 11). The charge which Casares's plot receives in this treatment is exacerbated by an increased emphasis on repetition, flowing from the influence of Alain Robbe-Grillet (who wrote the script for *Marienbad* with Resnais) and the new form of the *nouvel roman* in France. This is material I am taking forwards elsewhere.
31 Annette Michelson, 'Toward Snow' (1971), reprinted in P. Adams Sitney (ed.), *The Avant-Garde Film: A Reader of Theory and Criticism* (New York: New York University Press, 1978), pp. 172–83.
32 Annette Michelson, 'About Snow', *October*, 8 (Spring 1979), pp. 111–25; p. 118.
33 See Roland Groenenboom, 'A conversation with Tacita Dean', in *Tacita Dean* (Barcelona: Museu d'Art, 2000), pp. 80–106; p. 104.
34 An earlier precedent, perhaps, is supplied by Chantal Akerman's *News from Home* (1976), which is discussed by Maria Walsh in chapter 5 of the present volume, in terms which are relevant to my discussion here.
35 Rosalind Krauss, *A Voyage on the North Sea: Art in the Age of the Post-Medium Condition* (London: Thames and Hudson, 1999), pp. 52–53.

9 The projective shift between installation art and new media art: from distantiation to connectivity

Christine Ross

In one of the most influential assessments of the emergence and development of the projected image in the 1960s and 1970s, Chrissie Iles, in her catalogue essay for the Whitney's exhibition, *Into the Light: The Projected Image in American Art 1964–1977* (2000–1), convincingly situated early projective installation as a hybrid of the white cube and the black box, at the intersection of Minimalism and cinema. The installations of the 1960s and 1970s to which she refers (by Robert Morris, Dan Graham, Anthony McCall, Paul Sharits, Anastasi, Barry La Va, Peter Campus, and Yoko Ono, among others) adopt Minimalism's engagement of the spectator 'in a phenomenological experience of objects in relation to the architectural dimensions of the gallery', where space is transformed into a perceptual field.[1] In projected-image installations, the Minimalist model of space is mixed, she argues, with cinema's own model of space – 'the dark, reverie-laden space of the cinema' which tends to fix bodies in front of a single screen to enable their absorption into filmic narratives. Iles insists, however, that this new hybrid does not consist in a mere mixing. For the cinematic model is posited as broken apart by the Minimalist phenomenology of the pieces, which encourage 'movement, the sharing of multiple viewpoints, the dismantling of the single frontal screen, and an analytical, distanced form of viewing' – a phenomenology which turns the spectator's attention away 'from the illusion on the screen to the surrounding space, and to the physical mechanisms and properties of the moving image'.[2] The projected image might make space more elusive, but the spectator is invited to distance him- or herself from its absorbing effects. The projected image, in short, is a site that allows viewers to negotiate with possible confusions between the real and the fictional by being exposed to the mechanisms of illusion or by being made aware of the materiality of space in relation to the illusionistic image.

In the 1960s and 1970s, various aesthetic strategies were explored to elaborate these distantiations and screen-surrounding space connections. One of these strategies consisted in turning the apparatus of film projection into the artwork and, as such, in making visible the technological means of illusion, as in Anthony McCall's *Line Describing a Cone* (1973). This was McCall's first so-called 'solid light film', where conventional cinematic viewing was reversed by the introduction of a 16mm film projector in the darkened empty space of the gallery. Viewers were invited to watch a light beam emanating first as a line and developing gradually into a cone, while also attending to the projection of the beam first as a dot and gradually as a full circle on a distant wall. They watched, but could also interact with the light beam, interrupting its flow, walking into the cone, disappearing into it and reappearing on the other side. Thus the installation not only disclosed the hidden devices of cinematic illusion but also succeeded in unfixing the cinematic position of the spectator in front of the screen.

Another strategy was to explore closed-circuit video, a technology enabling the simultaneous filming and projection of images in real time, which would split and double the viewer's own image, as in installation works by Peter Campus and Dan Graham. In Campus's closed-circuit video installations, for example, the viewer experiences her image doubled, divided, reversed, or magnified, sometimes projected concomitantly with her mirror reflection. The main effect of such operations was to trouble the viewer's sense of cohesion, unity, and self-identity. In an installation like *Interface* (1972) – a work composed of a glass pane; a video camera located behind and directed toward the glass; and a video projector connected to the camera, placed in front of the glass and obliquely to the camera on the other side – the spectator circulates in the space in front of the glass. It is in that very space that she will experience the double mirror/screen function of the glass, the simultaneous reflection of herself and transmission of her projected image filmed by the camera in real time. In such settings, the spectator is confronted with two opposed images of herself: a black-and-white positive image (the video image) and a coloured negative image (the reflection). Video projection is thus the means by which the spectator engages in the act of perceiving the self-in-space, according to two irreconcilable (subjective/objective; internal/external) viewpoints. It facilitates the development of a critical attitude on the part of the viewer towards her own sense of self, and inhibits the tendency towards narcissistic blending of the self into one's own image.

This brief overview of some of the pivotal traits of the projected image as it developed in the 1960s and 1970s allows me to begin to formulate the shift I see happening in more recent forms of mixed/augmented reality projections combining real-world and virtual spaces. While the projected images of the 1960s and 1970s partook of an aesthetics of self-criticality, distantiation, and reality-versus-illusion, augmented reality (AR) art contributes to the shaping of an aesthetics of immersiveness, relationality, and real–virtual continuum. As I hope to show, it has come to act as a binding technology compensating for the unbinding operations of earlier forms of projected-image works and favouring the regrouping of users as communities and collectives rather than the dividing and distancing of the self.

To better appreciate this shift and before addressing augmented reality art proper, it is useful to contrast one of the key works made during the years of the emergence of projective installations – Dan Graham's *Present Continuous Past(s)* (1974) – with one of the most manifest non-digital forms of augmented reality projections: Olafur Eliasson's *The Weather Project* (2003). This comparison, between two installations exploring mirror reflections and projection to very different ends, helps to highlight the main characteristics of the projective shift. More crucially, it will help to formulate a clearer hypothesis concerning the nature of this shift.

The earliest of these two works, *Present Continuous Past(s)* (figure 9.1), consists in a closed-circuit video installation whose structural set-up is orchestrated to delay the transmission of images initially taken by a surveillance camera. The setting includes one video camera facing a mirror wall, one monitor located below the camera, an additional lateral mirror wall, and a microprocessor. Graham offers a precise description of the installation as one that simultaneously turns the spectator into an object but also a subject of perception:

> The mirrors reflect present time. The video camera tapes what is immediately in front of it and the entire reflection on the opposite mirrored wall. The image seen by the camera (reflecting everything in the room) appears eight seconds later in the video monitor (via a tape delay placed between the video recorder, which is recording, and a second video recorder, which is playing the recording back). If a viewer's body does not directly obscure the lens's view of the facing mirror the camera is taping the reflection of the room and the reflected image of the monitor (which shows the time recorded eight seconds previously reflected from the mirror). A person viewing the monitor sees both the image of himself or herself of eight seconds earlier, and what was reflected on the mirror from the monitor eight seconds prior to that – sixteen seconds in the past (the camera view of eight seconds prior was playing back on the monitor eight seconds earlier, and this was reflected on the mirror along with the then-present reflection to the viewer). An infinite regress of time continuums within time continuums (always separated by eight-second intervals) within time continuums is created. The mirror at right angles to the other mirror-wall and to the monitor-wall gives a present-time view of the installation as if observed from an 'objective' vantage exterior to the viewer's subjective experience and to the mechanism that produces the piece's perceptual effect. It simply reflects (statically) present time.[3]

Graham's account specifies quite clearly how *Present Continuous Past(s)* elaborates the interpenetration of past and present times – live, recorded, and projected. The entry of the spectator into the room is the trigger by which

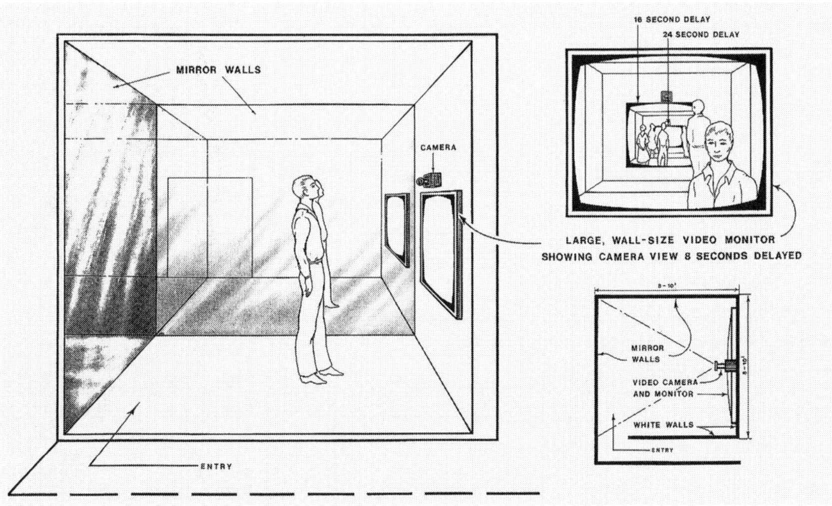

Dan Graham, *Present Continuous Past(s)*, 1974. Mirrored wall, video camera and 9.1
monitor with time delay, 96in x 144in x 96in/244cm x 366cm x 244cm (overall).
Courtesy of the artist and Marian Goodman Gallery, New York.

this interpenetration is launched. Although installation art has often been defined as participatory (for example, in Julie H. Reiss's and Claire Bishop's studies of the genre), in this work the recording, transmission, and postponing mechanisms are set off by the viewer whether she wills it or not.[4] The monitor projects to the viewer her own image but delays its transmission and inserts it into a regression of images within images within images, a regression ensured by the reflection of the images in the mirror wall facing the camera. The installation thus institutes the spectator as a split subject, spatially divided between her mirror reflection over there and her body over here, but also temporally split between past, present, and future. Simultaneously, however, she sees a present-time view of herself in the reflections of the lateral mirror wall. She may also discontinue the recording and delaying process by blocking the lens's view of the facing mirror. The mirror projection of the self and the blocking of the electronic projection of the self provide the possibility of seeing oneself seeing and the implicit possibility of figuring out the recording, delaying, and projective mechanisms of the installation.

The phenomenology of Graham's work is complex. A phenomenology of the lived body is established, one that posits the inseparability of the spatial and the temporal in the perceptual experience of the art object by emphasising what Maurice Merleau-Ponty designated as the paradoxical role of the mirror image: an image that 'forces me to leave the reality of my lived *me* in order to refer myself constantly to the ideal, fictitious, or imaginary *me*, of which the specular image is the first outline'.[5] The result of this is that the spacetime of

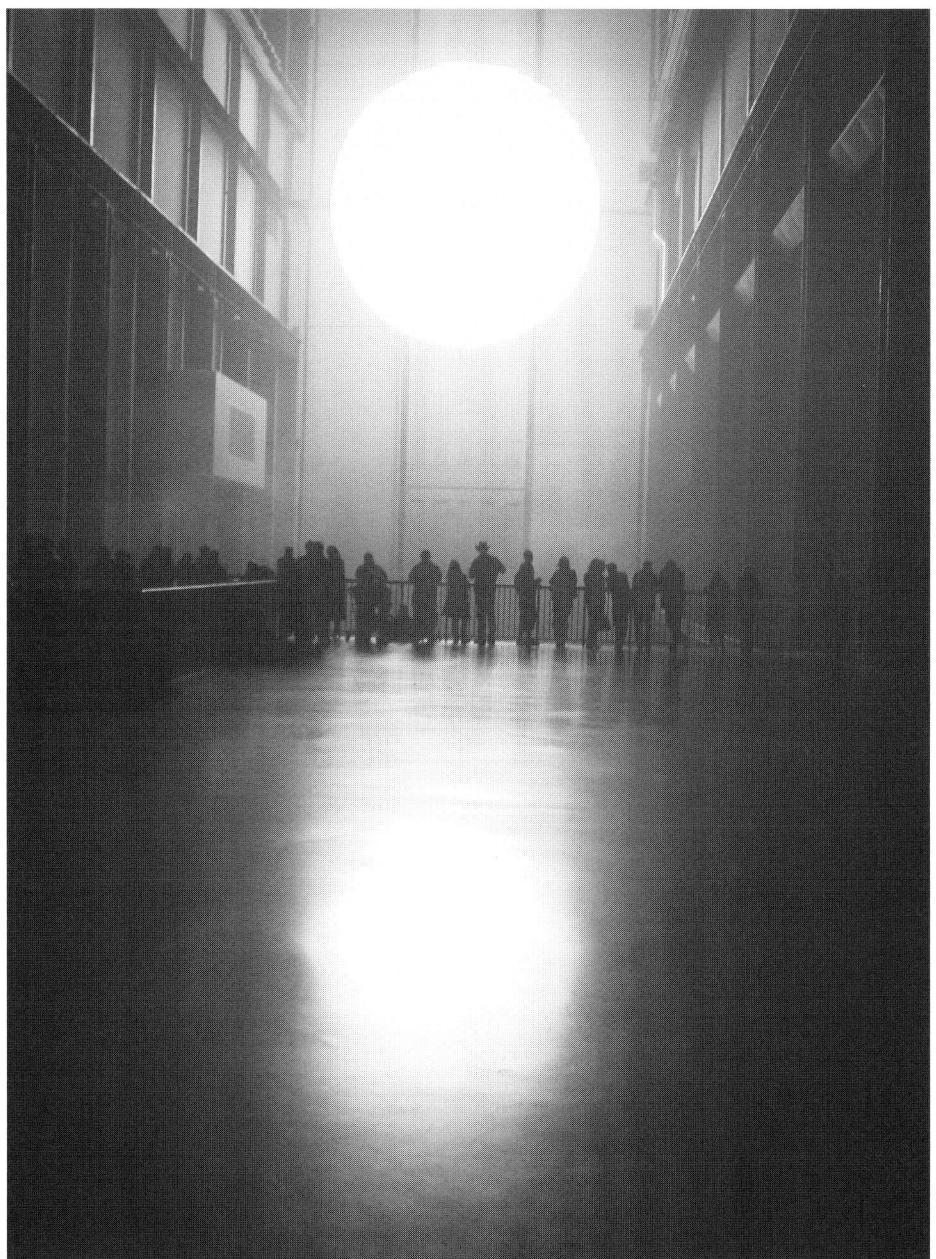

9.2 Olafur Eliasson, *The Weather Project*, 2003. Monofrequency lights, projection foil, haze machines, mirror foil, aluminium, scaffolding. Installation view at Turbine Hall, Tate Modern, London (The Unilever Series), 2003. © 2003 Olafur Eliasson. Courtesy of the artist, neugerriemschneider, Berlin, and Tanya Bonakdar Gallery, New York.

the video image and the spacetime of the room are disclosed in their interdependency, opposition, and possible reconciliation. But at the same time the spectator's sense of space and time is split and confused – 'virtualised' rather than grounded, in an experience which contrasts notably with that provided by contemporary Minimalist sculpture.

Twenty-nine years later, Olafur Eliasson assembled *The Weather Project* (figure 9.2) specifically for Tate Modern's Turbine Hall. The installation presented a gigantic semicircular screen covered with hundreds of monofrequency lamps radiating yellow light which was made to appear, through a play of mirrored reflections, as a full spherical sun – a glowing disc suspended from a mirrored ceiling. The disc was inserted in an environment of drifting patches of mist to create a microclimate as if of a sun in moving clouds. The mirrors lining the ceiling not only created the top half of the sun but also doubled the height of the space, whereas the fog refracted the light in ways that blurred the boundary between the space and its reflection. The mirrored ceiling also allowed viewers to see themselves as minuscule black shadows in space, surrounded by other visitors and immersed in the monumentality of the installation, in the 'spectacle' of the fabricated landscape. As pointed out by art historian James Meyer, the phenomenology at play here was clearly different from that invoked in the 1960s and 1970s by artworks engaged in self-criticality and institutional critique. It took the form of an event in relation to which spectators were constituted as a 'mass audience':

> Something unexpected happens to spectators of *The Weather Project*. We lie down – and lose ourselves, become part of, indeed become, the spectacle before us. The phenomenological practices of the '60s and '70s, to which Eliasson's work is sometimes compared, prized an active spectator – one who could "see" and, in seeing, make informed decisions. But *The Weather Project* delivers a mass audience that cannot fail to be overwhelmed by the magnitude of the installation itself: The museum is not so much "revealed" as transformed into a destination, an event.[6]

The kind of phenomenological experience provided by Eliasson might be thought to have some key features in common with that supplied in Graham's *Present Continuous Past(s)*. Both works use reflections to merge the spectator's 'real' space with some 'illusory' content, and so confuse the spectator's spatial (and, to an extent, temporal) orientation. However, they also substantially differ. The viewers of Graham's work are not constituted in the kind of spectral collectivity, or 'mass audience' as they are by Eliasson's. Furthermore, while the mirrored ceiling of Eliasson's work allows viewers to see themselves seeing, this self-reflexivity does not necessarily extract them from the realm of the specular or of the spectacular. Why? Namely because they are immersed in the environment, unlike the viewers in Graham's work, who can more easily distance themselves from the projection. Indeed, the spectators of *Present Continuous Past(s)* have a frontal relation to the projected images and a lateral relation to some of the reflected images; they also have the opportunity to block the regressive re-projections of their own image.

It is not that *The Weather Project* prevents the spectator's awareness of her own bodily position in space in relation to others, or that she is blind to the mechanisms of the illusion of the projected sun (these are apparent and can effortlessly be observed by the visitors). Rather, the installation unfolds a real–virtual continuum which is substantially different from *Present Continuous Past(s)*'s real-versus-image dynamics, made out of delays and image regressions. Scale also matters here, consolidating a sublime effect in *Weather* from which it is difficult to detach oneself. Finally, the voluntary or involuntary character of viewer participation is substantially different in the two pieces. Graham's work catches the viewer's image whether she wills it or not, while the audience of *The Weather Project* sought its reflection out, growing throughout the exhibition, between October 2003 and March 2004, to reach a reported record crowd of two million visitors, immersing spectators who wilfully – interactively – spent time there to form small, ephemeral, and spontaneous communities. This last point also helps to highlight that *The Weather Project* alerts us to something which is an important feature of contemporary digitally based AR (augmented reality) works, namely, that projection is not simply about a projected or reflected image as in its 1970s counterpart. Projection refers to the act of thrusting an image outward or forward but also light, mist, and smell (even, as we will see, voices, heartbeats and emotions). These non-iconic forms of projections are endemic to recent media projections.

The securing of a real–virtual continuum that does not sharply separate the real from projection; the embrace of the condition of the 'society of the spectacle' (defined by Guy Debord's assertion that 'everything that was directly lived has moved away into a representation'); the shift from 'subjection' to 'participation' or 'interactivity'; the move from a concern for the subject's false sense of unified self to a concern for the shaping of mass communities, gatherings, and collectivities; the shift from self-reflexivity to immersion; the increase of polysensorial receptivity through the deployment of non-iconic projections: these features which are all found in Eliasson's *Weather Project* are also among the key attributes of current digital projections in augmented reality art.[7] As stipulated above, the installation does not rely on digital technology (it was made out of lights, projection foil, mirror foil, aluminium, scaffolding, and a haze machine), but I understand it to partake of the same actual–virtual overlap, real–illusory spatial confusion, and audience-projection interaction dynamic as AR digital projections.

These specifications allow me to formulate my main claim: projection in new media art, especially in digital and non-digital augmented reality artistic practices, is inseparable from a binding impulse. Grounded in the development of community forms of public art, relational aesthetics, and mobile technologies, media practices of the 2000s use projection for the sake of connectivity. In digital forms of augmented reality, this binding impulse will be confirmed by the activation of interactivity, the interactivity between users and between users and machines, which systematically implies the formation of communities. But Eliasson's non-digital *Weather Project* already says it all: projection – the mirror reflections which allow the sun to complete its circle and allow the spectators to see their projected images, as well as the projection of mist that works to hold the whole as a tactile experience of a unified landscape – has passed from a self-reflexivity/distantiation/reality-versus-illusion logic to an immersion/interactivity/real–virtual continuum/holding-together device.

Augmented reality art projections

Since the early 1990s, the confirmation of mixed reality (MR) or augmented reality (AR) over virtual reality (VR) in a variety of domains – medicine, military training, robotics, education, communications, entertainment, tourism, design, and art, to name the most obvious – has increased awareness of how difficult it is to separate the real and the virtual, and how they in fact exist in a continuum. The engineer Paul Milgram introduced the concept of the 'virtuality continuum' to describe the unbroken scale ranging from real to virtual environments, with augmented reality and augmented virtuality located 'anywhere between' the two ends of the spectrum:[8]

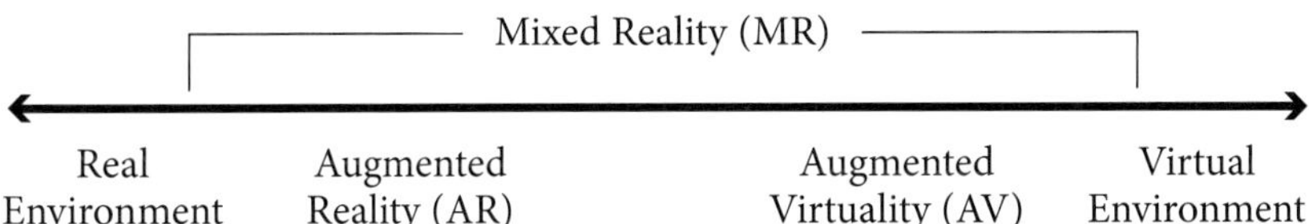

As Milgram's schema specifies, the real–virtual continuum – the unbroken scale ranging from real to virtual environments – is the foundational assumption of digital forms of augmented reality. AR builds up a continuous succession between the real and the virtual, in which the two categories tend to lose their distinction in relation to one another.

The concept of the real–virtual continuum is the foundational assumption of any AR system – and I borrow here Ronald Azuma et al's definition of augmented reality as a system which 'supplements the realworld with virtual (computer-generated) objects that appear to coexist in the same space as the realworld'.[9] AR was developed primarily to compensate for the restrictions of VR, namely its purportedly 'total' immersion of the user in a synthetic world. Yet AR does so not by discarding the virtual but by connecting it to the real, adjusting as it were the virtual frame of reference to what the user sees and hears. It does so, moreover, not simply by adding computer-generated information to space but by adding data to the user's sensory perception of space. In medical applications, for example, a surgeon can now wear a head-mounted display (HMD) device equipped with a semi-transparent visor which fuses his or her perception of the patient's body with the preparatory study of the internal anatomy projected on the screen.[10] In automobile applications, AR visualising systems enable the projection of GPS cartographic information on the car's windscreen, allowing the driver to see the outside environment through a constantly updated map of the area. Mixed, composite, or augmented reality is thus, as much as Minimalism ever was, a 'real-world' perceptual paradigm. Considering that the definitive (yet still unachieved) goal is 'to create a system such that the user cannot tell the difference between the real world and the virtual augmentation of it', the perceptual motivation underlying AR research carries several technical challenges, notably the imperative to perfect the panoply of technologies that converge to assemble a mixed real–virtual continuum for the observer-participant, from audiovisual (head-mounted, wall-mounted, handheld) display and playback devices to human–machine interface systems to body-tracking, sensing, and surveillance instruments, one of the most difficult technical challenges being the requirement for the computer to track where the user is looking and determine what he or she is seeing in order to augment his or her view.[11] This connectivity with perception has been from the start the impetus of AR explorations.

A derivative of installation art and virtual art, augmented reality art allegedly 'enhances' site by de/un/re-specifying it. It does so by connecting spectators to these sites through networking systems (mobile phones, GPS, the internet), sensing, tracking, and surveillance technologies, and by simultaneously projecting the detected data (sound, voice, images, different forms of bodily and environmental data) within the extended site. The projection of dynamic data is inseparable from the extraction of data enabled by the detection and geo-localisation technologies. This is how the real–virtual continuum is produced and maintained. Its productivity, moreover, most often lies in the connection it establishes between users. These traits become more explicit when we consider some of the key augmented reality environments produced in the last five years or so. Seiko Mikami's *Gravicells: Gravity and Resistance* (2004), for example, proposes a platform covered with panels of string-like lines that deform as the sensors underneath react to the participant's weight, tilt, and velocity. The changing platform (whose changes intensify when there are at least two spectators reacting to one another) is calculated by GPS systems that register the changes in the space, a calculation displayed on different wall screens that enhance the real-time dynamic between image, body, gravity, sound, and light. We might think also of Usman Haque's *Evoke* (2007), an animated projection on the façade of York Minster which lights up in response to the voices of the nearby public. An equally technologically sophisticated example is Stelarc's ongoing prosthesis project, *The Extra Ear (or an Ear on an Arm)* initiated in 1997, which famously involves the construction of a prosthetic ear out of soft tissue and flexible cartilage; its grafting (through a series of cosmetic, reconstructive, and orthopaedic surgeries) to one of the artist's arms, and its projected transformation into a communicational device. The ear will be made not to hear, but – through an implanted sound chip and a proximity sensor – to emit sounds addressed to nearby spectators, and will eventually be connected to a modem and a wearable computer to broadcast RealAudio sounds to which the spectator will be invited to reply through internet connection.

As these examples indicate, and as I shall go on now to show in more detail, AR projection as it is most often used by artists betrays ultimately a desire for connectivity through participation; a collectivity which is, however, enabled by non-participatory, i.e. unidirectional and panoptical, technologies of surveillance and detection. It also heavily relies on interactivity – the spectators' experience with technology. Interactivity ensures the triggering of projection which in turn ensures the constitution of anonymous and temporary communities, whose model varies from work to work but is likely, as we will see, to be unitary and amenable. Finally, it raises a fundamental question about projection: does interactive induced projection produce ways of perceiving which represent alternatives to those enforced by our ordinary experience, or does it merely sustain the mode of perception in which individuals are required to engage in a society of pervasive computing?

Inter-agero ergo sum

As the art of projection moves away from its reality-versus-illusion and related distantiation operations to embrace real–virtual continuum and immersive-inclined strategies, it propels spectatorship in a relational logic that can easily counter the perceptual potential of AR. Art critic Nicolas Bourriaud, the initiator of the concept of relational aesthetics, defines relational art as an artistic practice which takes, as its theoretical horizon, 'the realm of human interactions and its social context, rather than the assertion of an independent and *private* symbolic space'.[12] Its central theme is 'being-together': that is, the 'encounter' between the viewer and the artwork, together with the 'collective elaboration of meaning'.[13] In AR practices, interactivity is explored to produce projections whose main function is precisely to shape such collective deployments. I want to examine here five AR environments – by artists Lincoln Schatz, Rafael Lozano-Hemmer, Kazuhiko Hachiya, Mathieu Briand,

and Christa Sommerer & Laurent Mignonneau – to identify the modalities by which projection can be explored aesthetically to produce more or less complex community formations. More fundamentally, I will argue that the potential of AR as a perceptual paradigm lies in its ability to suspend its projection-*for*-connectivity/projection-*for*-collectivity impulse by favouring instead the inter-perceptuality or inter-sensoriality of these sites. In making this argument I will rely on Jean-Luc Nancy's notion of community as a practice of inoperativeness. The productivity of this notion lies precisely in its insistence on recognition of the several unsatisfying (redundant, reactive) forms of interactivity and projection in AR artistic practices, as it also lies in the questioning of the problematic 'communities' which are supposed to derive from such interactive projection settings.

The projection-*for*-community impulse through surveillance technologies may take the form of generative multi-channel video installations, such as those devised by Lincoln Schatz. In his installations, cameras capture images of public spaces, notably lobby environments and construction sites of specific buildings, which are then transformed and combined by specific software with stored images from the past. In *Here* (2007–), for instance, an arrangement of two interactive video walls (9ft by 9ft) commissioned for the entrance of One Arts Plaza in the Dallas Arts District are each composed of screens which display stored digital video images of the lobby (the images are initially stored as Quick Time files on Mac) in four overlapping layers, merging past with present and building as it were a fluid memory of the space and its visitors over time. From the moment the building opened, two cameras (one for each wall) began recording and storing daily collected images of the lobby. This process is planned to last at least eight years. Each video wall displays a different version of the same event and visitors are invited to react to these images as their own image appears on screen. The images pulled from the memory database are continuously recombined and manipulated in ways that make their repetition statistically unlikely. Supporting such projections is the promise of the establishment of a virtual community of visitors and passers-by, upon whose bodies a sense of community or being together is gradually built over time.

A similar example of this projective 'community' function, one that relies on the banking of data destined to interact with new entering data, are Rafael Lozano-Hemmer's *Pulse* works (2006–). Lozano-Hemmer's AR environments rely on the use of sensors that measure the heart rates or voices of passers-by to convert them into light beams projected in the public space as other passers-by simultaneously engage with the sensor devices. *Pulse Park* (2008) (figure 9.3) is surely the most emblematic work of the series, comprised as it was of a matrix of light beams moving and crisscrossing over the central oval field of Madison Square Park in New York. The intensity of the beams was modulated by sensors installed at the north end of the Oval Lawn that

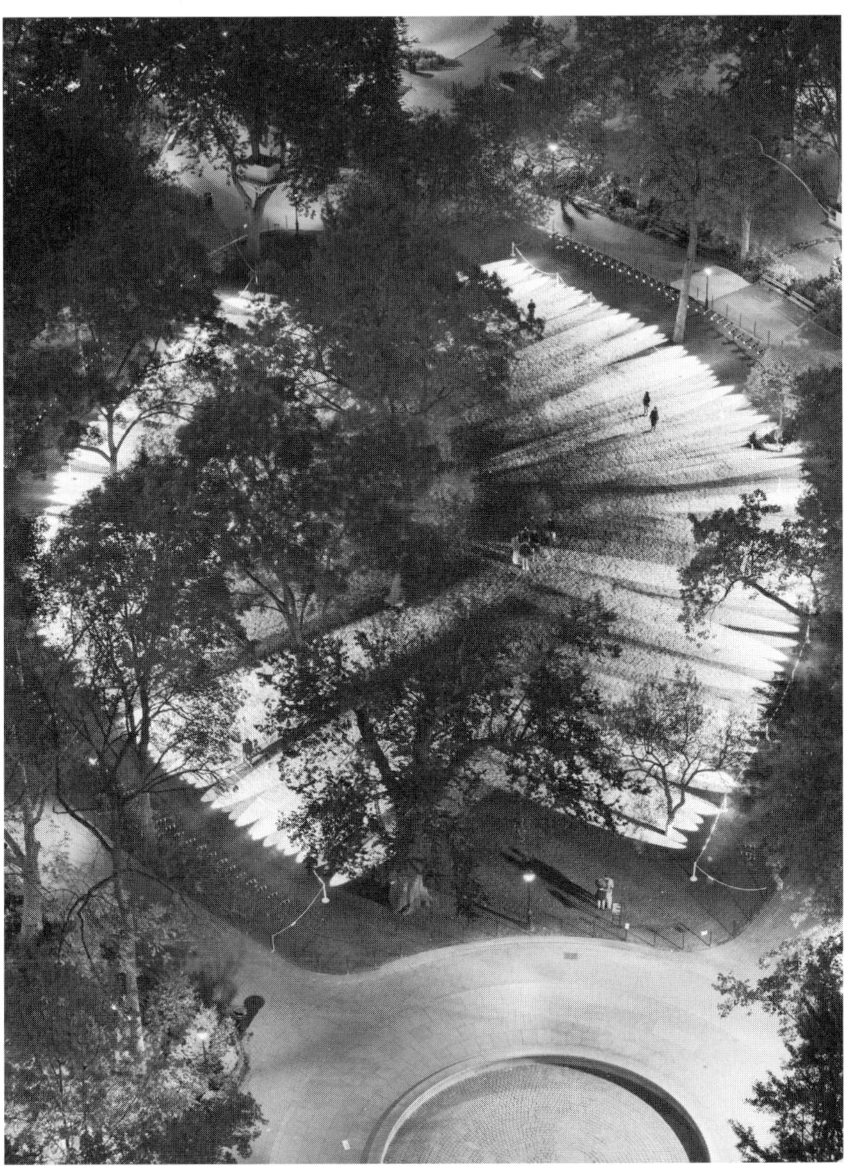

Rafael Lozano-Hemmer, *Pulse Park*, 2008. Madison Square Park, New York City. Heart-rate sensor, computer, DMX controller, custom software, dimmer rack, 200 Source Four spotlights, generator, dimensions variable (the lawn is an oval measuring 80m x 60m). Photo by James Ewing. Courtesy of the artist. 9.3

measured the heart rate (more specifically, the systolic and diastolic activity) of the visitors, which could then be translated and visualised as pulses of moving light beams projected by spotlights placed along the perimeter of the lawn. As each user made contact with the sensor, a light beam emerged to intersect with other light beams set off by other participants. According to Lozano-Hemmer, the result was 'a poetic expression of our vital signs, transforming the public space into a fleeting architecture of light and movement'.[14] But, although the heartbeats were indeed poetically translated into light through touch – and as such were productive of an interesting synaesthesia that let users see what was haptically generated – the translations were somewhat disappointingly homogeneous. The only differences between light beams lay in their pulse, and differences between pulses were minimal at best. Poetic expression was also inseparable from the institution of a virtual community of light-beam substitutes of the self, a virtual community triggered by the interactivity of participants who did not necessarily relate to each other otherwise. Projection, in this sense, is, in fact, the making of a dematerialised community, whose components (light beams) are akin to one another and whose form is not easily altered by the users. In contrast to other relational architectural works by Lozano-Hemmer, such as *Voz Alta* (2008), where the interactive devices allow participants to add their own personal stories to the installation, the constituency of the lit community was only marginally controlled by the users: participants could only manage the direct presence and memorised presence of the light beams by holding or letting go of the sensors. Although the artist specifies that the recording of the participants' pulses was 'immediately converted into light pulses by the computers' and that participants were surrounded by two hundred heartbeats, these were not heartbeats but highly mediated translations of heartbeats whose pulsing configuration was clearly predetermined by the network of sensors.[15]

Similarly, *Pulse Front* (2007) was a matrix of light over Toronto's Harbourfront, made with light beams projected by twenty robotic searchlights. These were exclusively controlled by a network of sensors that measured the heart rate of the participants. As Lozano-Hemmer's description specifies, 'ten metal sculptures detected the pulse of people who held them: the readings were immediately converted into light pulses by the computers and also determined the orientation of the beams. When no one was participating, the matrix showed the heart rate recordings for the last ten people who tried the interfaces.'[16] Hence, although the presence of users is required to activate the sensors, this interactivity is in fact a response to a predetermined sensing system, and this considerably nuances the actual level of interactivity involved in the participants' 'making' of light projections. In addition, once again the virtual light-beam communities only slightly modify their shape under the influence of the users, which is only to a very slim extent under their control.

All of these works may be said to share in what Julie H. Reiss and Claire Bishop have called installation art's aesthetic of participation.[17] Indeed, spectator participation may well appear to be more intensive in augmented reality art. However, as I hope to have shown, the extent of the spectator's willed participation in many of these works (I am referring here especially to the works of Schatz and Lozano-Hemmer) is really quite limited, and cannot obviously be identified with a more 'active' as opposed to 'passive' stance. The key rule underlying or triggered by AR projections is, certainly, interactivity – they are the very site of affirmation of an *inter-agero ergo sum* ('I interact, therefore I am') – but one is left with a sense of not having much control over the outcome of the projection. It is also crucial to emphasise that projection here (the generative projection of all the visitors of One Arts Plaza in the Dallas Arts District who will be filmed by the hidden cameras as they enter the lobby, as well as the light projection of visually translated heartbeats detected by the sensor technology laid out in Madison Square Park) forms collectivities which are quite poor in intersubjectivity. They lack in intersubjectivity what they gain in numbers of participants. The resulting communities are a conglomerate of at least two anonymous users, whose constituency is governed by laws of expansion and projection of personal data into the public sphere, so that the isolated participant might be inserted into a collective 'anyone + anyone + anymore'.

These collective formations are not automatically innovative, as they often simply correspond to an ephemeral gathering of individuals interacting within a preset environment. Sited but not belonging to a specific site, connecting but most often through technologies which enable connection at a distance, they fall more into the category of what Manuel Castells, in his study of the social uses and social effects of wireless communication in everyday life, has designated as 'ad hoc groupings', which find their 'technological platform in this capacity to call for action or … for sharing – in instant time'.[18] Required to interact; destined to sustain what individuals are required to do in a society of pervasive computing, namely, to insert himself or herself in a standardising logic of instantaneous community formation; anonymous yet celebrated in his or her embodied response to the site; allegedly 'in direct contact' with the immediate environment yet exceedingly mediated: the spectator turned user is solicited as a *destinataire* (recipient) in ways that do not necessarily produce alternative, redistributed, or critical ways of perceiving.

Poly/inter-sensoriality

It is imperative to underline, however, that some environments are more responsive, imaginative, and diversified. As I hope to show below, the exploration of perception in current AR research – including the switching of percepts between users, the switching of senses from one organ to another, and polysensoriality – does allow for new forms of user relationships. In artworks based on these experiments, the operation of projection is, productively, complicated. There is a whole area of technological experimentation in the field of AR research which is dedicated to translations, multiplication, or intertwining of the senses, notably the work of Carson Reynolds, Alvero Cassinelli, and Masatoshi Ishikawa, from the Ishikawa Komuro Laboratory, and their *Aural Antennae* (2008–): a portable device which translates sound impulses into vibro-tactile stimulus. By swapping audio sensation for haptic sensation, the compact device can be worn as an electronic travel aid for the hearing-impaired. The wearable computing system *Haptic Radar/Extended Skin Project* (2006–) by the same team, which translates visual data into vibro-tactile cues, allows users to feel distant objects on the surface of their skin. *Fingersight* (2006–) (more technically called *Fingertip Visual Haptic Sensor Controller*) by George DeWitt Stetten and Roberta Klatzky from the University of Pittsburgh is a device that maps texture detected by reflected laser light to vibrations felt on the surface of the finger. These inventions are crucial, as they project data in ways that diversify and complicate perceptual and sensorial relations to the environment instead of standardising them or forcing them towards the formation of behavioural collectivities, which discourage intersubjectivity, creativity, and heterogeneity. In AR art, similar research informs the work of Kazuhiko Hachiya, Mathieu Briand, and Sommerer & Mignonneau.

Kazuhiko Hachiya's *Inter Dis-Communication Machine* (1993), for example, designed to be used by two participants or more, requires that each user wears a machine equipped with an HMD (head-mounted display) and a winged backpack. The backpack is equipped with a battery (7.5V), a TV tuner, and a transmitter. A TV antenna is installed inside the wings. The machine uses radio waves to send the video image. Each HMD has two monitors and a video camera but only displays to the user the other user's view of the surrounding space. As participants exchange their visual perspectives, they thus see the immediate environment as the other sees it: differently. Hachiya explains that the machine was indeed created to inject in the user a 'double identity self' as well as 'perceptual confusion over the way in which they see the world. But at the same time the work strongly encourages the participants to recognise what they can see through one another's eyes so that they establish a physical and psychological unity while they are invited to involve themselves with the work.'[19] Projection becomes a modality by which two individuals can connect while being exposed to different views of a shared space.

Exploring a similar yet more complicated device, Mathieu Briand devised for some of his recent installations head-mounted display devices to be worn by users who can then click on a button to swap instantaneously their views of the environment with other participants, seeing as it were through the eyes of the other. Equipped with a battery-powered, audio-video helmet – a head-mounted display device composed of a built-in video camera on top and a visor located in front of the eyes that doubles as a small screen – the visitor to Mathieu Briand's *SyS*05.ReE*03/ SE*1/MoE*2* (2002) or *UBÏQ: A Mental Odyssey* (2006–) circulates 'hesitantly' in the exhibition space, seeing his or her environment through the visor but also, after clicking on a button attached to a handheld device which activates the swapping of views with other participants, private views of other helmeted visitors circulating elsewhere in the same space at the same time.[20] Most vehemently in *UBÏQ* in its MIT List Visual Arts Center version of 2006, real time is a condition of possibility for altered perception in a space of self and other, in which private views become public and are replaced by another's view. The system is only operative if two, three, or four users are engaged in the process, here and now, so as to allow perceptual substitution. This is why Briand – who stipulates that the experience of real time is the main stake of his work – prefers the term 'lived time' to that of 'real time':

> if no one is there, there is no image. The exhibition was conceived like this so that the visitor is always at the heart of a work and no longer just facing an icon … Personally, I try to conceive works within which the visitor becomes a receiver-emitter, systems that don't lead the viewer to a truth or a response, but rather lead the self to introspection.[21]

The uniqueness of *UBÏQ* lies in the fact that the work displays perceptual activity on the users' individual visors in the form of micro-projections. It displays it not to propose a similar view of the world but different views, delaying, splitting, and switching them, in situations where one never really knows for sure whose view is being displayed. Interestingly, the delaying mechanisms of *Present Continuous Past(s)* are not far away here, indicating that the rupture between video-projective installations of the 1970s and more recent digital forms of AR installations is not as radical as may initially be thought – a point to which I will return in my conclusion. This is Briand's thrust, for sure, when he declares that, in his work, 'our usual sense references are perturbed, but it is this destabilisation that allows us to discover new things. This is the emission/reception that I'm talking about', and says that he wants 'to branch out into alternative connections in the brain', enabling the user to 'apprehend the world differently through new perceptions and dive into the *inframince*'.[22]

What is crucial to emphasise here is how these works explore interactive projections for the development of communities which can't hold as a homogenised whole. Projection is a hiatus that both links the participants but also marks their difference. The same must be said about Christa Sommerer &

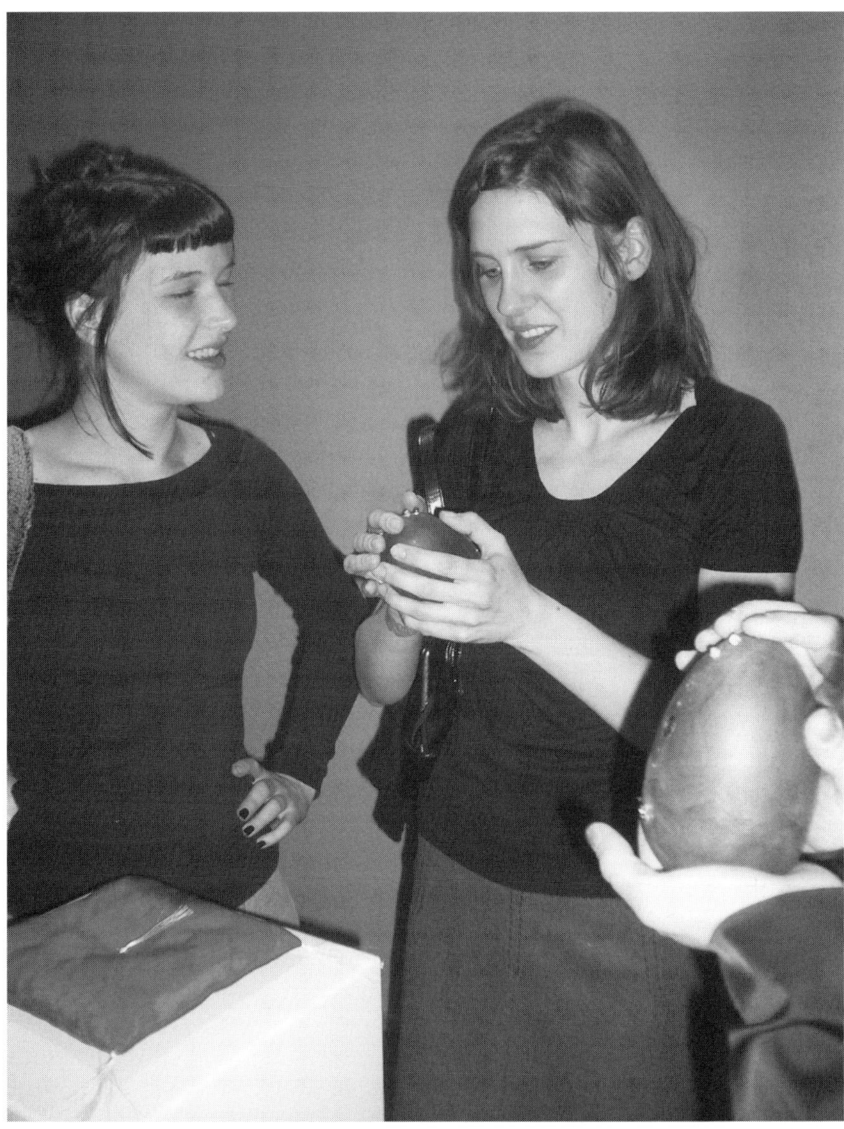

9.4 Christa Sommerer & Laurent Mignonneau, *Mobile Feelings II*, 2003. Two users exchanging their heartbeats at EMAF Osnabrück. Interface device contains a pulse and a touch sensor, a breath sensor, a micro-ventilator, a micro-motor (inside a yellow box), two LEDs, microcontrollers and a Bluetooth module (both inside the blue box). © 2003, Christa Sommerer & Laurent Mignonneau. Supported by France Telecom Studio Créatif, Paris and IAMAS Gifu, Japan. Photograph by Laurent Mignonneau. Courtesy of the artists.

Laurent Mignonneau's *Mobile Feelings I* and *II* (2003–4) (figure 9.4), which invites users to hold 'mobile feelings' phone devices equipped with sensors, vibrators, ventilators, and micro-bio-electrochemical systems that capture their heartbeat, blood volume and pulse, skin conductivity, sweat, and smell: when the devices are held by several participants, a user can select another user and receive that person's bodily sensations, through a vibration, a pulse, a slight stroke, a small wind or humidity. Within each device a Bluetooth module will either establish a direct connection between the devices in a range of 10m or communicate with a PC or PDA connected to the internet or to a mobile phone network. These connections allow the devices to communicate with each other wirelessly and send information to remotely located users. The work reproduces the private–public situation of mobile phones – a reduced sense of privacy combined with the unintentional witnessing of people's private lives. It explores the ambivalence of sharing personal information with an anonymous audience. The innovativeness of these devices lies in the fact that their set-up allows participants to communicate with strangers not, as is now habitually the case, via voice or images, but through atypical body sensations, including vibrations, smell, and sweat. The emphasis put on the tactile experience is also interesting as it reduces but never eliminates the sensory input channels of vision and sound. These channels are constantly negotiating with tactility, even more so in cases when users are strangers remotely located in relation to one another. For Sommerer & Mignonneau, the main objective is 'to get media art off the walls and out into people's lives', by exploring 'novel forms of mobile communications' that might as well include smell and sweat as more private ways of 'feeling and communicating with each other over distance'.[23] The integration of otherwise unperceivable sensorial experiences opens the possibility of exploratory forms of intersubjectivity.

The communities that emerge from such AR projections are communities made out of participants who can never easily settle into a resolved connection, precisely because of the need to decipher the nature of the tactile sensations and bodily properties communicated by the devices. The artists may well say that '*Mobile Feelings* devices allow remote users to feel each others' heartbeat and breath from a distance' almost 'instantaneously' and that the 'strong sense of bodily connection through these devices' is 'similar to "holding each other's heart in their hands" and feeling the other's heartbeat and strength', but users are in fact situated in bodily projections which continuously need adjustment, negotiation, and interpretation. The allegedly 'immediate' haptic feedback is after all a translation of the frequency and strength of the user's heartbeat or breath which is itself initially received via the wireless Bluetooth and relayed as data to the actuator.[24] There is nothing direct, instantaneous, homogeneous, and immediately binding or reflexive in the experiencing of these communicative devices. I believe this to be a strength. As in Briand's *SyS*05.ReE*03/*

*SE*1/MoE*2* and *UBÏQ: A Mental Odyssey*, as well as in Kazuhiko Hachiya's *Inter Dis-Communication Machine*, projection (the projection of views of a shared space; the projection of bodily data in a shared space) is set up so that the proximity, directness, and waning of distance it is assumed to establish are thickened, discontinued, and reconnected, re-distanced, re-mediated, and interrupted by the user's intersensorial acts of adaptation to culturally denigrated bodily properties. There is no community resolution here, although there is intersubjectivity processing in real time and what literary critic Steven Connor, when speaking of inter-sensoriality, has called a complexion, 'an indefinite series of integrations and transformations' through the mixing of senses (smell, touch, sound, and vision).[25]

Interactivity – and I follow here Jens Jensen's definition of the term as 'a measure of a media's potential ability to let the user exert an influence on the content and/or form of the mediated communication' – is necessarily contingent, and its productivity as a condition of possibility for community projection has limitations and undesirable consequences.[26] As Slavoj Žižek has pointed out, the uncanny double of interactivity is interpassivity. Whilst spectators of mixed or augmented reality art are now invited to interact with the screen and such relationships might seem to have put an end to the passive consumption of artworks (for example, in some of the works described above, the spectators shout, move, touch, hold, select, put on HMD helmets, and 'participate actively in the spectacle'), these consumptions create situations 'in which', as Žižek says, 'the object itself deprives me of my own passive reaction of satisfaction (or mourning or laughter), so that it is the object itself that "enjoys the show" instead of me, relieving me of the superego duty to enjoy myself'.[27]

Supporting this view, new media specialist Erik P. Bucy has empirically shown that interactivity is not so much located in the properties of technology and communication settings but instead mostly in the user's experience and perception of interactivity. The user might perceive that he or she is participating in a 'meaningful two-way exchange without ever achieving actual control over the content' or when the exchange in fact lacks communicative reciprocity or behavioural opportunities.[28] This perception varies from one user to another, depending heavily on the user's skills and experience in advanced information. Thus, the assumption that two-way communication is necessarily desirable and that it leads to more knowledge does not hold. Interactive settings may increase frustration and confusion and reduce memory when they demand too much time, expertise, and cognitive resources of the user. More importantly, in light of AR's community projections, as Bucy argues, 'at low levels of interactivity, such as that afforded by new media, a certain level of sociality and civic engagement may be cultivated, leading to norms of reciprocity and possibly the formation of social capital … As the information environment becomes ever more interactive, individualised, and fragmented, however, shared experiences across unlike groups may diminish, encouraging selfishness and self-indulgence.'[29] Interactivity is thus not automatically participation- or sociality-prone. AR artworks are not immune to such fluctuations, but can address them well in works which don't simply equate interactivity, progressiveness, and community.

I have argued here that the shift from real-versus-virtual to real-virtual continuum projective installations, and from self-reflexive projection to projection as a means for or a result of interactivity, becomes problematic when saturated by interactive demands and when it leads to uniform conglomerations of users. It is a fact that, as is clearly the case in the poly/inter-sensorial work of Hachiya, Briand, and Sommerer & Mignonneau, projection is a means of sociality, exchange, and community when interactivity is not an end in itself, when it allows for difference, perceptual shifts and permutations, exploratory forms of synaesthesia, and intersubjectivity. As the work of Jean-Luc Nancy has succeeded in demonstrating, the formation of communities requires *désoeuvrement* (inoperativeness) – gaps, *dissensus*, diversity, innovations, delays – to prevent their turning into homogeneities mobilised by problematic operations of inclusion and exclusions.[30] New media projections of images, sounds, smells, light, bodily sensations are at their best when they are open to *désoeuvrement*. As such, they gain in complexity when they integrate some of the delaying practices of earlier projective installations, such as those set into play in Graham's *Present Continuous Past(s)*. Therefore, the historical shift in contemporary projection art does not have to be oblivious to the projection devices that precede augmented reality. In fact, it is not. As it remembers and reuses these earlier paradigms, however, AR typically changes the function of delay between projection and spectator, moving away from the goal of self-reflexivity and the disclosure of the split subject, to rethink interactivity and to propose intersubjective forms of community.

Notes

1 Chrissie Iles, 'Between the still and moving image,' in Iles, *Into the Light: The Projected Image in American Art 1964–1977* (New York: Whitney Museum of American Art, 2000), p. 33.

2 Iles, 'Between the still and the moving image.'

3 Doug Hall and Sally Jo Fifer (eds), *Illuminating Video: An Essential Guide to Video Art* (New York: Aperture Foundation, 1990), p. 186.

4 Claire Bishop, *Installation Art* (London/New York: Routledge, 2003); Julie H. Reiss, *From the Margin to Center: The Spaces of Installation Art* (Cambridge, Mass.: MIT Press, 2001).

5 Maurice Merleau-Ponty, *The Primacy of Perception*, ed. James M. Edie, trans. Carleton Dallery (Evanston, Ill.: Northwestern University Press, 1964), p. 136. On Merleau-Ponty's positing of the continuity of internal life and external material

world, see Dorothea Olkowski and James Morley (eds), *Merleau-Ponty, Interiority and Exteriority, Psychic Life and the World* (New York: State University of New York Press, 1994).

6 James Meyer, 'No more scale: the experience of size in contemporary sculpture', *Artforum*, 62:10 (Summer 2004), p. 222.

7 Guy Debord, *Society of the Spectacle* (Detroit: Black & Red, 1983), no. 1.

8 P. Milgram and A. F. Kishino, 'Taxonomies of mixed reality visual displays', *IEICE Transactions on Information and Systems*, E77–D (12) (1994), pp. 1321–29.

9 Ronald Azuma, Yohan Baillot, Reinhold Behringer, Steven Feiner, Simon Julier, and Blair MacIntyre, 'Recent advances in augmented reality', *IEEE Computer Graphics and Applications*, 21:6 (November/December 2001), pp. 34–47; accessed online at www.cs.unc.edu/~azuma/cga2001.

10 J. P. Mellor, *Enhanced Reality Visualization in a Surgical Environment* (Cambridge, Mass.: MIT Press, 1995).

11 Jim Vallino, 'Introduction to augmented reality', online publication, www.se.rit.edu/~jrv/research/ar/.

12 Nicholas Bourriaud, *Relational Aesthetics* (Dijon: Les Presses du Réel, 1998), p. 14.

13 Bourriaud, *Relational Aesthetics*, p. 15.

14 www.lozano-hemmer.com/english/projects/pulsepark.htm.

15 www.lozano-hemmer.com/english/projects/pulsefront.htm.

16 www.lozano-hemmer.com/english/projects/pulsefront.htm.

17 '[I]nstallation art from its inception in the 1960s sought to break radically with the paradigm [of traditional painting and sculpture]: instead of making a self-contained object, artists began to work in specific locations, where the entire space was treated as a single situation into which the viewers enter. The work of art was then dismantled and often destroyed as soon as this period of exhibition was over, and this ephemeral, site-responsive agenda further insists on the viewer's first-hand experience … Instead of *representing* texture, space, light, and so on, installation art *presents* these elements directly for us to experience. This introduces an emphasis on sensory immediacy, on physical participation (the viewer must walk into and around the work) and on heightened awareness of other visitors who become part of the piece … [T]his need to move around and through the work in order to experience it *activates* the viewer, in contrast to art that simply requires optical contemplation (which is considered passive and detached)'. Bishop, *Installation Art*, pp. 10–11. See also Julie H. Reiss, *From the Margin to Center*, p. xiii.

18 Manuel Castells, Mireia Fernandez-Ardèvol, Jack Linchuan Qui, and Araba Sey, *Mobile Communication and Society: A Global Perspective* (Cambridge, Mass.: MIT Press, 2007), p. 249.

19 Ars Electronica Archive, Prix Ars Electronica 1996, accessed on-line at www.aec.at/en/archives/prix_archive/prix_projekt.asp?iProjectID=11264.

20 Gregory Volk, 'Back to the Bosphorus', *Art in America*, 90:3 (March 2002), p. 45.

21 Mathieu Briand, in Evelyne Jouanno, 'Mathieu Briand: hacking contemporary reality', trans. Rosemary McKisack, *Flash Art*, 37:238 (October 2004), p. 115.

22 Briand, in Jouanno, 'Mathieu Briand', pp. 115–16.

23 www.interface.ufg.ac.at/christa-laurent/WORKS/FRAMES/FrameSet.html.

24 Gerfried Stocker, Christa Sommerer, and Laurent Mignonneau (eds), *Christa*

Sommerer and Laurent Mignonneau: Interactive Art Research (Vienna: Springer-Verlag, 2009), pp. 202, 207.

25 Steven Connor, 'Intersensoriality', talk given at the conference on The Senses, Thames Valley University, 6 February 2004, online publication, www.bbk.ac.uk/english/skc/intersensoriality/.

26 Jens F. Jensen, 'Interactivity: tracking a new concept in media and communication studies', *Nordicom Review*, 19:1 (1998), p. 201. Jensen reconfirmed his definition in 'The concept of interactivity – revisited: four new typologies for a new media landscape', *ACM International Conference Proceeding Series*, 291 (2008), p. 129.

27 Slavoj Žižek, 'The interpassive subject', *Traverses*, no. 3 (1998), online publication, www.lacan.com/zizek-pompidou.htm. I thank Darin Barney for referring me to this important text.

28 Erik P. Bucy, 'Interactivity in society: locating an elusive concept', *The Information Society*, 20 (2004), p. 376.

29 Bucy, 'Interactivity in society', p. 379.

30 See Jean-Luc Nancy, *The Inoperative Community* (Minneapolis: University of Minnesota Press, 1991).

Index

Notes: 'n' after a page reference indicates the number of a note on that page; page numbers in *italic* refer to illustrations.